I0569865

CHASING MY NORTHERN LIGHTS

Traveling Life's Unpredictable Road Where
Adventure And Introspection Blur

THOM BARRETT

ISBN Hardcover: 979-8-9909823-2-1
ISBN Paperback: 979-8-9909823-0-7
ISBN Electronic: 979-8-9909823-1-4

Library of Congress Control Number: 2024914983

Publishing Consultant: PRESStinely, PRESStinely.com

Portions of this book are works of nonfiction. Certain names and identifying characteristics have been changed.

Printed in the United States of America.

Thom Barrett
www.livinglifewhiledying.com

To those kindred spirits who, alongside me, journey through life with the keen awareness that our time on this magnificent blue marble is fleeting. This book is dedicated to you—the brave souls who choose to savor each day and every moment with the intensity and appreciation of a fine wine. May we all embrace the beauty of our experiences, the depth of our connections, and the richness of each moment granted to us.

Preface

This book is a sequel to my previous work, *Living While Dying*, which detailed my journey with prostate cancer. In this volume, I share a travel narrative that captures one of my significant travel adventures during my ongoing battle with the disease. It chronicles a seven-month journey of overlanding and skiing, a venture embarked upon in 2022–23. Much of this book contains dated, immersive excerpts from my travel journal. Travel has assumed a vital role in my life since being diagnosed with prostate cancer in 2016. It allows me to embrace the present fully, engage in enriching activities, and revel in the world's offerings. This form of escapism also serves as a welcome reprieve from the constant reminder of living with the disease.

I'm currently facing stage IV prostate cancer, a condition typically seen as incurable. My struggle with this disease began back in 2015, and it has gradually progressed through various stages until April 2023, when it was confirmed to have reached stage IV. The statistics paint a grim picture, with the five-year survival rate for stage IV prostate cancer being about 28 percent.[1] This suggests the possibility that I might not reach my 70th birthday. However, as the saying goes, "There are three kinds of lies: lies, damn lies, and statistics."

Numbers don't always capture the full scope of individual experiences. Theoretically, I might have only five years remaining, but I am resolute in not spending them idly on my couch, lost in what-ifs, or brooding over my fate. My resolve is to fully utilize every moment I have. I believe that by actively living and maintaining an

---

[1] "Prostate Cancer," Johns Hopkins Medicine, accessed January 23, 2024, https://www.hopkinsmedicine.org/health/conditions-and-diseases/prostate-cancer.

optimistic mindset, I can enhance the quality and perhaps even the quantity of time left to me.

Being on the road is where I find my happiness. The freedom it offers, the chance to explore new places or revisit old favorites— it's what fuels my spirit. It's about embracing the unpredictability of the road, gaining wisdom from every twist and turn, and finding solace in the untamed beauty of our planet. I intend to remain a road warrior for as long as possible, welcoming friends and family who share my passion for the journey.

Admittedly, life on the road isn't all sunshine and roses, especially as I battle (and now live with) this disease. There are tough days when lifting my head seems impossible or when the pain becomes an unwelcome companion. Yet, the possibility of witnessing a mesmerizing sunset or sunrise, stumbling upon that iconic moment where mountains meet the sea, or sharing a profound interaction with a fellow traveler—that's what motivates me to lift my head from the pillow and take that next step forward.

What Does This Epic Journey Entail?

Aboard my slide-in camper (my "adventure home") and towing my trusty Jeep, I embarked on an unparalleled adventure. The trip unfolded in five distinct segments:

1. A month-long exploration across Canada, from Ontario to the Yukon, to experience the country's rich diversity.
2. Overlanding in Alaska, a land renowned for its sheer majesty and varied landscapes, encompassing the Inside Passage, Southcentral, Interior, and Southwest regions, each offering unique experiences.
3. Traverse British Columbia's Cassier Highway, explore the Inside Passage via ferry, and discover the wonders of Vancouver Island.

4. Skiing adventures spanning British Columbia, Alberta, Montana, Idaho, Utah, Colorado, and Wyoming.
5. A serene return journey, highlighted by fly-fishing in Wyoming and Montana.

This book is multifaceted in its intent. At its core, it narrates my personal journey navigating life with prostate cancer, demonstrating that it's possible to cultivate extraordinary experiences and treasured memories even amidst the disease's adversities. Confronting life's challenges is less daunting when set against the backdrop of the magnificent Rockies or similar breathtaking landscapes, a testament to how our environment can significantly alter our experience of hardship.

There were days so overwhelming that all I could muster was to lie still and absorb the beauty outside my camper window, drawing strength from the serene views and the companionship of my faithful dog. Additionally, this book is a guide detailing the methodology behind selecting my destinations and the resources that facilitated my overlanding adventure, aimed at empowering others to embark on their own journeys of exploration and healing. The appendices at the back of this book provide these details.

People often inquire about the motivation behind my travel style. Simply put, immersing myself in the wonders of Mother Earth instills a deep sense of awe and an appreciation for the natural world. Whether it's the Northern Lights, towering waterfalls, vast prairies, or the daunting mountain ranges, each offers a profoundly moving spectacle. This pursuit of natural wonders fuels my adventurous spirit, inviting me to explore new landscapes, cultures, and personal challenges. Nature is my place of worship, evoking feelings of peace and a profound connection to something greater than myself. In our urbanized and digitized existence, venturing into remote natural environments allows me to disconnect, reflect, and find solace.

I acknowledge my privilege of being able to travel; I understand this isn't possible for everyone due to various constraints, like mobility or financial limitations. I hope this book offers a vicarious escape, a momentary respite in your own journey, whatever battle you may be facing.

"Winter's crispness beckons journeys inward, where the warmth of self-reflection resides."
– Unknown

Table of Contents

Introduction

A Lifetime of Adventure

My name is Thom, but my friends call me "Guyius" or "Big." I don't think the nickname is because of my size, though I am 6'3" and weigh about 250. I like to think it is because I have a "go big or go home" mentality. I am in my late sixties. When I am not traveling and am home, I like to consider myself a furniture designer and maker. When I retired, I built myself a workshop. I need to point out that it is not just any "workshop." The place has a bigger footprint than my house, sports a full basement, and an office over the shop. At first, I had a dream of being a kayak builder, and the shop was outfitted for exactly that purpose: twenty-foot ceilings to facilitate the storing of the kayaks. The woodworking machines are located along the exterior walls to allow for plenty of floor space for the kayaks to be built.

I had hoped to build a fleet of kayaks and sell them or rent them and provide guided tours of the various marshes, rivers, and bays on the cape. I quickly realized that with the amount of used plastic kayaks for sale or rent, and the price of plastic or fiberglass kayaks being far less than a custom-made wood kayak, this was not going to be an economical endeavor. I also realized that I did not have the temperament for retail. Tourists have their own special way of doing things that, if they were home, they would never do. There were too many rude know-it-alls and complainers for my taste. "Yes, there is a spider in your kayak, and no, you can't use another one. We are on an adventure trip, and this is the outdoors, after all; spiders do live out here."

After a year, I switched to being a furniture maker, and I am happy that I did. Some of my favorite moments are working in the shop, the garage doors wide open, the smell of the workshop's various wood smells interlaced with the salty morning air, and the morning light finding its way into the recesses of the shop.

Now, eleven years into retirement, I consider myself an adventurer or wanderer—depending upon the level of activity and location of my travels. Ever since I turned 40, adventure travel has seemed to be my thing. I am not by any means an adrenalin junkie, though I do like trying new sports or environments. The list of adventure trips I have been a part of is long. Some have been solo, others as part of a team.

I have scuba dived such places as the great barrier reef of Australia, Koko Crater in Hawaii, shore diving in Bonaire, boat diving Key Largo, spent ten days on a live-aboard while diving the Galapagos, and the Dos Ojos Cenotes of the Yucatan; backcountry skied or ski mountaineered in the Alps, Rockies, Chugash, Appalachia, and Green Mountains; rafting class-four rapids on the Snake, Dead, Nenana or Mendoza rivers; sea kayaking expeditions in Alaska, Belize, Exuma Islands, San Juan Islands, New Zealand or off the coast of Maine. It seemed that there was always an adventure I was either planning, participating in, or reveling in the afterglow of. Some of these trips included my daughters, especially as they grew older and started developing their own wanderlust that seemed to have enraptured me.

Currently, I travel with my trusted travel companion, Dexter. Dexter is one of those travel companions who loves to be on the road, excited to check out new places, and it's not uncommon for her to stick her head out the sunroof or window to let the sun warm her face or let the wind flow through her hair. She never complains unless it's time to take a bathroom break. Never do I hear the words, "Are we there yet?" "I'm hungry," or "I'm bored." Anyone traveling with children is aware of these refrains. None of these things from Dexter. She is just happy to be out there.

Dexter has spent most of her life on the road. She has already traveled to two countries, forty-five states, and seven provinces. All without a passport. Dexter is my three-year-old four-legged furry friend and is a beautiful black Labrador Retriever with lots of spirit, independence, and energy. She has spent so much time traveling and living in the truck's backseat that this has become her home. During the summer, while home, I keep the doors to the truck open so that the seats and interior do not get scorching hot. I cannot tell you how many times I have had to go searching for Dexter, only to find her in the backseat staring out the door, wondering what the commotion is all about. That's my dog—always hoping and ready for a road trip.

Why Travel Now?

I take these "walkabouts" because of a whole host of items. Realizing that I have more miles behind me than in front of me concerned me. Having the health issues of these past five years concerned me. Getting out of a bad marriage concerned me. Wondering what life is all about now concerned me. Wondering what my contribution is these days concerned me. Am I living the best life I can? It all concerned me.

This trip is about realizing who I am—trite I know—and where I want to go. With the health, relationship, and aging issues, I was forgetting what made me, me. While I haven't found all the answers yet—I have found a sense of calmness, contentment, and am re-invigorating the sense of curiosity and wonder that I had before. While I have had a fuller life than most, there is much more I would like to experience.

Being in such close quarters (as my camper is) forces one to take stock of what is important. Back home, I have all sorts of "things." Here in the camper, I can only have "things" that serve an immediate purpose. If it doesn't, I ask why I have it and what purpose it provides me. An interesting process that heretofore I had not undertaken.

As an example, I took way too much clothing and personal clutter along on this trip that I don't really use. Why did I bring them, and when do I think I will use them? An interesting process.

The individuals I encounter on my journey are reshaping my perspective, bringing clarity and new insights. I've met a diverse array of people, some seemingly anchored in a life of routine, hesitant to venture beyond the familiar confines of their small towns. They live within the bounds of safety, reluctant to embrace the unknown. Yet, others embody the spirit of transformation, boldly closing one chapter of their lives to begin anew. These are the adventurers who have made daring choices, like selling their homes, embracing minimalism, and charting a course toward a life markedly different from their past.

Risk, I've learned, is a concept that each person navigates differently. While some embrace it, eagerly seeking to discover and engage with the wider world, others prefer to tread cautiously, safeguarding what they have or aspire to attain. Neither approach is inherently right or wrong; they are simply different paths shaped by individual experiences and desires.

As for me, at this juncture in my life, I am drawn to the path of risk. I yearn to explore, immerse myself in new experiences, and absorb all I can from the vast tapestry of life. There's an urgency in this quest, a recognition that the time may come when I no longer possess the ability, the desire, or the chance to pursue such adventures.

Therefore, I embrace this phase with open arms, eager to see where this journey of risk-taking and exploration will lead me.

Thom Barrett

VISUAL JOURNEY!

Dive into the captivating landscapes of *Chasing My Northern Lights*. Scan this QR code or visit www.livinglifewhiledying.com/booksresources to access full-color, high-resolution images related to the locations and adventures described in my book. Let the visuals enrich your reading experience, guiding you through the mesmerizing odyssey of my journey.

Section 1

Planning the Adventure

Expedition's Prelude: A North American Odyssey

In the heart of a dreamer, a journey takes shape,
A grand expedition, an escape.
Across North America's vast domain,
From sun-drenched beaches to plains of rain.

Maps sprawl across the table wide,
Marking a path for the long, joyous ride.
Fall's tapestry in the East unfolds,
Winter's majesty in the North holds.

Each point on the map, a story to tell,
Of cities, forests, where spirits dwell.
The thrill of vistas yet unseen,
From azure coasts to valleys green.

Planning for seasons, a dance of time,
Fall's leafy trails, winter's frosty climb.
Spring's bloom waits in the journey's wake,
Each phase, a new memory to make.
The gear is gathered, each detail keen,
For trekking, skiing, and places in between.
The excitement of cultures, people to meet,
From bustling cities to quiet retreats.

With each step, a discovery anew,
Of oneself, of the world, in a view.
This tapestry of travel, rich and vast,
In each moment, lifetime's contrast.

Adventures planned under autumn's moon,
Departure awaits, can't come too soon.
The road calls with its endless allure,
In every mile, life's essence pure.

Adventure Traveling versus Casual Traveling

Several years ago, I asked my brother John to join me for a "ski vacation" in the Alps. I was young and adventurous, as was he. I had wanted to go in May—and he thought it was a bit late in the year, but since it was "Europe," maybe their ski season was a bit longer. This seemed plausible since we had skied Matterhorn together in July 1981 and encountered white-out conditions skiing. When he asked what ski area, I just mumbled Chamonix or Zermatt. What I didn't tell him immediately was that we were going to "ski" the famous "Haute Route." It would be a six-day traverse across the mountains and glaciers between Chamonix and Zermatt. This is ski mountaineering at its best, high in the mountains, hut to hut, with long climbs and stunning descents. A great example of adventure traveling.

I just told my brother that it would be an exciting time, and that he needed to be in great shape. What I didn't tell him was that we had avalanche training planned as part of the first few days of the trip; he would need his experience in rappelling, be able to ski tour for hours at a time (while carrying a 65lb backpack with all our equipment and necessities), learn to be proficient with self-arrest (using your ice axe to stop you from sliding off a cliff), and that we would descending steep slopes on fresh powder (or hard-packed or icy conditions) with a full backpack.

This is one of a few times when I was not entirely honest about what we were to accomplish on our trip. Since then, I have learned that I need to be clear with folks and that they understand what they have agreed to when they travel with me. For me, travel can come in one of two general types, and each has its own purpose and benefit and offers unique experiences and joys.

- Adventure travel is about the thrill, challenge, and immersive experience in often rugged environments.

- Casual travel leans more toward relaxation, comfort, and easy exploration of a destination.

All in all, he was a good sport, and we had quite the adventure. However, it was a while before he would go on a trip with me that he, himself, did not organize. We did go on trips afterward based more on casual travel (which he organized), like scuba diving in Bonaire (where our condo came with a cook and a maid) or fly-fishing in Jackson Hole (each night we ended up in the Four Seasons).

That said, I love to adventure travel—the more rugged and remote, the more I find myself alive.

Overlanding and Boondocking

Overlanding is a unique blend of remote travel, off-roading, and camping, a passion that originated in the early 1900s with Australia's development of long-distance travel routes.[2] It's an art form that involves setting out on remarkable journeys to explore uncharted or lesser-known areas. This kind of adventure means embracing the unknown, committing to a path of discovery, and immersing oneself in a variety of cultures and landscapes.

Envision a journey where you navigate through rugged landscapes, cross tranquil bodies of water, and experience the wonder of nature's beauty—this captures the spirit of overlanding. It's a way of life characterized by self-sufficiency, a deep-seated love for adventure, the skills of survival, and the joy of discovering stunning environments and engaging with different cultures. Overlanding isn't just a way to travel; it's a journey into the heart of adventure and self-discovery.

Boondocking involves camping in your camper without any hookups. This requires "boondockers" to be self-contained and bring their own water supply, power system, and wastewater management. "Dry camping" or "wild camping" are other ways to describe this type of camping. Boondocking is normally free, though sometimes a permit is required. I often wondered where the term" boondocking" originated and was surprised to learn that the expression is from the Tagalog (Filipino) word bundók ("mountain"). I always thought that the term "boondock" was an American idiom applied to an out-of-the-way area considered backward and unsophisticated by city folk. You learn something new every day.

---

[2] Eleonor Segura, "What Is Overlanding? An Automotive Overview of The Awesome Activity," MotorTrend, November 30, 2020, https://www.motortrend.com/news/what-is-overlanding/.

My rig is built for off-roading and boondocking, which I plan and love to do as much as possible. When you boondock, it's just you, your camper, and the wilderness around you (if you are not boondocking in a Walmart parking lot, which happens from time to time).

The Rig

The rig we travel in is the result of years of experience as road warriors. It is not the most fuel-efficient, but it has seen some rugged terrain and challenging weather. Since my travels usually include travel in the worst winter conditions, this rig has proven itself time and again. The rig consists of a slide-in truck camper with my Willy Jeep flat towed behind the truck.

The truck is a Chevy Silverado 2500HD with the Z71 package and other off-road necessities, like a bull bar and additional lighting. It is also equipped with two batteries: a starter and a deep cycle. They are separated via a battery isolator so that one does not drain the other when there is a problem. I pulled out the back seat, and in its place is a DIY cabinet full of the tools that I would need on the road and a place for Dexter to stay.

The camper is a NuCamp Cirrus 820 and is equipped with features such as dual propane and dual battery compartments, a motorized eight-foot side awning, an air conditioner, and Titan electric jacks with remote control. I also installed a hundred-watt solar panel (that I am looking to expand before the next road trip in 2024) and upgraded the standard batteries. It has all the needed amenities: bathroom, hot water, kitchen with a stove and fridge, comfortable sleeping quarters for two and Dexter, a table with a pair of captain chairs, radiant heating system, an outstanding stereo system, cell enhancer, Skylink hookup, and a moonroof to watch the nightly shows across the sky while you sit comfortably in your bed. The Jeep contains the necessary toys for the trip: skis, downhill (both powder and rock) and backcountry, fly-fishing gear, snowshoes, camping gear, and a winch.

The Jeep is a Willy Wrangler equipped for the off-road: heavy-duty shocks and road rails, locking rear differential, high clearance fenders, skid plates, performance tires, tow hooks, performance brakes, a bull bar, additional lighting, modified interior, a rooftop tent for those overnight offroad excursions, and a nomad kitchen (which has a stove, sink, table, and all of the utensils necessary for cooking and eating). The Jeep is used during extended stays when I set up camp. Depending upon where we are, its use is varied. My favorite pastime with the Jeep is rock crawling and fly-fishing.

Both vehicles are outfitted with a winch, axe, shovel, tow ropes, first aid kits, traction pads, and Hi-lift jacks. Given that both will be used for traveling at some point, I needed to have them equally equipped for self-rescue and safety. See Appendix A for the specifics on each of these items.

The Northern Lights

Since I started down this path of adventure travel, which was back in 1996, seeing the Northern Lights (NL) had not been high on my bucket list; there were a lot more things that I wanted to do. Lately, seeing the NL is something that I wanted to say I had finally witnessed. The captivating photos I had seen and folks' experiences about this extraordinary event made it something I needed to experience for myself—this celestial dance across the night sky. Thus, the Northern Lights or Bust Tour originated.

For those who may not be aware, the Northern Lights, also known as the aurora borealis, are natural light displays that predominantly occur in the high-latitude regions around the Arctic and Antarctic. These displays are caused by charged particles from the sun colliding with the Earth's atmosphere.[3] The scientific explanation is that the sun emits charged particles into space, which travel toward Earth. These events are referred to as solar winds. When these charged particles hit our atmosphere and collide with oxygen and nitrogen, energy in the form of light is released. The colors we see result from this.

Fascinatingly, the variety of colors and patterns displayed by the Northern Lights are influenced by the type of gas—oxygen or nitrogen—and the altitude at which the collisions occur. Oxygen, when high in the sky, tends to emit deep red hues, while at lower altitudes, it may give off vibrant green or brownish-red shades. Nitrogen, on the other hand, is responsible for producing vivid blues and purplish-reds. Green is typically the most observed color, but the auroras can also dazzle with red, yellow, blue, and violet. The Northern Lights manifest in an array of patterns, from diffused glows to arcs, rippling curtains, or even shooting rays that illuminate the night sky.

---

[3] "Aurora," National Geographic, accessed January 24, 2024, https://education. nationalgeographic.org/resource/aurora/.

These lights are not just confined to high latitudes; during intense solar activity, they can often be observed further south than usual.

Equally intriguing are the myriad of myths, legends, and stories that indigenous and ancient cultures have woven around the Northern Lights. These celestial phenomena have been interpreted as omens, spirits, or even the souls of ancestors. For instance, many Inuit tribes view them as the spirits of the deceased playing with a walrus skull or as the spirits of the animals they hunted, reflecting deep-seated beliefs and cultural interpretations about the afterlife.

The allure of the Northern Lights, for me, lies in witnessing this majestic natural wonder steeped in such rich cultural lore.

The Plan, the Tools, and the Result

Planning a journey sparks a thrill in me, almost akin to the adventure itself. It's a deep dive into the details of this journey, uncovering hidden gems, which usually ends up stirring a longing to embark sooner. The process of researching, envisioning the sights I'll witness, the experiences awaiting me, and strategizing the most fulfilling path is exhilarating. Through this exploration, I discover the rhythms of the place—the ebb and flow of its busy seasons and the secrets of its lands, be it BLM (Bureau of Land Management) or national/state forests (these provide great opportunities for dispersed camping). I gather insights from fellow travelers thru their blogs, painting a vibrant picture of what lies ahead. Preferring solitude over crowds, I aim for the quieter off-season, and my frugal nature seeks the charm of camping without cost. Each step in this planning journey is a building block to an adventure tailored to my tastes.

My ritual of preparation is a blend of old and new, transforming my workspace into a personalized command hub. I begin by decluttering my office, creating a clean slate. In anticipation, I gather books and ideas related to my upcoming journey. The core of my ritual involves spreading out extensive maps of Canada and the USA, especially detailed ones of Alaska, British Columbia, and the Yukon, across tables and walls, vividly depicting the landscapes ahead. A prominently displayed large monthly calendar provides a timeline and visual anchor.

This arrangement not only visually stimulates but also serves as a tangible reference throughout my planning process. I then integrate digital tools into this physical landscape, utilizing apps like Google Maps (www.google.com) for routes, Road Trippers (www.roadtrippers.com) for discovering unique spots, Onx Off-road (www.onxmaps.com) for remote trails, Trip-It (www.tripit.com) for keeping the details of receipts for transportation, campgrounds, etc. handy on the web. This combination of tactile and digital elements creates a comprehensive and immersive planning experience, setting the stage for my adventure.

The primary hurdle for this journey involved gathering precise details about dispersed camping sites, road closures, and accessible off-road trails during winter months—especially given that "winter" varies widely, with snowfall starting as early as September in some regions. Additionally, establishing a central theme or focus for the trip is crucial. While a two-week holiday might naturally form its own narrative, embarking on a multi-month tour necessitates a more targeted approach. Concentrating on specific interests or activities can significantly reduce the stress of feeling obliged to explore every available option in each area visited. For this trip, the themes were clear: traversing exciting highways and byways, conquering summits and passes, exploring unbeaten paths, delighting in the thrill of skiing, and savoring exquisite food and drink in the most unique locales. These themes don't just guide my journey; they promise a rich tapestry of adventures waiting to unfold.

On the road, my journey is assisted by a suite of digital tools. Allstays Truck and Travel (www.allstays.com) becomes my guide, pinpointing fuel stops and rest areas with ease. Campendium (www.campendium.com) lends its crowd-sourced wisdom to discover spots for free camping, essential dump stations, and, if necessary, RV parks. Google Maps, with its treasure trove of maps pre-downloaded for offline use, ensures I'm never truly lost. And, of course, my truck's integrated GPS navigation stands as my steadfast companion, leading the way through twists and turns. Together, these tools form the digital convoy that keeps my road adventure smooth and informed.

One crucial tip I'd emphasize about using Campendium is always to check the date of the review. I learned this the hard way one evening. Exhausted and in need of a spot to boondock, I turned to Campendium and found what seemed like a perfect location just ten miles away. Generally, Campendium has steered me right.

But that night, after navigating a long and bumpy dirt road in the dark, with snow beginning to fall, I was greeted not by a welcoming campsite but by a locked gate leading to a private road. The once-open land for dispersed camping was no longer accessible. A glance back at the review revealed its age—it was several years old. I hadn't checked the date, a simple step that would have saved me the trouble. Despite this mishap, I still find Campendium reviews quite trustworthy; it's just a matter of ensuring their freshness.

Trip Route Planning Results

The overall trip route is as follows. This is what I had planned to accomplish.

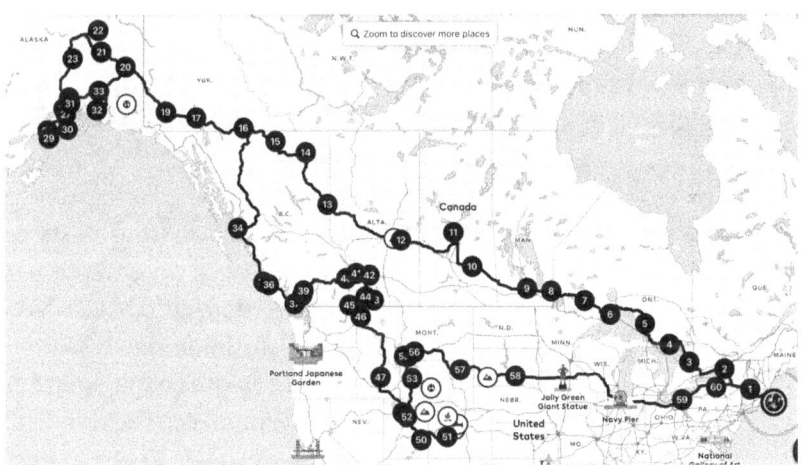

Insurance

Most may not consider this topic when they embark on a road trip, aside from making certain that their AAA is up to date. When you are traveling, as I will be, certain types of travel insurance may be required. Since I will be embarking in a foreign country, it's important to be well-prepared with the appropriate types of insurance to ensure your safety and financial security. Contained in the appendices is a brief write-up of the types of insurance typically recommended. For me, I was interested in the following types of insurance:

1. **Medical Insurance:** Perhaps the most critical insurance for any traveler. Ensure that your policy covers medical expenses for injuries or illnesses that might occur abroad, including medical evacuation if necessary. Not all domestic health insurance plans cover international travel. My insurance would treat any claims as out-of-network, so I didn't need to purchase a separate travel health insurance policy.

2. **Emergency Evacuation Insurance:** This covers the costs of transportation to a medical facility in case of an emergency, especially vital if you are traveling to remote or underserved areas like the Yukon, Alaska, and British Columbia. It's often included in travel medical insurance, but check the specifics of your coverage. Since I wasn't planning on the medical insurance, I did purchase a plan from Faye.

3. **Accidental Death and Dismemberment Insurance (AD&D):** This insurance pays a benefit if you die or are dismembered in an accident while traveling. It's a grim thing to consider, but it can provide important financial support to your family in the worst-case scenario.

4. **Adventure and Sports Coverage:** If your expedition includes activities like mountain climbing, off-roading, backcountry

skiing, or other high-risk sports, make sure you get a policy that doesn't exclude these activities. Standard travel insurance might not cover accidents occurring during "adventure activities."

Before purchasing any insurance, it's important to read the fine print and understand what is and isn't covered. It's also a good idea to purchase your insurance from a reputable company and to carry proof of your insurance and their emergency contact numbers with you during your trip. In addition, consider the stability and healthcare infrastructure of your destination, as this might influence the type and extent of coverage you need. Always plan for the unexpected and make sure you're covered for any eventualities that could occur while you're away from home.

During this trip, I had to visit the ER twice in Canada and once at a First Nations trauma center. My insurance did treat it like an out-of-network claim.

Objectives of the Trip

We (Dexter and I) will head north from Cape Cod, then travel across Canada, and then north again to Alaska. The plan is to ultimately make it to Alaska by late September or early October. We will leave my home on Cape Cod in September 2022 and return sometime in May 2023.

I have several objectives for this trip:

1. Revel in the beauty of the Northern Lights.
2. Venture off the beaten path to explore various roadways rich in history and unique challenges.
3. Embark on a skiing adventure across Canada and the Western USA, experiencing the thrill of downhill skiing and the serenity of backcountry skiing in at least twenty-five different areas (both lift-served and backcountry).
4. Engage with the tranquil sport of fly-fishing in the pristine rivers of Montana and Wyoming.
5. Explore and appreciate the diverse natural beauty of ten different state or provincial parks.
6. Embrace the freedom of boondocking, immersing myself in nature whenever and wherever possible.

I don't like making things so rigid in the planning that it stops spontaneity while traveling. I do like knowing what the options are as much as possible. Normally, if the destination is very busy or too touristy, I avoid the location entirely. Crowds are not my thing at all. That is one reason I like traveling in the off-season and winter.

While in Alaska, we will spend a month (weather permitting) traveling to Denali and over to the Kenai Peninsula, and then spend time in Homer, Valdez, and Hines before heading south again. After Alaska, there is a whole other game plan in play that will take us down the west coast of BC. Then the ski portion of the trip begins, including the

Powder Highway of BC ("Powder Highway" is the nickname given to the legendary snow-blessed route along Canada's 95A, which consists of a 630-mile loop through interior British Columbia's Kootenay Rockies and connects over sixty different powder providers), and then down to Idaho, Utah, Colorado, Wyoming and finally Montana. When spring sets in, then it's fly-fishing in Montana and Wyoming.

The goal is to have magnificent photos and compelling stories documenting my chase and capture of the Northern Lights. I am beyond stoked.

The following is a summary of general topics that I considered when planning this multiple-month overland excursion. You may want to develop your own general checklist when planning your overland trip.

1. **Objectives and Itinerary**: Define the purpose or objectives of your trip. Outline your intended route and major destinations. Decide on the must-visit places and those that can be skipped if time or resources are constrained.

2. **Duration and Timing**: Decide the length of time you'll spend at each location and consider the best time of year to visit each place on your itinerary, considering weather conditions, tourist seasons, and local events.

3. **Transportation and Logistics**: Determine how you will move from one place to another. Consider the logistics of border crossings if your expedition is international. Plan your route carefully, considering the availability of food, fuel, propane, road conditions, emergency or medical clinics, and potential places to pull out.

4. **Budget**: Establish a realistic budget, considering all possible expenses such as transportation, accommodation, food, per-

mits, gear, emergency funds, and insurance. Determine how you'll manage expenses and track your spending throughout the journey.

5. **Accommodation**: Whether you decide to use RV parks, campgrounds (like KOA), boondocks, hotels, or a mixture of each, planning is necessary. Booking accommodations for at least the initial part of your journey, or for places where you expect high demand, would be wise.

6. **Communication Plan**: Establish a plan for staying in touch with family and friends. Consider how you will access the internet, phone networks, or satellite communications. Set up a regular check-in schedule.

7. **Equipment and Supplies**: List all the gear and supplies you'll need, including clothing, camping gear, navigation tools, first aid, cooking equipment, and any specialized items relevant to your expedition's objectives. Consider the weight and space limitations of your transportation method.

8. **Permits and Documentation**: Research and obtain any necessary visas, permits, and other documentation required for your destinations, especially if you're venturing into protected or sensitive areas.

9. **Health and Safety**: Assess the health risks in the areas you'll be visiting and get any required vaccinations or medications. Learn about the local wildlife and how to coexist safely. Determine what safety gear and training you might need and plan for emergency situations, including having a reliable way to communicate and navigate.

10. **Insurance**: Obtain appropriate travel insurance that covers the entire duration of your expedition and all the activities you plan to undertake. This insurance should include medical

insurance, emergency evacuation insurance, accident and death and dismemberment insurance (AD&D), and adventure and sports coverage.

11. **Cultural Research**: Understand and respect the cultures you'll be visiting. Learn about local customs, language basics, and laws to ensure a respectful and smooth interaction with local populations.

12. **Environmental Considerations**: Plan to minimize your environmental impact. Understand the "Leave No Trace" principles and how you can apply them throughout your journey.

Section 2

Traverse across Canada

Canadian Tapestry: A Journey's Melody

From east to west, a journey's call,
In Canada's embrace, we find our all.
First, Ontario's waters clear,
With lakes and falls that draw us near.

In every ripple, a story told,
By shores where tales of old unfold.
Niagara's thunder, a mighty sound,
In its spray, our spirits bound.

Onto the prairies, fields of gold,
Where skies and lands in beauty hold.
A vastness so profound, so pure,
In these open arms, we feel secure.

Horizon meets the traveler's gaze,
In these wheat seas, one could laze.
The sun sets in a prairie fire,
Painting scenes that never tire.

Then rise the mountains, peaks so high,
Their majesty piercing the sky.
Rockies stand in regal grace,
In their shadows, our hearts race.

Snow-capped guardians of the land,
Beneath them, our petty worries stand.
Each vista a breathtaking sight,
In their presence, we find our light.

But more than scenes, it's people's warmth,
That makes this land of the north.
In every town, a friendly face,
In Canada, we find our place.

A Homecoming of Sorts

I am one of those individuals who have migrated to the US based on their folks' decisions. Born in Windsor, Ontario, in 1956, we moved to Detroit, MI, in 1963 and have spent sixty years living in the USA. Consequently, I do not have the same familiarity with my birth country as I do with the United States. Exploring every province and territory of Canada has been a longstanding ambition of mine. In recent years, my travels have concentrated on areas closer to home, particularly the Maritime provinces: New Brunswick, Nova Scotia, Prince Edward Island, and Newfoundland. These regions have been my playground for kayaking, camping, and hiking, allowing me to delve into their natural beauty and geological marvels.

My travels in the maritime provinces have led me to some extraordinary experiences: I've walked along the ocean floor at Hopewell Rocks in the Bay of Fundy at low tide, admiring the impressive rock formations that rise above; I've journeyed along the Cabot Trail, absorbing the stunning views of Cape Breton's rugged coastline and highlands; the vivid red sandstone cliffs have enchanted me, the remarkable dune formations, and the wetlands of Prince Edward Island; I've explored the iconic lighthouses and the rugged granite coastlines with their unique rock structures in Nova Scotia; and I've kayaked through the majestic fiords of Gros Morne in Newfoundland. Each of these adventures has been memorable and unique.

This year, the focus of this segment was the journey from Ontario to British Columbia and then the Yukon on my way to Alaska. Traveling across Canada is an immersion in some of the world's most breathtaking natural wonders. The journey began from my hometown of Marstons Mills, MA, which is a village based on the East Coast in a place called Cape Cod. The Cape is known for its wide expanses of sand, dunes, picturesque lighthouses, iconic fishing villages, and quaint, weathered-shingle homes.

Chasing My Northern Lights

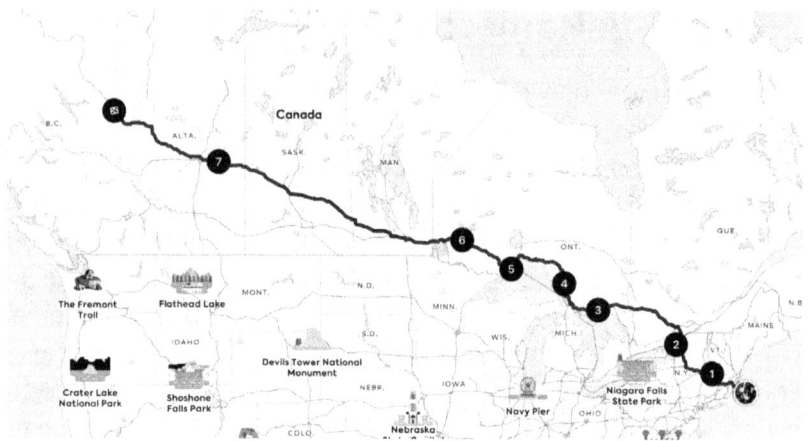

The Adventure Begins

Date: September 6, 2022
Weather: 68°F Wind 9 mph Humidity 93%
Location: Marstons Mills, MA, USA

Today marked the initial phase of the journey, a "shake-out" trip designed to stay relatively close to home, covering just two hundred miles, in case any issues arose. Before setting out, both the truck and Jeep underwent their routine pre-trip maintenance checks. This included tire upgrades, oil changes, and a thorough inspection of the undercarriage. The Jeep's brakes were also replaced. My contact at Sullivan Tire confirmed that everything was in top condition, with both vehicles primed for the epic journey ahead.

For the first day, I chose to stick to the main highways—taking Route 495 to Route 90, and then following Route 22 through the Berkshires. While the scenic Route 2 (Mohawk Trail) along the Massachusetts, New Hampshire, and Vermont borders was an option, I opted for the faster route to expedite my entry into Canada. Having driven Route 2 countless times on my ski trips to Vermont, I was well-acquainted with its picturesque landscape. It's a route I highly recommend for anyone in the area during the fall, as its beauty is unparalleled.

The camper and Jeep were meticulously packed for an eight-month expedition across three seasons. Balancing the need for clothing, tools, and emergency supplies was a challenge due to limited storage space. I decided to purchase any additional clothing on the road as needed. Food essentials were stored, and recreational gear was neatly organized in the Jeep. Departing from home took longer than anticipated, especially when I encountered issues with the running lights on the Jeep. The problem was traced back to the electrical harness connecting the Jeep to the truck—a blown fuse and a ground wire not properly attached to the truck's frame. This hiccup was a useful test of my toolkit, which, I discovered, lacked an adequate variety of fuses. A quick trip to the hardware store to stock up on fuses was needed before hitting the road.

Our destination was Clarksburg, MA, a quaint town nestled in the Berkshire Mountains. We reached Clarksburg State Park smoothly. The truck and Jeep performed well, the tow bar was effective, and Dexter, my canine companion, was content. The drive from Cape Cod to Clarksburg was picturesque, capturing the essence of Massachusetts, from the coastal charm of the Cape to the rolling hills of central Massachusetts and the idyllic small towns and mountain vistas of the Berkshires. Thankfully, by taking Route 495, we avoided the usual traffic snarls near Boston.

As I drove, various thoughts preoccupied my mind: had I secured everything at home? What would become of my garden? Was the outdoor water supply turned off? These concerns led me to consider creating a home-close-out checklist for future trips, which has been included in the appendices at the back of this book. At least I wasn't fretting about leaving an iron on; the one I own isn't for clothes but for woodworking, used to smooth out dents in wood. I knew it was off as I had brought it along for ski maintenance to apply wax.

I remember I had to send a few texts in the morning, informing friends that my garden was ripe for harvesting, especially the potatoes, peppers, and tomatoes. I also needed to contact my brother, David, to check if he could ensure the outdoor water was properly shut off. The last thing I wanted was to return to burst pipes in the winter.

I also realized I hadn't thoroughly researched the camping area at Clarksburg State Park, where I stopped for the night, as most facilities were already closed by September. Only water was available. This was a reminder to better check the amenities of future state parks before setting out.

The evening sky was overcast, so a campfire was off the table tonight. I always carry my solo stove bonfire for times when there's no available fire ring or if the existing one is unusable due to snow, rain, or debris. It's quite efficient, accommodating both wood and dura flame logs. But I planned for an early night anyway since the next day was set to be long. My goal was to cross the Canada/USA border and reach Kingston, Ontario, in time for a multi-day kayaking adventure around the Thousand Islands National Park. I also wanted to scout the area before embarking on the kayak trip.

However, I realized after a night's sleep that the new mattress cover I installed wasn't to my liking. The leather was too slippery and cold for comfort, so I made a mental note to pick up a flannel sheet. Another issue was the lack of Wi-Fi at the park, limiting my ability to check weather and travel conditions. I need to ensure that my cell signal enhancer connects automatically in the future—another lesson from this shake-out run.

The morning brought a serene start to the day. With coffee brewing and its aroma filling the camper, I enjoyed a stunning lakeside view from my parked camper. Sipping coffee while looking out over the water was a wonderfully tranquil way to begin the day.

Thousand Islands National Park

Date: September 7, 2022
Weather: 75°F Mostly Cloudy
Location: I-81, Alexandria Bay, Ontario, Canada

Today marked the significant transition to the USA/Canada border. I couldn't help but feel a bit anxious about the possibility of Canadian immigration conducting a thorough search of my camper and Jeep. My concern wasn't about finding anything illicit; rather, I dreaded the prospect of a lengthy stop and the hassle of reorganizing the camper post-search. I recalled a similar experience last year at the Montana/Canada border, where the inspection lasted a few hours. The border guard was all business, devoid of friendliness. The atmosphere grew tenser when I was directed to a separate area for further questioning, with commands like "Do this," "Go here," "Open the Jeep," and "Stay here while we search the camper."

As I heard them rummaging through my belongings, my imagination conjured images of a chaotic camper interior, with belongings scattered and overturned. Being an "old hippie" with a truck camper, long hair, and a beard, I seemed to fit some stereotype they were wary of. They found nothing of concern except for some food items I should've thrown away and some weed paraphernalia—neither of which was illegal. I received a warning about the food, which they confiscated, but thankfully, the camper wasn't left in disarray.

This time, as I approached the checkpoint between New York and Canada, I took precautions. I cleared the fridge of any produce, meat, or perishables, limited my alcohol to one bottle, and removed all weed-related items. Prepared for the worst, I hoped for a smoother experience at the border.

Once I regained cell service and confirmed my route, I realized the checkpoint was further than anticipated, yet conveniently just a few miles from Thousand Lakes National Park. The drive through Massachusetts and New York was picturesque, with the forests still brimming with greenery as autumn hadn't yet begun to cast its colorful spell.

Crossing into Canada meant driving over the St. Lawrence Seaway via the Thousand Islands Bridge. The bridge offered stunning views, though navigating it with my rig required full concentration, especially as the wind made the drive slightly challenging. Thankfully, the crossing was smooth and without incident.

Approaching the checkpoint, I couldn't help but feel a flutter of nerves, uncertain of what lay ahead. It was a relief to know that Covid tests and the previously mandatory online forms were no longer required. The border guard I encountered was a pleasant surprise—friendly and smiling. She inquired about my well-being, my plans in Canada, and the duration of my stay. Before I knew it, she wished me a good day, and I was through the checkpoint. This smooth and hassle-free experience was unexpected but very welcome. I was relieved to have passed through customs without any complications.

Upon my arrival at the national park, it appeared quite deserted. Luckily, I managed to catch a ranger leaving a building. He was incredibly amiable, confirming that most park services were indeed closed for the season, which was attributed to staffing issues and a general slowdown. He helpfully suggested a few activities in the area, mainly focusing on scenic hikes and viewpoints, which was excellent advice. This was my second interaction in Canada, and like the first, it was with someone friendly and engaging.

Next, I headed to the kayak rental shop, only to discover it was also closed. A quick check of my emails revealed that my planned, guided kayak tour had been canceled due to Covid cases, leading to the shop's closure. This left me with some unexpected free time, which was a welcome break. After a busy summer, some unplanned rest days seemed like a blessing. Back at the campsite, Dexter and I took a leisurely walk to appreciate our surroundings and ponder the next few days. I even set up my hammock and indulged in a peaceful nap. The campsite was tranquil, with no one around, and the weather was pleasant at seventy-eight degrees, with partial cloud cover.

I found myself torn between annoyance and relief regarding the kayak trip cancellation. I was frustrated at the lack of communication and alternatives offered, yet part of me was relieved. The prospect of avoiding the discomfort of a dry suit, uneven camping terrain, and spending time with strangers was somewhat appealing. In hindsight, since I hadn't checked my email earlier, I acknowledged my part in this and chose to appreciate the unexpected break.

Chutes Provincial Park

Date: September 9–11, 2022
Weather: 78°F Clear
Location: Sables-Spanish Rivers, Ontario

The landscapes in Ontario present a stark contrast to those of New England. Here, the terrain is richly verdant, teeming with dense forests and abundant water bodies like lakes, rivers, and ponds, though it lacks the mountainous backdrop of New England.

Navigating has been quite straightforward, thanks largely to my truck's GPS-based navigation system. My cell service, however, has been less reliable, with limited coverage and slow data speeds. This makes downloading maps or gathering information from the internet a task that requires foresight. I plan to make the most of Wi-Fi spots whenever they're available.

I've just reached Chutes Provincial Park, nestled in Sables-Spanish Rivers, Ontario, and conveniently situated only a kilometer from the Trans-Canada Highway. The park is beautifully set up, offering a picturesque drive leading to the campsite. I'm looking forward to exploring its hiking trails, which promise captivating views of waterfalls and the river gorge.

The park's intriguing history stretches back to the early 20th century.[4] In those days, loggers cut down trees during winter, laying them on the frozen Aux Sables River. With the arrival of spring, as ice and snow melted, thousands of pine logs were sent floating down the river. Logging chutes were constructed to manage difficult sections,

---

[4] Meg Cossmann, "This Ontario Park Is a Scenic Winter Escape with Waterfalls and Rapids," blogTO, February 4, 2023, https://www.blogto.com/travel/2023/02/chutes-provincial-park-ontario/.

like the main falls in Chutes. These structures, often narrow and sloped, made of wood or metal, were essential in rugged terrains where traditional transportation was impractical. They facilitated the movement of logs from higher to lower areas or directly into waterways, reducing friction and ensuring a smooth descent.

The historical significance of these chutes is noteworthy. They efficiently transported logs to mills and rivers for downstream floating or loading areas. Their design varied, from simple straight paths to more complex ones with turns and controlled descents.

It's fascinating to learn how integral lakes, rivers, and other waterways were to loggers, not just for transportation but also for storage, minimizing fire risks, cleaning logs, and preventing premature drying. Cargo mills used floating log booms to store logs before milling.

Though the use of logging chutes has declined with modern advancements, their role in the history of logging, particularly in areas with challenging landscapes, remains a significant chapter. It's an intriguing thought, being at Chutes Provincial Park, where these innovative structures once played a vital role.

Once Dexter and I had settled into the campsite, we set out to explore the campground, with Dexter eagerly leading the way along the path to the falls. As we neared the falls, a distinct humming sound greeted us, growing louder with each step. I even noticed a slight vibration underfoot as we walked. Reaching the falls, we were enveloped in a light mist and the deep rumble of cascading water. The falls themselves were a series of tiered cascades, each forming its own pool before flowing into the next—a truly picturesque sight, enhanced by the emerging amber and yellow hues of the surrounding foliage.

As I walked along the rocky edge, Dexter contentedly played in the water near the shore, wisely choosing not to venture too deep. Our journey along the Twin Bridges Trail, following the Aux Sables River upstream, was a visual feast of rapids, cascades, and waterfalls. The trail wound along the river, offering several vantage points and lookouts. The sunlight, filtering through the trees and catching in the mist, created a twinkling effect that was simply enchanting. Pausing to absorb the magic of the moment, I felt deeply connected to the surrounding beauty.

Gradually moving away from the falls, the thunderous roar softened to a gentle, rhythmic flow of water. Returning to our campsite, we were greeted by a beautiful sunset, rounding off our day perfectly with a serene campfire. It was a fitting end to a day filled with natural wonder.

Lake Superior Provincial Park

Date: September 15–17, 2022
Weather: 32°F Rainy
Location: Old Woman Bay, Ontario

The morning's plan was to brew a cup of coffee, hook the Jeep to the truck's tow bar, and leave early for Lake Superior Provincial Park. For some reason, the routine of connecting the Jeep to the truck's towbar was a bit more challenging than usual. I do not know if it was that I had only one cup of coffee, or that I didn't have my usual breakfast of toast and peanut butter, but it took longer than normal. Our early start was no longer an early start, and I wished I had grabbed something to eat. Nonetheless, the drive from Chutes Provincial Park to Lake Superior Provincial Park was enjoyable. We saw sprawling boreal forests with their mix of spruce, pine, and deciduous trees. One of the aspects of this trip through Ontario that I was not prepared for was the number of freshwater bodies. They ranged from rushing rivers to tranquil lakes, often right along the highway. The rugged terrain of the Canadian Shield, with its striking rock formations, is becoming increasingly apparent as we drive north.

Lake Superior Provincial Park, located in the Northern Ontario wilderness, is on the edge of Lake Superior. The park is extremely rugged—a vast wilderness on the edge of forested hills, crystal clear lakes, tumbling streams, and a rocky coastline. This Provincial Park is a designated Dark Sky Preserve certified by the Royal Astronomical Society of Canada.

We were fortunate to have a campsite near the beach. As we spent the late afternoon hiking up and down the beach, Dexter was in dog heaven. She had a vast beach to run and play; there was not another soul to be seen but plenty of waterfowl to chase. During the evening, we sat on the beach and watched the shooting stars as Mother Earth presented her form of fireworks. It was a beautiful display. What a lovely, starry night.

Sleeping Giant Provincial Park

Date: September 18–19, 2022
Weather: 60°F Clear
Location: Thunder Bay, Ontario

Sleeping Giant Provincial Park is located on the Sibley Peninsula, Northwestern Ontario, just east of Thunder Bay, on Lake Superior. The seasonal community of Silver Islet is located on the southern tip of the peninsula. The primary feature of the park is the Sleeping Giant, which is most visible from the city of Thunder Bay. There is one National Park in the States that I have wanted to visit for a while, and this might be the closest I ever get to it—Isle Royale National Park. As the crow flies, it's only fifty miles away.

The drive from the Lake Superior Provincial Park presented stunning panoramic views of Lake Superior. There was a gradual change in elevation and, with it, an increase in views of the ruggedness of the Canadian Shield, with its rocky outcrops. The colors were really starting to change, and the golds were becoming more prevalent. As I approached the Sleeping Giant Provincial Park, glimpses of the peninsular and the hills that look like a sleeping giant could be seen.

When I arrived at the campsite, I must have spent twenty minutes looking for the electrical power for the site. I thought it was odd that the power set-up was on a different side than what I was used to in the US. When I did find it, I realized that my cord, which is usually long enough for most instances, was woefully short. Thankfully, I am used to boondocking and just settled in with a campfire. The next day, I went to the park ranger to see what I could do about my site, and they had long cords for rent. Apparently, I am not the only one that suffers from short cords. The site was right on the water, so I have nothing to complain about. All great.

Second day here—it is very peaceful. I have the good fortune to be in a protected campsite right on Marie Louise Lake with a gentle onshore breeze. I feel very lucky to have this serene time and space. I can see why this park is called Sleeping Giant—the hillside looks like someone lying down. This park is very pretty. The sunsets have been stunning.

Just down the road from the park, on the Sibley Peninsula, there is a village that remains from the silver mining days. Its claim to fame is that for fourteen years, it was the world's richest silver mine (1870–1884).[5] While mining has stopped, tourism appears strong. The rejuvenated Silver Islet General Store is a lovely iconic landmark that first opened in 1871. I had the good fortune to spend some time there with the owners, Sandy and Jeff Korkola. They purchased the property in 2021 and have done a great job of restoring the property. Sandy's family purchased the property in 1985, but unfortunately, due to family health reasons, the store closed in 2015. Now, the Tea Room is once again a vibrant café offering light lunches and homemade baked goods like pies and the delicious cinnamon bun. While I was there, Sandy's parents were manning kitchen duties. The ambiance was welcoming, and the treats were so good that I went there both days I was there to grab coffee and the infamous cinnamon rolls—not disappointed in the least.

As I often do when I am at peace, I think. Think about where I am and how I was able to get here. Today, I uncovered something that has been nipping at the recesses of my consciousness of late and was finally coming into perspective. It has to do with getting older and how to deal with the change.

When does one realize they are "older" and not physically able to do the things that they once did with ease? I, for one, have always been

---

[5] Elle Andra-Warner, "Iconic Silver Islet General Store and Tea Room Is Re-Opening," Northern Wilds Magazine, July 29, 2021, https://northernwilds.com/iconic-silver-islet-general-store-and-tea-room-is-re-opening/.

independent. I like to do things by myself that involve pushing the envelope of my skills to some degree—not solo climbing or base jumping, but kayaking in the ocean on solo expeditions, solo back-country ski trips, or hikes. This summer, when I took my seventeen-year-old nephew Troy out to kayak, we experienced some bad weather. Normally, it was not an issue, but when I tried to get back to shore, I realized I no longer had the strength to power my way through the waves, and it really concerned me.

I used to relish this, using the waves to propel me onto the shore and loving it. This time, I was fearful of broaching and flipping over and tried what I could just to power forward. When I finally beached on shore, I was shaking like a leaf. It forced me to take pause. I barely had the strength to take care of myself; forget about having the strength to help Troy if anything would have happened while he was in the kayak at sea. That has troubled me—not being able to physically take care of others if there is a problem. That has always been my thing—the guy with enough skill and strength to deal with anything and everything. I am no longer that—now, I am just a participant.

What I have also realized is that if I want to continue doing things like this, I need to seek venues that are more in line with my physical strength and rely more on my skills to a greater degree. For instance, instead of sea kayaking in rough weather, I should look for a smooth lake that would allow skill to take control and not just brute force. Or maybe move from a kayak to a canoe. Or maybe not at all.

I know that I do not want just to stop doing things. I need to adjust my expectations and pursue interests that are more age (strength) appropriate (now I understand why old guys like to play golf). Also need to come to accept that tranquility (safety) versus adrenaline rush should be the direction I pursue. Without realizing it, I did this regarding skiing last year. I spent most of my time on the blue and green trails and avoided the moguls, blacks, and double blacks. I still enjoyed the skiing and was still feeling challenged. So, that is a good example of the change in mindset I need to adopt. Another example is traveling in guided groups, such as with organizations like Vermont Biking Tours (VBT), the retail outfitter REI, or the National Outdoor Leadership School (NOLS). In the event there is a problem, others are around who will be able to assist.

Another solution is to work out and get stronger. However, I just do not have the drive to do that any longer. My body aches too much when I try to do things. It humbles me to realize that at 67, I just don't have it anymore. This is causing me grief and leading me into depression. Realizing that life, as I once knew it, is changing, and it is not easy for me to adapt.

That balance between adventuring and not putting myself at overt risk is what I should be striving for. And I seem to enjoy just sitting and reading a lot more than I ever have.

Dryden, Ontario to Minnedosa, Manitoba

Date: September 21–23, 2022
Weather: 38°F Clear
Location: Highway 16, Minnedosa, Manitoba

While Ontario seemed like it took forever to cross east to west, traveling through Manitoba will be a breeze. There were several places I wanted to see and visit in Ontario, but I can't say the same about Manitoba. My desire is to get to the Alcan (Alaska Highway) asap. Still about a thousand miles from Dawson Creek, BC, the start of the Alaska Highway. Based upon my calculations, we are five days away—based on an average of 250 miles per day (or about four hundred kilometers per day) and no problems.

I spent the night at a picnic rest stop that was a bit off the main highway. It was nice—right on a lake, and I was able to enjoy a beautiful sunset while enjoying a beer from the Sleeping Giant Brewing Company. Around 3 a.m., a truck came beside the camper and had lights and stuff going on. They were not in the least trying to be quiet. I was a bit worried that they may have been up to no good. There have been random killings in the Manitoba and Saskatchewan provinces of late—so I grabbed my weapon of defense, watched, and was ready to respond. Apparently, all the light activity was him setting up his tent to sleep in. I'm so glad to have the camper when I stop—all it takes is a walk out of the truck, and I just jump in the camper and go to sleep (of course, after the dog has been taken care of).

Now, into the harder (boring) part of the journey—pedal to the metal for the day. I am trying to cover as much ground as possible. I only have nine days until October—which is when I wanted to be in Alaska. I also want to enjoy aspects of the Alcan Highway. Tomorrow morning, I will need to go over the route to ensure that we are on course to meet the self-imposed deadlines. Some changes will need to be made with respect to mileage per day, etc. Currently, I am driving Route 16, also known as the Yellowhead Highway. This route offers an array of landscapes—from the prairies of Manitoba and Saskatchewan, the rolling hills of Alberta, to the mountainous terrain of the Northern Canadian Rockies. The route eventually ends in the Pacific coastal regions of Northern BC, but I will have long turned north on Route 43 to the Alaska Highway.

Today was the same as yesterday, and I suspect the same tomorrow and thereafter until I get to Northern Alberta. While driving along the Yellowhead Highway in Manitoba, I stopped at a brewery called Farmery Brew. What was interesting about this brewery is that it is an "estate brewery," meaning it grows the hops and barley used in its beer. This was the first time I had seen a brewery have vertical integration ownership. They brew quite a range of beers, and I grabbed a smattering of brews to taste over the next few days. They were all very good. It is worth stopping and checking out.

My nightly camping "sites" while traveling through these provinces were more of pulling off an exit and staying on the side of the dirt road. A few times, when I thought it was a little used road, it turned into what seemed like an interstate highway with all the eighteen-wheelers with their loads coming down these dirt roads from the various ranches or farms. As they say, a picture is worth a thousand words; here are a few photos of the vastness of Manitoba and Saskatchewan.

Vegreville, Alberta: An Interesting Day

Date: September 23–24, 2022
Weather: 67°F
Location: Highway 16, Vegreville, Alberta

The miles are accumulating—now through both Manitoba and Saskatchewan and currently in Alberta, still on the Yellowhead Highway. One thing I can say is that these roads are as straight and far as I have ever driven. Today, the Northern Lights or Bust Tour turned into a real adventure. It was Friday afternoon, and I felt the truck wobble. I thought I was having an issue with the Jeep, so I pulled to the side of the road. The tow hitch has not worked properly, and I thought the wobble had something to do with that.

I pulled over, did a walk around the rig, and didn't see anything wrong. Boy, was I incorrect. As I was pulling back onto the highway, I felt the back end of the truck lurch, make a loud sound, and then pull at the steering. I didn't overreact. Just kept the wheel steady, thinking that I just had a flat, until I saw a tire bouncing down the road in front of me. The darn tire took off toward oncoming traffic— thankfully, there was a big median between the lanes. The tire ended up down the road in the median. Given that I was in Canada, AAA nor Liberty Insurance was going to be of much immediate use. So, I called 9-1-1 and found my exact location, and they passed me along to the Royal Canadian Mounted Police, who provided the phone number to a towing company.

The tow company came forty-five minutes later. The fellow, Barry, didn't talk much. All business. He took care of loading the truck, with a few problems, given that the camper was still on the truck. It's no wonder he didn't have me take the camper off. After some quick thinking (and out-of-the-box solutions by Barry), he was able to take both the truck and camper while I drove the Jeep behind him. Unbeknownst to me, his boss already identified a service station to drop the truck off. When we arrived, the owner of the service station was already ordering parts and getting his guys organized.

When I arrived, I naturally wanted to speak with someone about the game plan. I was worried that given the time (4:00 on a Friday afternoon), they would push me off to Monday to start the effort. When I approached the owner, he was on the phone. He leaned over, looked at me, and said, "I can either talk to you or keep ordering your parts." It didn't take a genius to figure out what to do. I turned, asked the receptionist if there was a bar nearby, and she pointed me to Vito's.

From the moment the tow truck pulled into the station, someone was working the truck. By 6:00, the truck was operable—which was unbelievable news, given it was Friday and closing time. I had thought that both back tire rims were shot and the axle was thoroughly messed up. The driver's side tire had to be replaced with the spare, and the passenger side was still able to be used—though the passenger side was also showing the same problems. The issue was that all the studs and lug nuts on the driver's side and four on the passenger side were sheared off. How they removed the sheared studs was impressive and didn't take them much time.

Talk about the closeness of a small town. As I was waiting for the repairs, instead of sitting around, I went to Vito's and was having a beer when the phone rang from behind the bar. The server answered it, then looked at me and asked if I was Thom. She said it was the repair shop, and I needed to head over because they had questions. Since I was in the middle of my beer, I asked if it was okay to walk over and then come back and finish. She said of course. I headed over to the repair shop and dealt with the questions; they were making good progress. I was impressed they were working as diligently as they were, and it looked like they would be finishing this tonight.

While I was at Vito's lounge, I started chatting with someone named Rick, who was the supervisor of the local RV park and ran a bison ranch not too far from the lounge. Rick was an interesting character, and we had an enjoyable dinner together. He regaled me with stories of his past work experiences and offered a tour of the ranch, which I took him up on. You never know when you'll ever see a legit bison ranch again. After the tour, he let me park my rig at his place.

One thing I can say after being up close and personal with the bison is that, boy, they are big.

With the truck fixed and a good night's sleep behind me, I am ready to put in some miles. The drive from Vegreville, AB, to Dawson Creek, BC, is now approximately five hundred miles (around eight hundred kilometers), about two days away. The scenery is beautiful: rolling prairie landscapes with vast skies that never seem to end and sprawling fields with hay bales ready to be picked up and stored for the winter. As we continue west and then northwest, I am starting to see the transition from the prairies to forested land. We were fortunate to see a whole host of wildlife, mostly deer and elk, as we drove, though we did see a moose feeding along a river.

Observations

It's funny how you can be born somewhere and still be taken aback by its sheer size. Growing up in Ontario, I never fully grasped its vastness until someone pointed out that the entire state of Texas could comfortably fit within its borders. And who could have guessed that my home province boasts the longest freshwater coastline in the world? Beyond the majestic Great Lakes, Ontario is sprinkled liberally with thousands of smaller lakes and rivers, including the enchanting lake systems of Muskoka and the historic Rideau Canal, a proud UNESCO World Heritage Site that I've longed to kayak through. Imagine my disappointment when my planned kayak trip was canceled! I've made a mental note to return earlier in the season next time; I won't let another opportunity slip away.

What I cherish most about Ontario is the uncanny way it reminds me of home on the Cape. There's a certain charm to the quaint lakeside villages here, quite different from the fishing villages back home, but charming, nonetheless. The vast, open vistas of the lakes, especially when I stood on a sand dune along the shoreline of Lake Superior in the provincial park, almost tricked me into thinking I was gazing out over the ocean from the cliffs at Cahoon's Hollow. It took a deep, pine-scented breath to bring me back to reality—the familiar salty tang of the ocean was conspicuously absent here.

Now, onto the people! My experience in Ontario and Canada at large was like being enveloped in a cozy, amiable hug. It seemed as though smiles were the go-to form of exchange, with everyone ready and willing to extend a helping hand or spare a moment for a friendly chat. My escapade in Vegreville, AB, stands as a shining example of this warmth. It was this authentic, heartfelt kindness that truly marked my journey, making every moment spent here unforgettable and leaving me excited to plan my return.

Section 3

Alaska Highway

First Journey: Alaska Highway in Fall

In autumn's embrace, where the wild calls,
A road warrior heeds, to where horizon falls.
On the Alaska Highway, paths unfold,
A story of solitude, bravely told.

Wheels roll on tarmac, aged yet firm,
Through landscapes that make the heart squirm.
Mountains draped in auburn hues,
Nature's canvas, broad and diffuse.

The road stretches, endless, serene,
In the midst of a world so vast, so clean.
With each mile, a quiet peace,
In this wilderness, all worries cease.

Yet, in this solitude, there's a subtle fear,
Of the remoteness, so starkly clear.
Miles from the nearest soul or town,
In this vastness, one could easily drown.

But in this journey, there's a strength found,
In the echoing silence, a profound sound.
The road warrior, alone yet bold,
Finds a connection, deep and old.

The fall's crisp air, the eagle's flight,
Add layers to this tranquil plight.
The Alaska Highway, winding, long,
Sings to the heart a siren song.

It's more than a route; it's a passage of soul,
In the beauty of fall, he finds his role.
A warrior of roads, in landscapes immense,
Where peace and worry strike a balance intense.

Alcan Highway

The Alaska Highway, also known as the Alcan Highway, stands as a monumental route linking the contiguous United States with Alaska through Canada, a vital artery born out of historical necessity. Its construction, initiated in 1942 during the throes of World War II, was primarily driven by military strategy following the Japanese attack on Pearl Harbor on December 7, 1941.[6] This event heightened concerns about the vulnerability of North America's West Coast to invasions or attacks. Alaska, strategically positioned, was considered crucial for US military defenses to safeguard the mainland and potentially launch counter-offensives. The highway was envisioned as a direct, dependable conduit for transporting troops, military equipment, and critical supplies to defensive outposts in Alaska. It also supported the construction of airstrips and the Northwest Staging Route, a key air ferry route used to transfer aircraft from the US to the Soviet Union under the Lend-Lease Program.

The creation of the Alcan Highway was a testament to the collaboration between the United States and Canada. While primarily built by US military personnel, the road traverses Canadian territory, symbolizing the united wartime efforts of the two nations. The urgency for a secure route to Alaska spurred the remarkably swift construction of the highway. Work commenced in March 1942 and concluded by November of the same year, though subsequent improvements and paving extended well beyond its initial completion. The highway was officially opened to the public in 1948, transforming the connectivity between Alaska, the contiguous United States, and Canada. It became an essential overland link to the north, boosting travel, trade, and development in areas that had previously been isolated.

---

[6] "Alaska Highway," Encyclopædia Britannica, accessed January 24, 2024, https://www.britannica.com/topic/Alaska-Highway.

Today, the highway not only serves as a crucial infrastructure for tourism in Alaska and the Yukon, inviting travelers to immerse themselves in the breathtaking northern landscapes, but it also remains a symbol of resilience and strategic ingenuity. For many, including myself, journeying along the Alaska Highway is a once-in-a-lifetime experience. This true bucket-list adventure captures the spirit of exploration and the rich tapestry of North American history.

The highway begins in Dawson Creek, British Columbia, and ends in Delta Junction, Alaska. The original length of the highway was about 1,700 miles. However, over time, improvements and changes to the route have reduced its length to approximately 1,387 miles.

The Alaska Highway travels through varied landscapes, including dense forests, mountain ranges, and alongside rivers. Originally, the road was a rough, challenging trail, but it has since been improved and is mostly paved today. There are still some sections that can still be gravel or dirt, especially on side routes or during construction periods (which, during this trip, there were). While there are major towns along the route, such as Fort Nelson and Whitehorse, that offer full services, there are long stretches of the highway with limited amenities. I was advised to be well-prepared, especially in the more remote sections, thus my addition of the Jeep as my towed vehicle. There's nothing like having an alternate mode of transportation when things head south.

A publication known as *The MILEPOST* is a must if you are to travel this road. This publication describes itself as one of publishing's longest-running guides, starting in 1949, and has been guiding travelers to Alaska longer than Alaska has been a state.[7] This proved quite helpful to me as I traveled this historic highway.

---

[7] "About Us," The MILEPOST, March 24, 2023, https://themilepost.com/about-us/.

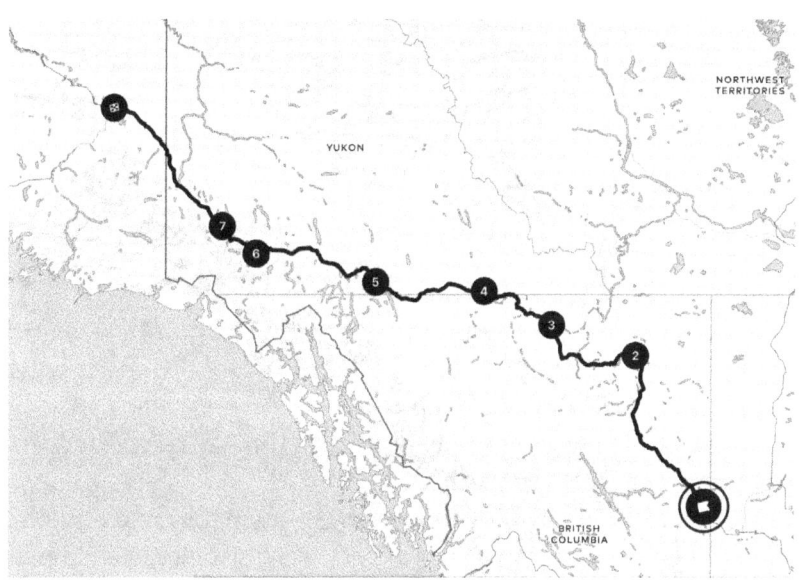

Dawson Creek

Date: September 26, 2022
Weather: 70°F Wind 8 mph Clear
Location: Dawson Creek, BC

Well, here we are, at Dawson Creek, the beginning of the Alaska Highway. I have heard about this highway for so long, with its myths, warnings, and the opportunities of a peaceful and serene journey. The upside for traveling at this time of year means fewer tourists, less traffic, and less competition for boondocking sights (though that is not a real issue given the vastness of what we are about to enter). The downside is that I can expect less assistance when things go south, and it is not uncommon for it to snow as I travel along the Alcan, especially at higher elevations. Overall, traveling the Alaska Highway in September offers a mix of scenic beauty, wildlife encounters, and a more relaxed atmosphere.

We are prepared, as best we can, for the changing weather conditions and limited services as we embark down the Alcan Highway. While I had a good idea of what to expect during September, November was a different story. Because of the approaching winter and the threat of some severe snowfalls, I changed my initial plans and decided not to take the Alcan back and head instead down the Cassiar and over to Prince Rupert so I could take the BC ferry to Vancouver.

We stayed at the Mile 0 RV resort—and it's nothing to really get excited about. Yes, it provides the basic amenities, which I availed myself of, such as a shower and laundry. I don't expect these amenities again until I reach Tok, AK. There is what looks to be an old western town next to the campsite, but it was not open while I was there. In the morning, I did get a great breakfast and coffee at the Beans & Barley. Their cinnamon bun was out of this world.

(I thought I had the best cinnamon bun at the Silver Islet General Store in Ontario, but this rivaled it.)

It's late September, and Mother Earth is painting such beautiful landscapes. I can't get over how the amber, golds, oranges, and yellows blend with the green, making an unbelievable backdrop as we motor along. I hope wildlife viewing will be optimal because of the lack of tourists. I will be on the lookout for bears, moose, caribou, and other animals as they prepare for winter. I will also be on the lookout for opportunities to view the Northern Lights. The clear, dark skies of fall will make for spectacular displays of this natural phenomenon. I cannot wait to witness this for myself.

As we head out of Dawson, it is 287 miles until our next stopping point, and from the folks at the visitor's center, we can expect it to be good pavement until Ft. Nelson.

Parker Lake Recreation Fort Nelson

Date: September 28, 2022
Weather: 3°F
Location: Alaska Highway Fort Nelson, BC

Things are starting to look more rugged and sparse. I can even see the rambling hills change to foothills as we approach the mountains. The only stops along the way were to let Dexter and I stretch our legs and take care of other business. There was not too much interest as we drove to Ft. Nelson beyond the crossings over rivers and creeks, with several bridges offering panoramic views of the surrounding landscapes. We boondocked at the Parker Lake picnic area; it was not too far off the Alcan. The drive to the lake was down a rather straight dirt road that was rich with autumn colors on both sides of the road. It was rather stunning with its amber and gold against the backdrop of blue skies, with the occasional cloud.

We had a great dinner and enjoyed the peaceful setting as I watched the sunset. During the night, we had a few visitors of the two-legged kind. It must be the local drinking or make-out spot for Ft. Nelson teenagers. Cars were coming and going throughout the night. I was half-expecting someone, once they saw the out-of-country license plate, to have a little fun at our expense. No one bothered us and left us alone. (Though I think if someone were to try something, Dexter would be barking, and she has a more deep growl bark. If you didn't see her, you would expect it to be a rather vicious dog.)

In the morning, as we watched the sunrise, we had another visitor while having coffee and taking in the lovely view of the lake. This was the four-legged variety and swimming in the lake. I couldn't tell what it was at first and initially thought it was a woodchuck. As I watched it effortlessly make its way along the shore, it noticed me, raised its flat tail, flapped it on the water, and was gone, leaving ripples of where it once swam. I quickly figured that I had just witnessed a beaver giving a warning "shout" to its posse, a first for me. Boy, it does make a sound.

As we headed toward Liard Hot Springs Provincial Park, the boreal forest continued to amaze with its black spruce, white spruce, lodgepole pine, aspen, and birch, each predominating according to the sogginess of the soil. The cloud cover was hanging low, especially in the valleys where the trees were no longer visible because of the clouds (or could it have been fog?). Bison were rather abundant, sitting or standing along the side of the highway, keeping to themselves. At one point, there must have been a herd of about seventy-five bison. Even Dexter kept her barking to a minimum, not wanting to attract the attention of the bison when we stopped to take pictures and just ogle at their enormity.

We stopped at the Muncho Lake Provincial Park for lunch and to stretch our legs. The visually stunning Terminal Range flanks Muncho Lake to the west and the Sentinel Range to the east, providing striking vistas.

Liard Hot Springs Provincial Park

Date: September 30, 2022
Weather: 50°F
Location: Alaska Highway, Watson Lake, BC

After a long day of driving, the hot springs were a nice diversion. The location is a primitive provincial park for camping. When I was here, there were very limited amenities, but the water was running, and the hot spring was open, which is what I really cared about. The hot springs are of ecological significance and are well known for their natural setting in a lush boreal spruce forest. The park has done a nice job of balancing the natural aspects with some convenience, like a sheltered area to change and a cement bench in the river for sitting while enjoying the hot spring. The walk to the springs is a lovely half-mile boardwalk across a marshy area. The lush plant life is influenced by the warmth of the springs, which in turn attracts wildlife like black bears and moose to forage for food. Staying on the boardwalk is required so that the local ecology is not affected and for your own protection. Sad to say that on this visit, there were no sightings of wildlife.

From speaking with folks that were there, I learned that one side of the river is a lot hotter than the side I was entering. You could feel the colder current coming from deeper in the river. If you moved the water just right, you were able to create a warm place by mixing the two water currents—hot and cold. The springs' water temperatures range from 105°F to 125°F, so you can find some really hot spots.

I was relaxed and at peace, enjoying the warmth as it soothed my tired muscles from sitting so long while driving. While I was enjoying my time in the springs, I thought that this would be a great place in winter to watch the Northern Lights. The challenge of enjoying the hot springs at the end of September, when the temps were somewhere around the high 40s, was getting out and dressing. I couldn't imagine what it would be like if it were below zero. I needed to keep this on the to-do list in case I happened to come back this way in the future.

I have been fortunate to have visited several hot springs on my travels: Strawberry Hot Springs in Colorado, the Boiling River in Yellowstone, Manly Hot Springs in Alaska, and Mystic Hot Springs in Utah, to name a few. Each of these springs has its own unique attraction. Some require a hike, others a 4WD, and others just a walk.

Someplace North of Watson Lake, Yukon

Date: September 30, 2022
Weather: 49°F
Location: Alaska Highway, Watson Lake, BC

Today's drive treated me to a captivating display of wildlife. I remain utterly awestruck by the sheer size of bison—colossal creatures that could easily rival the dimensions of my own truck. While perhaps not the most glamorous of animals, they exude a commanding presence with their imposing heads, humps, and robust shoulders. These magnificent beasts are among the largest terrestrial animals in North America. Male bison, or bulls, can tip the scales at a staggering two thousand pounds or more, while their female counterparts, the cows, are typically smaller, weighing around a thousand pounds. Their thick fur, which varies from dark near the head to light toward the rear, provides vital insulation against the harsh winter cold.

However, the weather soon took a turn, enveloping me in thick fog, reducing visibility to a mere five feet in front of my truck. A prudent decision would have been to pull over and wait on the roadside. Instead, I pressed on, creeping along at a cautious twenty-five miles per hour with my flashers activated, hoping that the flashing lights would signal my presence to any oncoming vehicles. It was a tense and nerve-wracking experience, and I couldn't quite explain why I continued driving. Perhaps it was the eerie solitude of the road that gave me a false sense of security, at least from the perspective of other vehicles.

Then, as suddenly as the fog had descended, it dissipated, revealing a startling sight. A herd of around sixty bison lounged peacefully by the side of the road. They seemed as if they could have easily chosen to hang out on the road itself. I had no choice but to stop, primarily to capture the moment with photographs, but also to calm my racing heart.

I chided myself for not fully comprehending the real danger of this highway: the unpredictable wildlife. They acknowledge no boundaries, and there were no fences to keep them off the road, at least not in the section I could see. This experience served as a valuable lesson: when visibility is limited, the best course of action is to stop. Just as you can't see where you're going, the wildlife can't see you either and may not move out of your way. A collision with a bison would have been a disastrous end to the day.

The ever-changing weather in the Yukon never ceases to amaze. One moment, I was navigating through dense fog, and the next, the radiant sunbathed everything in a warm, golden light. As I continued down the road, my attention was drawn to a mother black bear casually strolling along with her playful cub joyfully chasing butterflies. I reached for my camera on the passenger seat, but in the blink of an eye, the cub vanished into the wilderness, with its vigilant mother not far behind.

My journey also brought me to a fascinating manmade wonder I had read about in *MILEPOST Magazine*. I had initially underestimated its grandeur, thinking it might be a kitschy tourist attraction with just a few items. Little did I realize that the "Signpost" Forest in Watson Lake, Yukon, is a genuinely captivating place. Its origins trace back to the Alaska Highway Project of 1942, when US soldier Carl K. Lindley, while recovering from an injury in Watson Lake, was tasked by his commanding officer with repairing and erecting directional signposts.[8] During this process, Lindley added a sign pointing the way to his hometown, Danville, Illinois, which became a catalyst for

---

[8] "Watson Lake Signpost Forest - Yukon Territory Information," Yukon Territory Information - Your Guide to Exploring Northern BC, Yukon and Southeast alaska, May 26, 2020, https://yukoninfo.com/watson-lake-signpost-forest/.

others to follow suit. This humble act sparked a tradition that has endured for generations.

To illustrate the vastness of this "sign forest," in 1990, an Ohio couple contributed the 10,000th sign to the Signpost Forest, which has since burgeoned to house over 77,000 signs, with this number growing yearly as visitors continue to embrace the tradition. The dedicated town of Watson Lake meticulously maintains the site, adding more posts as the existing ones fill up. Visitors are encouraged and invited to bring their own sign to join this unique forest or create one at the visitor's information center.

As I explored the Signpost Forest, I stumbled upon remnants of equipment used during the construction of the Alaska Highway. Engaging in conversations with fellow travelers, I learned that in 1992, a time capsule and cairn were placed within the forest, set to be unveiled again in 2042. Even after spending about thirty minutes wandering through this captivating "forest," it became evident that covering even one-third of the area was a considerable feat. Some signs I encountered required substantial effort and meticulous planning, adding to the charm and uniqueness of this remarkable attraction. During my visit, I was pleasantly surprised to find several signs originating from the New England area, underscoring this extraordinary place's global appeal and magnetic allure.

This brings back memories of a remarkable island that my daughter Caroline and I had the privilege to explore while scuba diving in the Galapagos Islands. Our underwater adventure led us to Post Office Bay, a place with a fascinating history that has served as an informal mailing station since the 1700s, a concept that initially relied solely on a humble barrel and the goodwill of sailors and adventurers.[9]

---

[9] Eric Grundhauser, "This Post Office Is Actually Just a Barrel," Atlas Obscura, September 17, 2015, https://www.atlasobscura.com/places/post-office-bay.

The tradition of Post Office Bay was first established by whalers in the 18th century, as they set sail from England and the United States on their arduous expeditions in search of whales. The Galapagos Islands became an essential stopover for these seafarers, providing a crucial source of food and water to sustain them during their lengthy hunting journeys. However, the deep longing these sailors felt to connect with their loved ones back home gave rise to something truly unique.

On Floreana Island, a simple barrel was strategically placed, serving as a makeshift mailbox. Outbound whalers would leave letters inside, hoping for the goodwill of fellow mariners to carry them to their destinations on their homeward voyages. Remarkably, this system operated without any postage fees; it relied solely on the trust that the person who retrieved your letter would ensure its safe delivery.

What makes this story even more captivating is that Post Office Bay's age-old tradition is still alive today. Of course, the participants have changed—now tourists, not whalers, visit the island. They come to see if this time-honored communication system still works, leaving their postcards and letters in the barrel, waiting for fellow travelers to help fulfill their wishes and maintain the legacy of this incredible place. It's a testament to the enduring power of human connection and the sense of adventure that continues to thrive in this remote corner of the world.

Teslin River

Date: October 3, 2022
Weather: 54°F Mostly Cloudy
Location: Highway 1, Yukon

The Teslin River, located in the southern Yukon Territory and northwestern British Columbia, Canada, stretches for 393 miles as it meanders from its source. A few miles upstream of Johnsons Crossing, Teslin Lake narrows, and water rushes out from its northern end. From this juncture, the river continues its journey until it converges with the Yukon River approximately 125 miles downstream. Interestingly, despite being labeled as a tributary of the Yukon River, the Teslin River is, in fact, the larger of the two watercourses. Speaking with locals indicated that this becomes abundantly very clear when you reach the point of confluence situated at the abandoned village of Hootalinqua.

As I stand on the bridge at Johnson Crossing, I can't help but appreciate the vast expanse of the river, spanning several hundred yards. The Teslin River, often described as a tranquil waterway, is typically rated as Class I-II, making it a perfect choice for a mild paddling experience. While I desired to kayak during this trip, the approach of winter made it less than ideal. However, this setback only adds to my motivation to return to the Yukon.

My previous experiences in Alaska had already kindled my curiosity about spending more time in the Yukon Territories. The sheer vastness of this territory is awe-inspiring. One of my long-held aspirations has been to kayak the Yukon River, although embarking on such a journey solo feels a bit daunting these days. The combination of the Teslin and Yukon rivers offers a more manageable alternative, condensing the adventure from four months to a ten-day excursion.

I had come across the remarkable story of London writer Adam Weymouth, who spent an incredible four months canoeing the entire Yukon River.[10] Originating in the coastal mountains of Canada, this majestic river flows a staggering 1,979 miles northward in a sweeping arc, eventually meeting the Bering Sea. Along its course, it meanders through the Yukon-Charley Rivers National Preserve for 128 miles. Weymouth's journey was marked by encounters with bears, treacherous crossings, and weeks without encountering another human soul. Moreover, it allowed him to explore the profound relationship between the Yukon people and the diminishing salmon population they rely upon for sustenance. This epic two-thousand-mile odyssey was the foundation for Adam's book, *Kings of the Yukon*.

As much as I'd love to undertake such an epic adventure, it's no longer a viable option for me, and it's not solely due to my age, although being sixty-seven may play a part. The primary reason is that I can't afford to be away for that extended period without my necessary treatments for prostate cancer, nor can I risk being too far from immediate medical assistance if the need arises. Nonetheless, the prospect of a ten-day trip along the Teslin and Yukon rivers is undeniably appealing and something I may consider for a future journey.

Tonight, we are nestled on the edge of Marsh Lake, and if this isn't the perfect boondocking spot, I do not know what is. The campfire crackles and dances, casting a warm, flickering glow amid the wilderness, keeping the chill that is setting in at bay. The night sky above is a canvas of infinite darkness, yet it is adorned with countless stars, their brilliance undimmed by any hint of cloud cover. It's a cloudless night of unparalleled clarity, and the heavens seem to stretch on forever.

---

[10] Adam Weymouth, *Kings of the Yukon: An Alaskan River Journey* (London: Penguin Books, 2019).

As I sit by the campfire, the embers send tendrils of golden light into the cool, crisp air, creating a cocoon of comfort amid the wild surroundings. The scent of burning wood mingles with the earthy aroma of the Yukon's forests, creating a sensory symphony that envelopes you in a deep sense of tranquility.

Gazing out across the lake's glassy surface, I can see the reflection of the stars above, doubling their enchanting presence. The lake's waters mirror the starry expanse, creating a surreal and awe-inspiring tableau, as if you were suspended between two celestial realms.

And then the night's true magic begins. Shooting stars streak across the sky, leaving ephemeral light trails in their wake. Each meteor appears like a fleeting wish, a brief but breathtaking moment of celestial wonder. The silence of the wilderness is punctuated by the occasional crackling of the campfire, the hooting of distant owls, and the lapping of water against the shore.

In this remote corner of the Yukon, far from the trappings of civilization, you find yourself connected to the universe in a way few places on Earth can offer. The campfire's warmth, the tranquil lake, and the shooting stars above create a profound and unforgettable experience, a night of serenity and wonder in the heart of the pristine wilderness. I had set up my hammock and was planning on watching the starry night, hoping to see the Northern Lights. I don't know if it was the swinging of the hammock, the fire's warmth, or the night sky's beauty; it wasn't too long before I found myself drifting off to sleep.

Last night, there was supposed to be a chance to witness the Northern Lights, but luck wasn't on my side. I woke up twice, once at midnight and again at four in the morning, and was treated to a breathtaking display of the starriest sky. It's become clear that I must set up my camera for future night stargazing.

My primary concern now revolves around the weather. I need a reliable means of checking the forecast. Neither the weather radio nor my phone is picking up any signals. I've pondered whether the Garmin InReach satellite communicator can provide weather information. The Garmin InReach is a fascinating device—it's a two-way satellite communicator that utilizes the Iridium satellite network for data exchange. After delving into the Garmin manual, I discovered it can indeed provide weather updates, which is quite a relief. It's satisfying when a plan comes together. I've been carrying this Garmin without fully utilizing its capabilities, even being able to send texts, as I did this morning. Now, my next task is to secure better maps for the area before I venture off the beaten path. At the moment, I lack digital maps with sufficient detail to navigate effectively. This is an oversight I should have addressed before embarking on this journey. Once I regain cell coverage, I'll research GPS-based mapping systems and download maps for Alaska, British Columbia, and the Yukon.

In moments of self-doubt, I've come to recognize the importance of taking a step back and reflecting. While my physical strength may not be what it once was, I've grown to appreciate the enduring adventurous spirit that resides within me—an eagerness to embrace new experiences. I'm currently undertaking a path less traveled, a privilege to explore solo, primarily through the wild landscapes of the Americas—a journey that not everyone would choose.

I find myself deep in the remote wilderness of the Yukon, surrounded by the vibrant colors of autumn, accompanied only by my faithful companion, Dexter, and my trusty camper. It's a solitary adventure that grants me the privilege of witnessing the awe-inspiring beauty Mother Nature generously bestows upon us. I am living out the dream I've cherished for so long, and I couldn't be more grateful for the opportunity to do so.

When I catch myself caught up in trivial worries, I remind myself of my extraordinary path. These moments serve as gentle reminders to pause, reflect, and regain perspective—rekindling my appreciation of the remarkable journey I've embarked upon.

Today, I will work on my skills flying the drone. The drone was brought because, when I am traveling the backroads and do not have a map of the area, the drone is to be used to check the road ahead of me to see if there are any obstructions or restrictions. There is nothing worse than getting stuck on a dirt road where there is no place to turn around, especially when you are towing another vehicle. The other benefit is capturing unique photos—or at least learning how to do so. So, when I do come across the opportunity, I will be able to take advantage.

Haines Junction

Date: October 4, 2022
Weather: 44°F
Location: Haines Highway, Stikine Region, Yukon

The drive from Haines Junction to Haines, Alaska, was undeniably beautiful. Although I wouldn't rank it among my top ten scenic drives, the snow-covered mountains on one side and rolling hills on the other, interspersed with serene lakes and meandering rivers, offered a picturesque landscape. My ultimate destination was the Tatshenshini-Alsek Provincial Park, a place of remarkable natural beauty.

Tatshenshini-Alsek Park is home to glacier-clad peaks, untamed rivers, the formidable presence of grizzly bears, and unique plant communities. Nestled in the far northwestern corner of British Columbia, a seamless connection forms between Kluane National Park and Reserves in the Yukon, Glacier Bay, and Wrangell-St. Elias National Parks and Preserves in Alaska. Together, these parks create the largest protected area on Earth, encompassing roughly 8.5 million hectares of pristine wilderness.

Today unfolded as one of those leisurely days, albeit not without a few hiccups along the way. Many places were closed for the season, making it challenging to find propane, which I desperately needed. Thankfully, the cold hadn't fully set in yet, although the morning greeted me with temperatures as low as thirty degrees and frost blanketing the ground. It seemed winter was swiftly approaching, at least in these northern reaches. Consequently, I had to ration my heat and stove usage until I could replenish my propane supply.

I encountered a couple of towing mishaps today. First, I had to put the Jeep on tow to start the day, and later, I found myself on a road I couldn't navigate with the Jeep still attached. It was a bit frustrating.

I realized I should have used my drone to scout the road before attempting it—a valuable lesson learned. Both instances took some time to resolve, and I realized I needed to find a more practical approach to dealing with the tow hitch and getting it connected. I suspected that disassembling the tow bar, thoroughly cleaning it, and applying fresh grease might do the trick. One of the struts appeared to be functioning, while the other seemed stuck, so I also needed to address that.

I've been quite pleased with my modifications to the camper. Adding a photo of my daughters has been heartwarming, as I wake up to their smiling faces every morning.

The captain's chairs I installed have proven to be remarkably comfortable, and the additional storage space above the stove has exceeded my expectations in terms of utility.

I found a relatively flat spot to camp for the night, and it was conveniently situated so I could turn the rig around without the need to detach the Jeep. The night sky appeared overcast, and I didn't anticipate much of a celestial show.

However, I was in for a pleasant surprise. The following morning, I spoke with someone who raved about the beauty of the Northern Lights the previous night. This revelation prompted me to extend my stay in the area, planning to rise at 2 a.m. to witness this captivating display. My camera was ready, poised to capture the ethereal dance of the auroras. Unfortunately, I was treated to another overcast evening. I must be doing something wrong—either at the wrong time or not giving it enough time. Patience is everything, I guess—something that I have never been in a high supply of.

One of my favorite moments during these travels is waking up in the morning and witnessing the mist rising off a nearby lake or river. As the temperatures drop, I have the opportunity to observe more of these mesmerizing scenes. They strike a delicate balance between beauty and an eerie, otherworldly quality that never fails to captivate me.

Today, my journey continues in the direction of Haines, with the hopeful anticipation of visiting the bald eagle preserve. Regrettably, I found myself growing restless during the drive, prompting me to pull over and search for a suitable camping spot around 4:00 p.m. While the drive had its moments of beauty, it didn't quite live up to my expectations. I couldn't help but think that had I embarked on this route a few weeks earlier, I would have been treated to the vibrant foliage that's said to grace this corridor.

My original plan had been to camp at Million Dollar Falls, but unfortunately, it was closed. I find it troubling when they don't tell you about closings before you trek down a single-lane dirt road. Not having the space to turn around nor the ability to back up because of how I have rigged my towing of the Jeep is more than frustrating. This unforeseen obstacle forced me to disconnect my Jeep so I could turn around, and needless to say, I wasn't thrilled about it. The campsite I eventually stumbled upon turned out to be a rather basic, flat area with enough space for maneuvering.

As I awoke the next morning, I was greeted by the presence of a few hunters and their guides, mounted on horses, and preparing to embark on their hunting expedition. It was undeniably a unique and intriguing sight to behold.

Destruction Bay

Date: October 6, 2022
Weather: 5°F Cold and Clear
Location: Alaska Highway

Destruction Bay is a charming little community nestled along the Alaska Highway next to the picturesque Kluane Lake. Home to about forty-three folks, it's situated nineteen kilometers southeast of Burwash Landing and boasts a unique history. Originally established as a construction camp for the Alaska Highway, this place earned its intriguing name from a ferocious windstorm that swept through the area back in the 1940s.[11]

I hadn't initially planned to make a stop here; my intention was to head straight to Tok. However, fate had different plans for me. When I pulled over to refuel, I discovered that Destruction Bay had a saloon, and that's where things took an unexpected turn. I decided to treat myself to dinner and a few beers. The saloon was a quaint little spot, and to my surprise, I had it all to myself. Its walls were adorned with a collection of old posters that probably wouldn't fly back home, adding to its unique charm. Of course, it didn't hurt that the views from the saloon were breathtaking. Perched atop a hill, it offered an unrivaled panorama of Kluane Lake.

After my evening at the saloon, I hit the road once more to find a spot to camp. Eventually, I stumbled upon a lovely site right alongside the lake—much to Dexter's delight. We took a leisurely stroll, basking in the glory of the stunning landscape. Dexter couldn't resist the allure of the water, and she had the time of her life, even though I

---

[11] "Destruction Bay," The MILEPOST, June 26, 2020, https://themilepost.com/communities/destruction-bay/.

wasn't thrilled about the idea of her being all wet in the camper—inevitably leading to that distinct "wet dog" smell. *Ugh!*

The following morning greeted us with a spectacular sunrise. Instead of snapping photos, I opted to lay in bed and simply soak in the beauty as it unfolded over the lake, with Dexter as my trusty companion. It was a lazy yet incredibly gratifying start to the day.

With Tok, Alaska, as my destination, I hit the road, tracing the route along the mesmerizing Teslin River. The autumn colors, the towering mountains, and the flowing river created a breathtakingly awesome tableau. I was even treated to the sight of a complete rainbow, arching across the sky in a vibrant display of colors—a truly magical moment along this incredible journey.

Observations

Leaving Dawson Creek, I was really excited about the prospect of traveling the famous Alaska Highway, though tinged with a hint of letdown. The town didn't quite match the postcard dreams in my head. But as I hit the road, the wilderness beyond embraced me, calming my spirit with its tranquil beauty. The Alaska Highway was everything I'd hoped. The further I traveled, the more the landscape bloomed into a riot of fall colors, turning every twist and turn into a breathtaking canvas of amber and gold. I often found myself pulling over simply to lose myself in the sheer wonder of it all.

The area around Atlin and Haines Junction was like something out of a fairy tale; nestled at the edge of the vast and wild Kluane National Park and Reserve in Yukon, it is a place where the stillness of nature speaks volumes. I'd whisper into the breezes, half-hoping for a reply from the ancient sentinels around me. The area is dramatically set against the backdrop of the Saint Elias Mountains, part of a range that includes Mount Logan, Canada's highest peak. I fell in love with these towering giants, covered in snow and ice, reflecting the pink and golden hues of the sunrise and sunset, creating a breathtaking vista that changes with the light.

The Liard Hot Springs was a godsend. Their steamy caress melted away the long hours of driving, refreshing my body and soul. I found Signpost Forest to be a very interesting area. Each sign, a story from a fellow traveler, made me feel part of a vast, adventurous family. I'd recommend that anyone heading that way take a sign of their own and leave their mark on this global tapestry.

As I reminisce about this journey along the Alaska Highway, I'm filled with a yearning for more. I envision myself kayaking down the Teslin and Yukon rivers, a tiny speck amidst the grandeur. I can almost see myself returning, camera ready to capture the fleeting dance of the Northern Lights. This part of the journey has really impacted me; it's a deeply personal chapter in this current journey, one that I'm eager to continue writing.

Section 4

Alaska

Alaskan Road Warrior: Winter's Prelude

In the land where Northern Lights play,
A road warrior finds his way.
Through the vast, untamed Alaskan wild,
Nature's rugged, unspoiled child.

His steed, a truck of steel and might,
Cuts through the day and into the night.
Mountains loom like silent giants,
In this realm, he's self-reliant.

The road, a ribbon through the trees,
Twists and turns with the greatest ease.
Each mile, a new discovery,
Alaska's heart, vast and free.

As winter whispers in the air,
The landscape dons a snowy flare.
He drives through towns, sparse and small,
Where the spirit of the frontier stands tall.

The oncoming cold, a daunting guest,
Puts the road warrior to the test.
Yet, in this challenge, he finds his peace,
In the wilderness, all worries cease.

Through the taiga, over streams,
His journey, like a waking dream.
The Northern Lights, a guiding blaze,
In Alaska's winter, endless days.

In this journey, there's a truth he's found,
In the wild, where life abounds.
The road warrior, in his quest,
Lives each day to its fullest.

Alakshak, Alaxsxaq, Alyeska: All Refer to "The Great Land"

Alaska, often referred to as "The Great Land," is a realm of unmatched adventures and breathtaking scenery, segmented into five unique regions: Inside Passage, Southcentral, Interior, Arctic, and Southwest. My numerous excursions to Alaska have consistently captivated me with its majestic beauty and vast expanses. In 2002, I embarked on an exhilarating few weeks of ski mountaineering, along with resort and heli-skiing in the Chugach Mountains and at Alyeska Ski Resort. My 2009 adventure entailed a two-week kayaking expedition through Prince William Sound, guided by the National Outdoor Leadership School (NOLS). In 2015, I dedicated two weeks in Anchorage to volunteer with Habitat for Humanity's Global Village program. Another remarkable experience was my 2017 road trip along the Dalton Highway, a five-hundred-mile journey from Fairbanks to Deadhorse in Alaska's North Slope.

Each journey has deeply influenced me, continually reigniting my eagerness to delve deeper into Alaska's stunning wilderness. Over the years, I've explored various regions of Alaska, yet the Interior and Southwest regions remained uncharted territories for me. This upcoming trip was set to focus on these two unexplored regions, promising new adventures and discoveries in the vast Alaskan landscape.

The Interior region is at the heart of Alaska, showcasing Denali, North America's tallest peak, and vast tundra expanses. This area is rich in wildlife, including grizzly bears, caribou, and the willow ptarmigan, the state bird. Here, you can witness phenomena like the summer's midnight sun or winter's Northern Lights. The highway connecting Anchorage to Fairbanks offers incredible views and access to Denali National Park and Preserve. The Interior, originally home to the Athabascan peoples, later attracted gold miners and fur trappers. Fairbanks, the largest city in the Interior, offers insights into Alaska Native and gold rush history, with diverse visitor amenities. Southwest Alaska encompasses the Aleutians, Bristol Bay, Kodiak Island, Lake and Peninsula boroughs, and parts of the Kenai Peninsula. It's an area defined by its rugged, remote beauty.

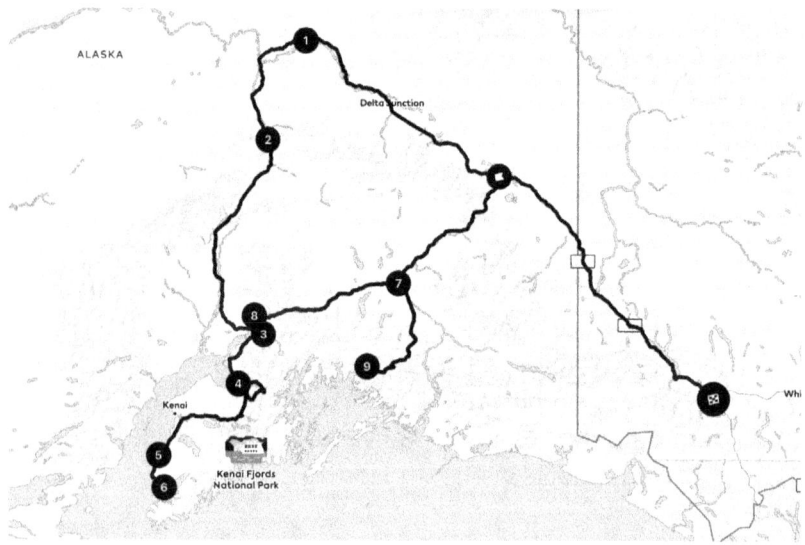

About Sixty Miles Outside Tok

Date: October 8, 2022
Weather: 37°F Foggy
Location: Alaska Highway, Tok, AK, USA

Today was all about the journey to the Canadian-USA border and the customs procedure that awaited me there. The drive from Destruction Bay to Tok unfolded like a magnificent tapestry, revealing breathtaking vistas that stretched across both the Yukon and Alaska. The rugged and untamed beauty of Kluane, with its towering mountains as a constant awe-inspiring backdrop.

As I drew nearer to the Canadian border, that familiar twinge of anxiety began to creep in. It's somewhat perplexing why I get so jittery when it comes to navigating customs, regardless of the location. You'd think that returning to Canada, my country of birth, would be a more relaxed experience. However, in a pleasantly uneventful manner, the border crossing turned out to be rather anticlimactic—an unexpected relief.

Once again, the customs process unfolded smoothly, and there were no complications or concerns regarding my resident alien card. It seems that up here, they are quite accustomed to travelers like me—those of us who are a bit older and possess the "infinite" resident alien card, as opposed to the newer ones that require updating every decade.

The town of Tok, I must admit, didn't strike me as particularly remarkable, at least from my perspective, having spent a total of just two hours there. However, I did manage to have dinner at Fast Eddie's and savor one of its renowned cheeseburgers.

As I was stocking up on supplies at the local general store, I found myself parked next to someone, and naturally, we struck up a conversation. He turned out to be an engineer working in the Kenai Peninsula, and he was headed home for the holidays. When I learned where his family lived, I couldn't believe my ears. Here I was, roughly 4,400 miles from home, and this gentleman's parents resided just two blocks away from me on Cape Cod. It was an astonishingly random connection that nearly knocked me off my feet. I couldn't resist texting my friend Steve to inquire if he knew the family, and to my astonishment, he did; he occasionally went mountain biking with the dad. It truly is a small world. We shared a pleasant chat, and he expressed his excitement about finally heading home after spending the past five years or so in Alaska. It's a reminder that you never know who you'll cross paths with on your journey through life, no matter how far from home you may be.

While on my journey from Tok, Alaska, to Chena River Hot Springs, I made an unexpected stop in Delta Junction. Originally, my plan was to head directly to the hot springs, but an alluring sound coming from the Big Delta Brewery lured me in its direction (that sound was the low mummer of "come have a cold one," which I could not turn down). I intended to have just one craft ale, but as I sat at the bar, engaging in conversations with fellow patrons, I found myself engrossed in a chat with none other than the head brewer himself, whose name also happened to be Thomas.

Thomas was a recent addition to the Delta Brewing team, bringing with him a wealth of brewing experience from his previous roles as the Lead Brewer at Crux Fermentation Project and a Brewer at Deschutes Brewery. During our conversation, we delved into the various brewing styles he envisioned for Big Delta Brewery. I also had the pleasure of meeting his wife, Sami, and our conversation was equally enjoyable.

To my delight, Thomas recommended a scenic place to spend the night right by the water. I was grateful for his suggestion, especially when the snow began to fall. After indulging in a few beers, I didn't want to be on the road, so finding a cozy spot for the night was a welcome respite.

Chena River Hot Springs

Date: October 10, 2022
Weather: 30°F Cloudy
Location: George Parks Highway, Chena River, AK

The Chena Hot Springs is nestled in the heart of Alaska's interior. This place is renowned for its geothermal hot springs and offers a wide range of relaxation and recreational activities. It's located at the end of Chena Hot Springs Road, about sixty miles northeast of Fairbanks. Beyond the soothing waters, it's also famous for being an excellent spot to witness the mesmerizing Northern Lights, especially during the winter months. Driving along the George Parks Highway toward Chena Hot Springs took me through some of Alaska's most iconic landscapes, providing moments of reflection amidst the breathtaking natural beauty.

Chena Hot Springs is quite a unique destination, blending its own charm with some industrial elements. One of the highlights for me was the bar and restaurant, which exuded a certain rustic charm I found inviting.

While I was at the bar, I had the pleasure of chatting with the owner, who happened to be having a coffee. He and his wife acquired Chena Hot Springs Resort from the State of Alaska back in 1998, with a commitment to preserving the resort's natural surroundings. Over the years, they've made several additions, including the construction of a new forty-room Moose Lodge and an outdoor hot springs rock lake, providing a serene and relaxing environment.

What struck me most was the owner's vision for the resort. They aimed to make it more environmentally friendly by harnessing geothermal technology for its power needs. To achieve this, they collaborated with engineers, developing innovative technologies that not only serve the resort but are also available to others in the state. Today, this technology powers the resort, and the onsite geothermal heated greenhouses produce lettuce and tomatoes for the restaurant. The resort has grown to employ over forty-five individuals year-round, even cultivating a variety of fruits.

Chena Hot Springs is a hub of activity, and its remote location is the primary draw. It's about an hour outside of Fairbanks. While I didn't partake in everything it had to offer, they had a range of activities like Northern Lights viewing, snowmobiling, and various winter outdoor pursuits. I had my doubts about viewing the Northern Lights due to potentially overcast skies, so I opted for the hot springs and a massage instead. Let me tell you, I was a bundle of knots, and the massage initially had me in pain. But after a few well-deserved beers, I was feeling as good as new.

Just Outside Denali National Park

Date: October 11, 2022
Weather: 21°F Sunny
Location: George Parks Highway, McKinley Park, AK

Today's journey from Chena Hot Springs to Denali turned out to be a pleasant drive, despite the ongoing roadwork. The route had its share of rough patches, with frost heaves and such, limiting my speed to around forty miles per hour in some areas. As I passed through Denali village, it struck me as a ghost town, with everything boarded up and a pervasive sense of desolation hanging in the air.

I'm taking a much-needed break today. I've come down with the flu, so I decided to pause, pick up some medication, and rest by the side of the road. Fortunately, I topped off everything (except the water) yesterday, so I'm well-prepared to continue when I'm back on my feet.

Last night brought some cold challenges as the temperature inside the cabin dropped to forty-four degrees while it was a mere five degrees outside. Once again, the camper heater decided to act up. However, this time, I was ready, having brought extra of the necessary liquid for the heater to function properly. I refilled the reservoir with the Alde fluid, and by four in the morning, it had warmed up to a cozy sixty-six degrees inside while it remained a chilly five degrees outside. The location where we're boondocking near Big Lake, just outside Denali, is quite special. Although we're parked in a pullout by the road, the views from every window in the camper are simply spectacular.

Yesterday, I fell seriously ill. It had been lurking around the edges for a while, but yesterday, a full-blown cold and flu hit me like a ton of bricks. So, today, I'm taking it easy in my camper, nursing myself with Dayquil, and getting some much-needed rest. It's already in the afternoon, and I'm feeling considerably better, thanks to the medication and some downtime.

Today, the temperatures have been frigid, ranging from four to eighteen degrees. However, inside the camper, it's a snug sixty-eight degrees. Dexter, my faithful companion, is taking it easy, too, with the occasional trips outside.

As I lay here, I find myself reflecting on the journey I'm on—both this trip and my battle with cancer. I've wondered if I'm being selfish by embarking on these solo adventures for extended periods. But I've come to a conclusion: this is my life, and I need to do what brings me happiness. (To clarify, being with my daughters also brings me immense joy.) The road is where I find that happiness. It's hard to pinpoint exactly where this happiness stems from. Perhaps it's the adventurer in me, always yearning to explore and embrace new experiences. Every morning, I wake up to a vista that is often breathtaking. My camper, though compact, has everything I need—a cozy refuge, storage for my belongings, a comfy sleeping space, and a spot to unwind. Plus, the cleverly positioned windows provide me with a multitude of views while I'm in the cab.

I keep asking myself why I haven't considered buying some property and building a cabin. But in many ways, being on the road accomplishes that dream for me, with the bonus of ever-changing vistas. While the cross-country drive from the East Coast can be a hassle, everything changes for the better once I cross the continental divide. The landscapes are stunning, the people diverse, the food unique, and the pace of life shifts. I suppose, at this stage of my life, mobility is paramount. There will come a time when I can't do this anymore, and then perhaps the idea of a cabin will make more sense. But then again, I always have the Cape—a lovely place in its own right.

Despite the challenges of dealing with cancer, I find myself content with my life, and for that, I'm grateful.

Knik River

Date: October 13, 2022
Weather: 19°F Fair
Location: South Old Glenn Highway, Knik River

I woke camped by the Knik River this morning and was happy that we had not floated away. I had spent the night worrying that I might have chosen the wrong spot to park. Considering that last night was Friday evening, and I was the only one parked out here, I had concerns that the river's tide might rise significantly. I had read about tide changes along the Turnagain River, comparing them to the infamous Bay of Fundy. I kept mulling over what I knew—seeing tire tracks everywhere, but no seaweed. If the tide were to come up so high, then there wouldn't be so many tire tracks unless this was a very popular area, which it wasn't. Another thing I was looking for was seaweed and the remains of sea creatures like crabs, but I couldn't spot any.

When I go on expedition kayaking trips and camp along the shore, I always make sure to set up above the highest point where you can see a line of seaweed washed ashore. Here, I didn't see any seaweed, which could mean two things: either the tide did get quite high, and the seaweed was closer to the road, or the tide simply doesn't reach where I was. (Later, I realized that I was on the Knik River, which was not tidal but glacier-fed, and there wouldn't be any tide to worry about.)

A brief stop at the visitor's center confirmed our proximity to the Knik Glacier. Situated on the northern fringe of Alaska's Chugach Mountains, this glacier stretches over twenty-eight miles in length and spans five miles in width, earning its title as one of central Alaska's magnificent ice rivers, often referred to as Alaska's "Sunny Glacier." My plan for the day was to off-road to the glacier in my Jeep. The starting point for the Knik Glacier Trail was Jim Creek, which was conveniently positioned across from where we had been boondocking for the past few nights. The trail leads us alongside the Knik River, which is sourced from the very glaciers I was poised to witness. This river's distinctive braided character is defined by a dynamic network of interwoven water channels that undergo constant shifts, sometimes changing within the span of an hour. I was envisioning creek crossings and awe-inspiring vistas offered by the open gravel bars as we set off to unveil the grandeur of the Knik Glacier.

Although my Jeep is equipped for river crossings, this might mark my inaugural experience with a true river crossing (to this point, my water crossings have been confined to creeks where the depth had not exceeded two feet). I heeded the advice imparted by locals regarding the ever-changing mud holes that may lie in wait. Anticipating the river and creek crossings, I approached this aspect of the journey with meticulous caution, ensuring a thorough assessment of the conditions before proceeding.

With Dexter by my side, eagerly sticking her head out of the window and sensing the forthcoming adventure, we uncoupled the Jeep from the camper and secured the camper and truck. Before crossing the Knik River bridge, we released some air from the tires, preparing ourselves for the challenge ahead. My objective was to maintain a safe distance from the muddy sections. The cold weather had rendered the mud somewhat crunchy, which worked in my favor. As I meandered through the trees, I approached the Knik River from a different angle, affording me a breathtaking backdrop of Pioneer Peak and distant mountains behind the glacier.

The trail veered northeast, away from the river and into wooded terrain. This section presented a tighter passage, necessitating a close watch against overflow and broken ice. The terrain eventually leveled out, becoming more open until I encountered a gorge. Surprisingly, the creek crossings proved to be less challenging than expected, thanks to the cold temperatures and the onset of freezing.

However, I remained cautious, avoiding complacency. We reached the glacier's terminus, but the terminal moraine posed challenges, prompting us to park and complete the remaining stretch on foot. Dexter reveled in the experience, thoroughly enjoying our journey.

I decided to spend one more night at the Knik River Recreation Use Area before setting out to the Kenai Peninsula, where I planned to explore places like Hope, Homer, and Seward. The current plan involved dedicating approximately a week to exploring the Kenai Peninsula and potentially taking a day ferry to Kodiak with the Jeep, contingent on weather conditions. From there, I intended to make my way to Valdez, Slena, and then back to Tok, with the possibility of a side trip to Chicken, Alaska.

As I savored a hearty breakfast of eggs, bacon, and a steaming cup of coffee, I enjoyed the view of the Knik River and the surrounding mountains. It truly was a breathtaking sight. After breakfast and tidying up the camper, Dexter and I embarked along the Seward Highway. This renowned highway is celebrated for its scenic, natural, historical, and recreational beauty. It holds the distinguished titles of a USDA Forest Service Scenic Byway, an Alaska Scenic Byway, and an All-American Road.

The initial fifty miles of the Seward Highway led us alongside the majestic Chugach Mountains and the shores of Turnagain Arm. Based on my discussions with locals, this stretch of road often provides sightings of beluga whales, Dall sheep, waterfalls, and eagles. I kept a close eye, and aside from the waterfalls (icefalls now), our journey that day didn't include such sights. Instead, our focus was on the roadwork that was causing occasional traffic stops. Nevertheless, the highway continued to wind through the mountains, offering us captivating views of the untamed beauty of Alaska.

While driving along the scenic Seward Highway, I found myself faced with a decision—take a detour and visit Hope, Alaska, or just continue on. It meant a seventeen-mile diversion, but I had the luxury of time, and I was eager to explore another of Alaska's historic gold rush towns. A few years back, I had the pleasure of visiting Skagway, Alaska, where I was captivated by how different interests had come together to preserve the late 1890s atmosphere. Klondike Gold Rush National Historical Park oversees more than twenty buildings in the Skagway Historic District, preserving the legacy of the Klondike Gold Rush and honoring the hardships of the stampeders. I wondered if Hope would share in the benefits of such cooperation and preservation.

I turned to Dexter for some sort of confirmation, and she simply gave me a sideways glance from her perch on the console between the front seats, her eyes darting around as we drove. I interpreted that as her way of saying, "What are you waiting for? Let's go!"

Hope: Kenai Peninsula

Date: October 15, 2022
Weather: 30°F Cloudy
Location: Seward Highway, AK

At present, Hope's population hovers around sixty residents, though I believe it swells during the summer months (much like Cape Cod used to). While there are several restaurants, most appear to be closed. Hope, in its heyday, accommodated as many as three thousand people, all lured by the promise of gold.[12] In 1889, a miner unearthed nuggets in nearby Resurrection Creek, which soon led to more discoveries in various streams, including Bear, Sixmile, Canyon, and Mills. This sparked the Turnagain Arm gold rush of the 1890s. According to local lore, the town got its name from the youngest gold rusher to disembark from one of the boats, seventeen-year-old Percy Hope. Whether or not the story is entirely true, the name certainly reflects the optimism that filled every prospector who arrived in Hope in pursuit of fortune.

Today, Hope feels like a town caught between identities, and I suspect that some of it is due to the offseason and boarded up. It feels like it is attempting to keep its history alive, but it doesn't seem to have much to work with. Unlike Skagway, where there is a good-sized town, Hope is a very small enclave on the Kenai Peninsula. Its attraction is its remoteness and peacefulness, with narrow lanes winding past old log buildings, exuding a laid-back atmosphere. I learned that during the 1964 Good Friday earthquake, most of the town was lost to rising waters and now stands as a tidal meadow with camping opportunities on the fringe.

---

[12] "Hope Alaska: An Original Gold Rush Town," ALASKA.ORG, accessed January 26, 2024, https://www.alaska.org/destination/hope.

The hundred-year-old Hope Social Hall remains a weathered log cabin that hosts community gatherings, dances, and weddings. The town, which consists of only a few buildings, was pretty boarded up. It looks to be a quaint place for a leisurely stroll on a summer evening with its shop and saloon, which advertises live music on summer weekends. Many of the homes that still stand today were constructed during the 1890s.

I tried the Creekside Restaurant but was somewhat put out when the cook/waiter/bartender asked for my ID. I thought, "Really?" The guy explained it wasn't for my age but because in Alaska, you're not allowed to drink due to a felony or similar reasons, and they mark your driver's license accordingly. I wondered if he was being difficult or just a millennial, playfully teasing a boomer. In either case, I was not interested in staying. I finished my beer and decided to check out another restaurant—the Dirty Skillet. Here, I ordered a beer without any questions asked, leading me to think that the guy at the Creekside might have just been a bit challenging.

I had initially sought out a pull-out spot recommended by the folks at the Dirty Skillet, but it was already occupied. Luckily, I stumbled upon another pull-out a bit further down the road, right by the river, with the majestic mountains serving as a breathtaking backdrop.

My health has been a bit of a concern lately. My lungs are congested, and breathing has become quite challenging, especially at night. I've resorted to sleeping in a seated position to prevent fluids from accumulating in my lungs and triggering severe coughing fits. These coughing episodes can get so intense that I end up feeling dizzy as a result. I've even experienced these bouts while driving, and it's a truly frightening experience. At times, I've had to pull over to the side of the road just to catch my breath and rest. While I do have a Covid test kit with me, I'm hesitant to use it because I'm currently quite far from any hospital. My hope is that I'll find cell service tomorrow so I can call my primary care physician for guidance. I also have albuterol on hand in case my breathing worsens, but

I'm reserving that for emergencies, which it might become if this condition doesn't improve.

Additionally, I'm still dealing with some tire issues. There's one tire with a slow leak, but I haven't been able to pinpoint where it is. I'm waiting for the rain to let up so I can tend to filling the tires. The air compressor I have isn't the greatest, but it'll have to do for now. I searched for a service station that could work on an RV while on the peninsula and was fortunate to find a place. I booked some time to drop off the truck, not only to have the tires fixed, but also to have an oil change and an overall checkup.

Ninilchik: Kenai Peninsula

Date: October 19, 2022
Weather: 47°F Cloudy
Location: Wayside Road, Ninilchik, AK

At times, I find myself pondering what the allure of spending the winter is in a four-hundred-square-foot space, accompanied by a dog (yes, even a sometimes smelly one). The answer isn't singular; it's a blend of various elements.

I relish waking up to the sight of a breathtaking view outside my window, knowing that all I need to do is roll over to take it in. I appreciate the self-reliance that comes with this lifestyle and the ability to handle things when they don't go as planned. Engaging in conversations with people who have trodden diverse life paths fascinates me, often revealing surprising similarities despite the vastly different settings.

Witnessing sunsets and sunrises in different environments and under varying conditions brings me joy. The freedom to move about without constraints is liberating, allowing me to explore physically and mentally. Above all, this way of life places me in a positive mental and emotional state. This state of mind keeps the thoughts of having cancer far recessed in the back of my mind.

There's not much room for accumulating possessions in a space of only four hundred square feet. What I collect must serve a purpose and see frequent use, emphasizing the value of simplicity and utility in my surroundings. This notion of keeping it simple is important, and I hope it finds its way into other aspects of my life.

As I continued along the Seward Highway, I decided to stop at Ninilchik, a quiet town just off the Sterling Highway, which boasts amazing views across the Cook Inlet. My decision is based primarily on the views and the fact that there was an area that allowed sufficient space for my rig, right on the beach. Dexter and I love where we are boondocking. She is enjoying the freedom of running on the beach, chasing the birds, and the ability to go for a dip in the water when she wants. I just love the views, the smell, and the walk along the beach. Across the inlet are volcanoes. What a majestic site. They drop right into the ocean.

Last night, I witnessed the most spectacular sunset. The entire sky was lit up as the sun set behind the volcanoes on mainland Alaska. It was so nice that I decided to spend another day, hoping to witness it again this evening. (What I am really hoping is that I will have luck and see the Northern Lights.)

After a couple of days of hanging on the beach and taking a few hikes, I continued along the highway on my way to Homer, AK. It was getting around lunchtime, and we passed what looked to be an interesting place to eat. I am a sucker for dirt bars and roadhouse saloons, so I had to stop. Upon entering and seeing a rather large trout hanging on the wall, fishing mags everywhere, and the smell of a wood fire, I was not disappointed. This rustic log roadhouse (Gwin's Lodge Restaurant) looks like it was built in the last century.

It didn't take long to get a discussion going with the bartender, who is also a local fishing guide, and he shared with me a bit of the history of the roadhouse. A couple, Helen and Pat Gwin, hand-built the roadhouse in 1952. Since then, it has grown to include rooms/cabins for rent and has become known for its fine cuisine (which I will agree with). I had salmon, and it was delicious. While it was fairly quiet when I sat down, things picked up quickly. You could tell that this was a popular place. Folks were sharing with each other what they were going to do now that the season was over and the planned trips to see family down in the Lower 48.

Homer: Kenai Peninsula

Date: October 20, 2022
Weather: 45°F Cloudy
Location: Sterling Highway, Homer, AK

Homer is renowned as the "Halibut Fishing Capital of the World." Nestled along the picturesque shores of Kachemak Bay, this coastal town boasts a relaxed, artistic ambiance that perfectly complements its breathtaking views of the bay and the surrounding mountains.

As I ascended a steep incline just before reaching Homer, I was completely unprepared for the awe-inspiring vista that greeted me at the summit. At this precise moment, I fell head over heels for Homer. For years, I had been searching for an elusive place where the mountains harmoniously meet the ocean, and Homer embodied that ideal. It possessed the comforting essence of home with its fishing village charm and sandy beaches, yet it also exuded the grandeur of mountains that gracefully descended into the tranquil bay.

Regrettably, my timing was off, as the season had drawn to a close, and most of the shops, galleries, and restaurants that typically line the picturesque strip of land just outside of Homer had shuttered their doors. Evidently, this place would be teeming with activity during the summer months. Fortunately, one establishment remained open, and I was grateful for it. The Salty Dawg, a quintessential dive bar, was alive and well. Much like any beloved dive bar, it had its share of colorful characters and lively patrons.

The Salty Dawg's history was as rich and diverse as the town itself. It began as one of the earliest cabins constructed in 1897, shortly after

Homer was established as a town.[13] Over the years, it served various purposes, including being the first post office, a railroad station, a grocery store, and an office for a coal mining company. In 1909, a second building was added, which functioned as a schoolhouse, post office, and grocery store. The late 1950s saw the merger of the two buildings, solidifying the Salty Dawg's place in Homer's history and lore.

While I was in the area, I obtained a dozen oysters from the Kachemak Bay Shellfish Co-op, which is located on the spit, and it was an enlightening experience that provided me with valuable insights. I engaged in a lengthy conversation with the individual managing the fish counter, who shared intriguing details about oyster farming in this region. One of the most captivating revelations was that Alaskan oysters do not naturally reproduce in these chilly waters; instead, oyster seed, known as spat, is procured from shellfish hatcheries in the contiguous United States. As per our discussion, the Kachemaks® brand of Alaskan oysters they offer originates from a hatchery in Washington state.

These Alaskan oysters possess distinctive qualities, marked by their sweetness, delicate shells, and gradual growth. They reminded me of Kumamoto oysters, but on steroids. They are carefully nurtured in trays suspended in Alaska's Kenai Peninsula's deep, glacial waters. This unique environment enables them to feed continuously on plankton in the pristine water, sheltered from the elements of scorching summer sun, freezing winter winds, mud, and sand. Consequently, Alaskan oysters exhibit uniform shapes with deep cups and plump, delectable meats, making them perfect for serving on the half shell.

Additionally, I discovered that Alaskan oysters rank among the safest available in the market, especially when compared to oysters from

---

[13] "History," Salty Dawg Saloon, accessed January 27, 2024, https://saltydawgsaloon.com/pages/history.

regions subject to harvest limitations due to public health concerns. The probable reason for this safety is the cold and pristine nature of Alaskan waters, where oysters are harvested from areas that rarely exceed fifty degrees.

What's more, the evolution of an oyster's flavor profile is based on changing seasons, weather conditions, age, reproductive cycles, and even its specific location within a small bay. Each oyster can deliver a delightful medley of flavors, starting with the initial salty touch on the palate, followed by a sweet burst as the silky, fatty lipids are released, culminating in a smooth and lingering sea tang.

You might be wondering why I've delved so deeply into the world of oysters. Hailing from Cape Cod, I thought I knew a thing or two about oysters. However, my experience of learning about oyster farming in Alaska left me fascinated and pondering the state of oyster farming on Cape Cod. Just five miles from my home lies the Cotuit Oyster Company, where I frequently purchase oysters. After doing some research, prompted by my visit to the local oyster farm, I found that the Cotuit Oyster Company boasts a rich history dating back to the 1850s and produces the oldest brand name of oysters in the USA.[14]

Shellfish cultivation on Cape Cod was a practice embraced by Native Americans and later by colonists. Captain William Childs transitioned from a life at sea to the life of an oysterman, eventually establishing one of the largest oyster businesses on Cape Cod. During those times, oysters were packed into wooden barrels and transported across the Cape in large wagons to the railroad depot in West Barnstable. They were shipped by rail to cities like Boston, New York, and others in the Northeast.

---

[14] "Home," Cotuit Oyster Company, Inc., accessed January 27, 2024, https://www.cotuitoystercompany.com/ourhistory.

In 1894, Captain Childs' son Samuel Childs embarked on his own oyster venture. He set up his oyster shanty at the present location of the Cotuit Oyster Company. These oysters from the Nantucket Sound side of Cape Cod are cultivated on one of the oldest oyster leases in the country, situated across Cotuit Bay from the town of Osterville, formerly known as "Oysterville." The oysters are initially started in mesh bags and then bottom-planted in the shallows of Cotuit Bay to enhance their shell strength and deepen their cups. Cotuit Oyster Company, Inc. leases five shellfish aquaculture grants in Cotuit Bay, totaling 33.83 acres, with each site serving various stages of the oysters' life cycle based on factors like predation, bottom type, and depth. Cotuit Oysters are known for their plump meats, moderate brine, and slightly sweet finish.

As I headed back toward Anchorage via the Seward Highway, an unfortunate accident brought traffic to a standstill. The sight was unsettling, with an emergency helicopter shuttling back and forth, indicating the severity of the situation. While waiting along with fellow motorists, a police officer tasked with managing traffic approached me. I couldn't help but wonder why he had singled me out from the long line of vehicles. The answer soon became apparent—I was the only one traveling with a camper and out-of-state license plates.

We struck up a conversation, and he informed me it would be several more hours before the wreckage could be cleared. With that in mind, he suggested an alternate route, albeit slightly longer, that was both remote and promised breathtaking vistas. I gladly accepted his recommendation and, in retrospect, was grateful I did. Following the officer's guidance, I found myself on Skilak Lake Road, leading me toward the stunning Skilak Lake itself. Intrigued, I decided to take a detour and explore the area. Skilak Lake, a part of the Kenai River system, also receives glacial runoff, thanks to the meltwater from Skilak Glacier. The water here is incredibly clear, adding to the lake's allure.

As the early afternoon sun began to cast its warm glow, I thought this spot would be perfect for boondocking. I set up camp, brought out my trusty solo stove, and kindled a comforting fire. Meanwhile, my faithful companion, Dexter, explored the surroundings, caught up in a whirlwind of intriguing scents. Settling into my camp chair, I relaxed by the crackling fire, completely immersed in the scene before me.

The view was nothing short of enchanting—snow-covered mountains stood tall, their mirrored images glistening on the tranquil surface of the lake. It was a mesmerizing tableau, one that transported me into a world of tranquility and natural beauty.

As I lost myself in contemplation, a hauntingly beautiful sound interrupted my reverie—the trumpeting calls of swans. High above, a group of trumpeter swans soared gracefully, seemingly blending into the low-hanging white clouds. Their aerial performance was spellbinding as they circled overhead, repeatedly landing and taking off in a mesmerizing display of avian grace.

The swans continued their intricate dance, seemingly performing for an eternity, before gracefully concluding their elegant display. This extraordinary moment served as a poignant reminder of the profound wonders that nature bestows upon those who pause to appreciate its beauty. And if witnessing the swans' dance wasn't already a remarkable experience, the evening's sunset added another layer of awe. The sky transformed into a breathtaking canvas of yellow and amber hues, offering a soothing and delightful end to the day.

As morning broke, I was treated to an even grander spectacle—a sunrise of unparalleled magnificence. Its natural radiance gradually bathed the entire landscape in a warm, fiery glow, leaving an indelible impression on my senses.

Glenallen

Date: October 27, 2022
Weather: 19°F Sunny
Location: Richardson Hwy, Copper Center, AK

Last night, I managed to find a campsite in a picturesque picnic area by a river. When I woke up this morning, I was greeted by the sound of a snowplow working to clear the area where I had parked. I needed to move my camper so they could complete their task, as it appeared that about four inches of snow had fallen overnight. While I was getting dressed, my nose began to bleed once again, a somewhat frequent occurrence lately. Unfortunately, this time, I couldn't get it to stop.

I shifted my camper and Jeep to a new location, then settled back into the camper to contemplate my next move. The recent string of nosebleeds had been worrying me, and I wondered if it was a sign that my blood pressure medication wasn't doing its job anymore. A bit of online digging hinted at a possible link between nosebleeds and high blood pressure. Concerned, I called my primary care physician, who recommended I visit an urgent care center. I dialed 9-1-1 to find the closest one, and they directed me to Crossroads Urgent Care, a facility under the umbrella of Cross Road Health Ministries. This ministry, established in 1956, has been offering healthcare in the Copper River Valley and Interior of Alaska, motivated by a mission of service in the name of Jesus Christ.[15]

Admittedly, I wasn't sure what to expect from this facility. At this point, I was open to receiving help from any quarter, including divine intervention. Fortunately, I managed to secure an appointment and was seen by a doctor who, interestingly, was a volunteer from Atlanta,

---

[15] "History," Cross Road Health Ministries, May 25, 2022, https://crossroadmc.org/history/.

Georgia, dedicating a few months each year to serve in Glenallen. Everyone I encountered there was kind and eager to assist.

The nurse attempted to draw blood from my arm, but dehydration made my veins elusive, forcing her to use a vein in my hand instead. The cause of my nosebleeds remained unclear, so they packed my nose with cotton and scheduled a follow-up for the next day to recheck my elevated blood pressure (which read 161/105) and to see if the bleeding persisted. They also took some blood to check for anemia. To keep an eye on my condition, I bought a blood pressure monitor, though the readings I got throughout the day were somewhat inconsistent.

While I was boondocking in the parking lot of the picnic area in Glennallen, the idea of embarking on a journey to McCarthy, a route steeped in legend among Alaskan locals, began to occupy my thoughts. After hearing numerous tales of this adventure, I found myself irresistibly drawn to the prospect. Most of the successful stories I encountered revolved around summer treks, while the less fortunate ones were about winter excursions. As I often say, a trip truly becomes an adventure when it presents challenges.

The journey to McCarthy was starting to take on the characteristics of an adventure, especially with the forecast predicting snow. The more precarious part of the trip lay beyond the town of Chitina, a place boasting a population of around 120 residents, located approximately thirty miles off the Richardson Highway. The spur road to Chitina can be found across from Pippen Lake, and as far as I could gather, it was paved.

Chitina sits on the banks of the Copper River, marking the boundary of Wrangell-St. Elias National Park. It was the ancestral home of the Athabascans for millennia, with the Ahtna Athabascan name for the region being Tsedi Na', signifying "Copper River."[16] However, the

---

[16] "History of the Wrangell-St. Elias Area," National Parks Service, accessed January 27, 2024, https://www.nps.gov/wrst/learn/historyculture/human-history.htm.

discovery of copper ore around 1900 brought about a transformative shift in the area's history.

If I were to proceed, my plan was to take the rig, park it at Pippen Lake, and then uncouple the Jeep, continuing from that point with the Jeep. According to the National Park Service (NPS) website, the road is described as a "winding road deep into the heart of Wrangell-St. Elias National Park and Preserve." It sounded interesting. Once a conduit to immense fortunes, it now serves as a gateway to stunning landscapes, vast wilderness, and adventure. For those willing to leave the comforts of pavement behind, this road offers access to many natural and historical wonders within the USA's largest national park.

Based on my research, the road retains vestiges of its railway origins, with remnants of railroad ties occasionally surfacing and the occasional spike, creating unexpected hazards. It's important to note that during the winter, no services are available near, around, or at McCarthy, which means you're on your own. While the McCarthy Road is open and maintained year-round by the State of Alaska, driving it during winter presents significant challenges, including snow, ice, slush, deep ruts, and mud. Despite my keen interest in pushing my luck and enjoying the trip to McCarthy, I realized I needed to take care of a few health issues first, namely this darn nosebleed. It was still occurring.

This morning was dominated by an urgent need to address my suddenly severe nosebleed. Rather than heading toward McCarthy or revisiting the ministry, I made the decision to drive to the ER in Palmer, a journey of about two and a half hours. With the bleeding intensifying, I couldn't risk the possibility of a serious hemorrhage, especially while being in the middle of nowhere.

The drive was fairly direct. Upon arrival and check-in at the ER, they promptly attended to me, cauterizing my nose to halt the bleeding, and advising a return visit in a few days for packing removal.

In moments like these, I'm reminded of the advantages of my nomadic lifestyle; wherever I am, my home is always with me. Being temporarily stationed in Palmer wasn't a hassle. I saw it as an opportunity to catch up on some everyday tasks: laundry, a much-needed shower, restocking essentials, and refilling propane.

During this unexpected pause in my travels, I took time to visit the NOLS branch in Palmer, reflecting on my summer of 2009 kayak expedition with the National Outdoor Leadership School. That adventure had us kayaking for weeks in Prince William Sound. The Palmer branch was where it all began: learning about the expedition, gathering supplies and gear, and embarking into the wild Alaskan frontier. It was an unforgettable journey that not only offered me a chance to experience Alaska's majestic wilderness, but also imparted crucial skills in expedition management.

Hatcher Pass

Date: October 30, 2022
Weather: 23°F Cloudy
Location: Fishhook Willow Road, Palmer, AK

Back in Palmer, I seized the opportunity to add some excitement to my journey with a ski mountaineering trip to Hatcher Pass in Alaska's captivating Matanuska-Susitna Valley. This area is named in honor of Robert Hatcher, a pioneering prospector who struck gold in these mountains in the early 20th century. I had previously explored Hatcher Pass in 2002 with my friend Fred, as part of our acclimatization for an extensive ski adventure in the Chugach Mountains. That expedition was an ambitious one, spanning from the slopes of Mt. Alyeska in Girdwood to heli-skiing in the Chugach, and even a bush plane airlift to the pristine Matanuska Glacier for four days of intense ski mountaineering. We set up our base at the Scandinavian Peaks hut, embarking on various peak-bagging excursions from there.

This time, however, my plan was more modest but no less exciting—a day-long ascent and descent of the slopes, serving as a perfect primer for an upcoming ski mountaineering trip in British Columbia. Before setting out, I meticulously inspected my gear, which had braved the elements atop my Jeep for a month. I tended to every detail, from removing rust from my backcountry skis to cleaning my ski touring boots, ensuring my climbing skins were ready, and checking all my avalanche safety equipment—beacon, shovel, probe, and essential warm clothing.

Eager to embrace the daybreak, I arrived at the Fishhook parking area just as the early morning darkness lingered, equipped with steaming coffee, a bagel, and my trusty headlamp lighting the way. Dexter, my faithful furry friend, remained in the camper, his suitability for the rugged mountain terrain uncertain in my mind.

I was thankful to find a beacon checkpoint installed by the Hatcher Pass Avalanche Center right in the Fishhook lot. Skiing solo, it was prudent to ensure my beacon was functioning correctly. Despite a low avalanche risk, as reported by the HPAC website, which I had consulted the day before, I wasn't keen on wishing I had checked my beacon amid an avalanche.

Today's challenge: Marmot Mountain, rising to 4,623 feet with a substantial 1,947-foot vertical climb from where I stood. With climbing skins fitted for the necessary grip, I began the season's first ascent. The steep climb had me questioning my choice almost immediately, but as I ascended, the reward became apparent. The Talkeetna Mountains, bathed in the emerging light of sunrise, unfolded in a breathtaking panorama, a memory etched forever in my mind.

Reaching the summit, I took a moment to relish my coffee and bagel, all while being enveloped in the magnificent vista. What followed was the day's pinnacle—the ski descent. After removing my climbing skins and adjusting my bindings, I faced the descent with anticipation. The slope presented a complex tapestry of icy patches, crusty snow, and sporadic grass tufts peeking through, making the downhill journey an intricate dance of adrenaline and precision.

Successfully completing my first ski run of the season at Hatcher Pass, under the challenging early season conditions, was a personal victory. Given the level of exertion required, I was worried that my nose would begin bleeding at any moment. Thankfully, it did not. This achievement marked a nice start to my ski mountaineering adventures, a day that beautifully blended the majesty of nature with my own determination and grit.

The experience of ski mountaineering in Hatcher Pass is a test of both physical stamina and technical skill. Despite its demands, the rewards are beyond measure. I found myself deeply gratified by my spur-of-the-moment decision to include Hatcher Pass in my journey. It allowed me to immerse myself in the awe-inspiring beauty of Alaska's pristine wilderness, leaving me exhilarated, albeit a bit weary from the adventure.

Valdez

Date: November 2, 2022
Weather: 0°F Snowy
Location: 329 Fairbanks Dr, Valdez, AK

Nestled at the head of a deep fjord in Prince William Sound, Valdez is a mesmerizing fusion of tidewater glaciers, majestic mountains, and a rich tapestry of wildlife, both on land and in the surrounding waters. The allure of Valdez beckoned to me, but I harbored concerns about what would be accessible during this time of year.

My research unveiled that Valdez is a highly sought-after winter destination, where several outfitters stand ready to guide adventurers in the pursuit of thrilling activities like heli-skiing, snowboarding, ice climbing, fat biking, and cross-country skiing within the rugged Chugach Mountains of Alaska. Valdez boasts an abundance of glaciated areas, offering a variety of terrains, from steep mountain faces to expansive powder bowls and lengthy couloirs—each one a unique treasure waiting to be explored. The snowfall in Valdez is legendary, with over three hundred inches annually within the city limits and an astonishing 600 to 900 inches in nearby Thompson Pass. For snow sports enthusiasts, the allure of fresh powder is incomparable. Valdez and the nearby Thompson Pass boast an extensive expanse of untouched backcountry wilderness, offering a playground for snow activities of every kind. Valdez provides the ideal setting to venture off the grid in pursuit of undiscovered and awe-inspiring adventures.

Despite the sensible warnings, especially with the anticipation of an impending snowstorm, I still chose to embark on the journey to Valdez, swayed by the advice of locals I had shared beers with the previous night. My departure this morning coincided with a blinding snowstorm that obscured visibility, with relentless snowfall shrouding the landscape. The weather forecast predicts clearing skies by Friday, so I'm hopeful that my stay in Valdez will prove worthwhile. Perhaps I'll finally have the opportunity to explore a museum or immerse myself in the culture of the local Indigenous community, though only time will tell.

En route to Valdez, I made a wise decision to pull over and spend the night as the snowstorm intensified. When I awoke, I was greeted by the sight of nearly a foot of freshly fallen snow. Concerned about the potential closure of the pass, I faced a challenge: lacking internet access, I did not know if it was open. I was already committed, so I continued to drive through Thompson Pass and Keystone Canyon. This presented a few challenges, yet the scenery was nothing short of breathtaking. I gained a newfound appreciation for Thompson Pass, renowned as the snowiest place in Alaska, receiving an average of five hundred inches of snow each year!

As I continued through Keystone Canyon, it became evident that this region is famous for its waterfalls. While many of these falls were already frozen, I could easily see why it's a prime destination for ice climbing. The icy road and limited opportunities to pull over made for a nerve-wracking journey, but my determination propelled me forward, ultimately leading me to Valdez.

During this journey to Valdez, I had the privilege of encountering remarkable wildlife. The sheer abundance of bald eagles in the Valdez area left me in awe. Furthermore, stumbling upon two moose leisurely traversing a game path was an unexpected and delightful surprise, adding a unique dimension to my adventure.

This town exists in a state of near hibernation, with only a handful of businesses remaining open to provide essentials like food, fuel, propane, and clothing. The tourist-centric establishments, however, have mostly closed shop, with the notable exceptions of the museum and visitor's center, which I surprisingly found myself exploring. It seems I've arrived in the shoulder season, an in-between time that's too chilly for summer pursuits and a tad early for winter activities.

A few days ago, the sun broke through, presenting a breathtaking scene. During a walk down to the docks, I was greeted by a mesmerizing interplay of light and shadow against a snowy canvas. The sun, a shy orb, barely pierced through the thick blanket of clouds and fog enveloping the town. Amidst this overcast sky, a delicate layer of mist weaved its way around the masts of the boats, casting them in an ethereal glow. The distant mountains, visible only as silhouettes through the mist, added to the scene's serene beauty. There was an undeniable chill in the air, enhancing the wintry tableau.

In this quiet moment, it was easy to imagine the docks bustling with energy in the warmer months of spring and summer. But for now, the streets lay so deserted that one could fire a cannon down the center without risk of disturbance—a stark contrast to the vibrant life I envision here in the town's peak seasons.

On my visit to town, I decided to take Dexter for a stroll and chanced upon the Dock Point Trail. The kiosk sign promised breathtaking views of Harbor Cove, the Duck Flats wetlands, and a rich array of wildlife. The trail, winding along a peninsula, includes a steep section but conveniently loops back, allowing hikers the option to hike clockwise to bypass the tougher ascent.

Our walk turned out to be a wildlife enthusiast's delight. The highlight was witnessing a convocation of eagles perched in the trees and on shoreline stumps. One eagle seemed to eye me curiously, as if questioning my presence. Observing these eagles was mesmerizing. Each would majestically launch into flight, wings unfurling and catching the wind like sails. The way they ascended with such ease, effortlessly soaring above the landscape, was a sight to behold. Their flight was smooth and swift, gliding through the air and shifting from a high soar to a rapid dive in an instant, a testament to their hunting skill and agility. Watching these magnificent birds, each seemingly trying to outdo the last in an aerial ballet, was a profound reminder of nature's splendor.

However, our exploration of the peninsula was cut short due to the deep snow, which made walking challenging as I kept post-holing (sinking) into the snow. But Dexter found her joy, leaping into snowbanks and playfully burrowing through tunnels, making the most of our winter adventure.

One evening, I decided to explore the local scene and found myself at Valdez Brewery. As I stepped inside, I was immediately struck by its spacious, bright, and welcoming ambiance. The place was a hive of activity, with a few folks huddled together and engaged in deep discussion. Others were sitting along a long table with sketch pads and pencils in hand, looking with interest at what appeared to be the instructor. A real sense of community was apparent within the first few steps of the taproom.

As I walked to the bar, the aroma of hops and barley was thick in the air. The brewery offered an impressive array of brews. I was immediately drawn to the Hippy Ridge Hazy pale ale. It was not because of the brewer's description of the ale but because I view myself as a bit of a hippy and the type of pale ale was New England, reminding me of home. The other beer I sampled and really enjoyed was the Spruce Springsteen with real spruce tips, a true Alaskan twist.

What set this brewery apart was its heartfelt commitment to the local arts scene. The walls were adorned with an array of creative works by local artists, turning the taproom into a vibrant gallery. As I wandered through, sipping my Hippy Ale, I was captivated by a particular painting. The artwork, created by Raeann Kruger, a local Valdez artist, depicted a solitary figure ascending a snowy valley. This scene struck a chord with me, evoking a sense of solitude and resilience against the harsh yet serene Alaskan landscape.

Raeann's painting transported me to the very scene it depicted. The solitary figure, battling the elements while finding peace in the solitude, mirrored feelings I had experienced in my own outdoor adventures. It was as if the painting was speaking directly to my soul. I later learned that Raeann owns an art studio in Valdez, which she described as "the dreamiest piece of property with the cutest little cabin." She calls it a "zenful" art studio, a slice of heaven where her creativity and motivation soar. Learning about her passion and dedication to her art made the painting even more meaningful to me. Her work can be seen at Off the Hook or the Tsaina Lodge and on facebook.com/raeanntheartist.

While my visit to the brewery began as a casual outing, it turned into an experience of connecting with local culture and art. The combination of unique Alaskan brews and the discovery of Raeann Kruger's inspiring artwork made the evening at Valdez Brewery one that I would remember for a long time, particularly because I purchased the painting, and it now sits prominently on my wall. It serves not only to remind me of this night but also of the many ski mountaineering trips I have made where I was that lone figure navigating the valley while a snowstorm was in full force around me.

The trip out of Valdez was tinged with a touch of apprehension due to an impending snowstorm and my concerns about crossing Thompson Pass. I acquired some tire traction pads during my stay in Valdez on the off chance that the roads were now icy, given the few sunny days we had, and now that the temps were dropping. When we left, the sun was shining, highlighting the mountains and the majestic panorama looking out over the harbor. I noted a lone cargo ship anchored, mist coming through the valley, and the mountains coming to an end in the harbor. A tugboat was moored to the cargo ship, making it unclear if the ship was getting ready to set sail or was in the process of unloading. I did not see any human activity, though.

As I drove along the Richardson Highway out of Valdez, I could see the mountains with blasts of wind moving snow about the peaks.

Glancing in my rearview mirror, the scene transformed dramatically. Behind me lay the harbor, where mist danced gently around the boats, creating a serene tableau in stark contrast to the road ahead.

As I drove through Keystone Canyon toward Thompson Pass, I was in store for some frigid temperatures and wind gusts. Each turn on the highway brought me deeper into the mountains, and I could feel the gusts of wind as they shook my rig, and the snow squalls appeared before me. Despite its beauty, I refrained from lingering at any one spot for fear of getting stuck. It was getting late in the afternoon, and I did not want to drive in the dusk or dark.

Along the route to the pass, I was treated to the captivating sight of numerous waterfalls or ice falls. Each one is a little different from the other. Some were a mixture of ice and gushing water, others were frozen solid, and some appeared to be ice tunnels with the water cascading through them. The range of colors, from opaque to greenish blue, was captivating.

Meanwhile, the sky was engaged in its own drama. Clouds rolled in swiftly, challenging the sun's dominion. Though the sun fought back, it was soon reduced to a muted, white orb struggling to shine through the thickening veil. My very cautious pace, necessitated by the icy conditions under my tires, afforded me a silver lining. It allowed me the luxury of time to absorb and reflect upon the magnificent spectacle of nature that was currently unfolding around me, as well as the changes in weather over the past few days in Valdez.

Observations

My journey through Alaska was a tapestry of unexpected thrills and awe-inspiring sights, far surpassing what I had envisioned. Embarking on this adventure at the beginning of "winter" presented its unique challenges, yet it unveiled Alaska's raw beauty in a rare and enchanting light. By far, the sight of majestic mountains, draped in a cloak of snow and ice and plunging directly into any number of bodies of water, Turnagain Arm, Kachemak Bay, Resurrection Bay, or Prince William Sound, has been indelibly imprinted in my mind. The robust fishing boats dotting the foreground added a layer of rugged charm to the scene.

Be it in Homer, Seward, Girdwood, or Valdez, each location unfurled its own brand of wonder, captivating my senses. The back roads of Hatcher Pass in Willow, AK, were as breathtaking as they were demanding, offering vistas that seemed untouched by time. A personal highlight was my off-road trip to Knik Glacier, an experience that brought me face-to-face with nature's grandeur.

Revisiting the NOLS facility stirred a bit of nostalgia within me. It was a delightful reunion with the branch manager, evoking cherished memories of summer days spent on the Prince William Sound, where friendships were forged amidst nature's splendors.

However, the journey wasn't without its trials. An unrelenting nosebleed was a stark reminder of the contrasts between rural and urban healthcare in Alaska, an experience that broadened my understanding of life in these remote parts.

Despite the journey's richness, I harbor a tinge of regret; the Northern Lights remained elusive, their ethereal dance just beyond my reach. And then there was the road less traveled to McCarthy, a path I chose not to tread, a decision prudent yet tinged with wonder about what might have been. My Alaskan adventure, woven with marvels and what-ifs, remains unforgettable during this journey.

Section 5

British Columbia

Mountains Our Sentries

In British Columbia's grip and November's chill,
Along the Cassair, a journey's thrill.
A path less traveled, through vastness we glide,
Mountains our sentries, in silence, they preside.

The snow lays its blanket, a white, endless shroud,
On roads seldom whispered, in landscapes unbowed.
The beauty, a sharpness, both wild and refined,
In isolation's embrace, a peace we find.

Days stretch without seeing another soul pass,
The world seems forgotten in frost's icy glass.
Yet beneath the cold quiet, a heartbeat, a song,
Of nature's enduring, where all things belong.

Mountains stand majestic; in snow caps, they dress,
A backdrop of splendor in stark wilderness.
The Cassair whispers of mysteries untold,
Of stories in silence, of legends bold.

Here, in the remoteness, a journey unfolds,
Where the soul meets the sky, and the earth holds.
A road less traveled, where the wilds caress,
In British Columbia's November, we confess.

The sense of isolation, a gift, not a weight,
In the vast, snowy roads, we find our own state.
A drive through the Cassiar, under skies so wide,
In the heart of the wild, we find where we reside.

British Columbia: Part 1

As this segment of my journey unfolds, the brisk November air ushers in the stark reality of winter—a winter that would be deemed profound and unyielding in other parts of the world. The Alaska Highway now beckons me southward, snaking through towering evergreens. Their branches, laden with the season's first snow, sculpt a landscape that feels almost otherworldly in its tranquility. It's a stark transformation from just a month ago when the same road was a ribbon through a kaleidoscope of fall colors, and the air tinged with an almost tangible warmth.

Now, a penetrating cold slices through my clothing, a relentless reminder of temperatures that have nosedived past the zero mark. Snowbanks, majestic and unyielding, flank the roadside, their crisp edges melting into a slick and deceptive pathway. Vigilance is paramount, as the hidden ice beneath the tires can betray my senses, subtly coaxing the vehicle to hasten its pace. Thankfully, the steady hand of cruise control helps maintain a constant speed, an invaluable ally in these conditions.

My exploration of British Columbia is set to unfold in two distinct chapters. The first will immerse me in the experiences of the Cassair Highway, the BC Ferry system, and the rugged charm of Vancouver Island. The second chapter will lead me from Vancouver along the Powder Highway and the BC Ale Trail, weaving through a tapestry of ski resorts, quaint microbreweries, and breathtaking vistas. Navigating the Cassair Highway promises a fresh challenge, especially now, as winter's grip renders many communities into off-season mode, their services sparse and infrequent.

My departure from Alaska was marked by preparation, ensuring essentials like food, propane, water, and emergency supplies were in good supply. Advisories have cautioned that this journey is not for the faint-hearted in November, marrying the stark beauty and isolation of the Canadian wilderness with the relentless demands of winter travel. I brace myself for the rigors of the road ahead, tempered by the anticipation of encountering stunning, untouched winter landscapes and the profound solitude of the remote wilderness. I am thankful that my planning before embarking on this trip was thorough. There will be minimal cell service on this road. Having the InReach communicator relieves some of my anxiety in the event there is a problem.

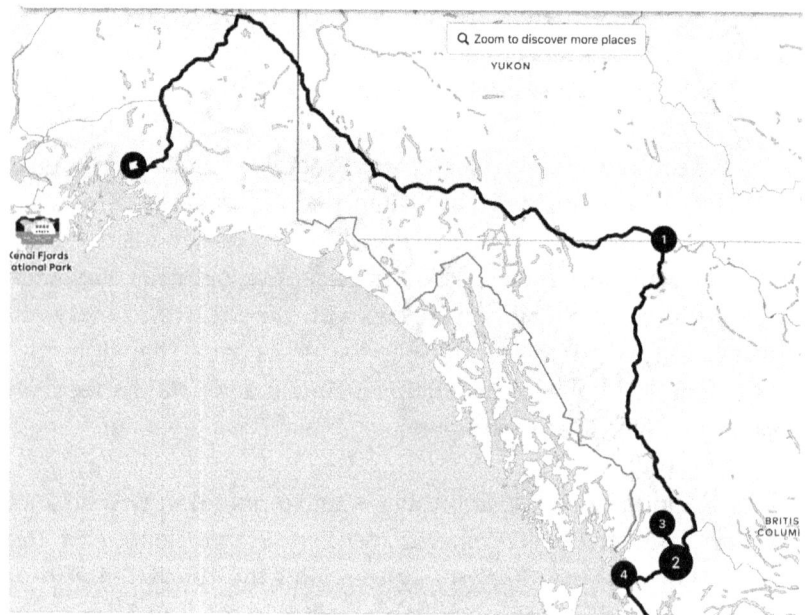

Cassiar Highway

Date: November 10, 2022
Weather: -21°F Overcast
Location: 69831, Äì69839 Cassiar Highway,
Stikine Region, BC, Canada

Today marks the inaugural leg of my Cassiar Highway odyssey. The Cassiar Highway, also known as Route 37, extends for approximately 450 miles through awe-inspiring mountainous landscapes, winding through a picturesque terrain featuring rivers, lakes, and glaciers. While traveling this route, I came across several communities, many of which were in off-season mode. Considering the distance to cover and my vehicle's fuel efficiency, which isn't the best, I'll have to make at least two refueling stops, three to be on the safe side.

I've discovered a wonderful feature along this highway—rest areas. Each area is equipped with a map station that provides valuable information about the facilities available along the way, such as what mile marker to expect rest areas, what services are provided, if any, and if they are seasonal. This resource will be extremely helpful as I continue my journey on this highway. After checking out the first kiosk, I noticed that only three service areas have gas along the next 450 miles.

The reason behind embarking on the Cassiar adventure, aside from seeking the challenge and appreciating the natural beauty, is my decision to take the BC ferry from Prince Rupert through the Inside Passage to Port Hardy on Vancouver Island. The prospect of embracing the unfolding scenery from the ferry's cozy interior, far removed from the escalating snowstorms on the highway to Vancouver, holds a unique allure. It offers a much-needed respite, a peaceful interlude in my journey without halting my progress toward Vancouver.

The road, flanked by dense forests and distant mountains, weaves through a landscape draped in heavy overcast. The path is alarmingly narrow, with snow and ice adding treacherous elements to my journey. I find myself driving cautiously, my hazard lights flickering in a rhythmic dance. Though the road is devoid of other travelers, I keep them on, an instinctive gesture to signal caution amidst these challenging conditions.

An hour has passed on this solitary road, and not a single vehicle has crossed my path. The remoteness is both astounding and eerie. As expected, cell service is non-existent, a likely scenario for the remainder of this route. Fortunately, my old phone, repurposed as a music vault, is brimming with tunes. The melodies of the Modern Jazz Quartet fill the cabin, offering a soothing contrast to the starkness outside. Their rhythms accompany my thoughts, which inevitably turn to emergency scenarios. The likelihood of losing traction on this icy, uneven road looms large in my mind. With little to no shoulder, just a sheer drop-off, a skid could mean a significant plunge, with the attached Jeep potentially exacerbating the situation. Here, in this isolated territory, roadside assistance is a distant dream.

I take solace in my prior planning. Should my truck falter or become ensnared, the Jeep stands ready as an alternate escape. Both vehicles boast their own sets of winches and essential survival gear: blankets, warm clothing, food, water, a flashlight, first-aid supplies, a shovel, an ax, a heat source, and tire chains. Barring any catastrophic damage to the camper, it provides a haven against the harsh, frigid weather. Dexter, my faithful companion, adds a comforting presence to the mix.

One oversight, however, lingers in my mind: I have yet to inform anyone of my travel itinerary and when I'll emerge back into the realm of cell service. This lapse in communication must be addressed promptly.

In terms of technology, my constant companion for this part of the journey is the ever-charged InReach satellite communicator, always attached to my hip. Utilizing the Iridium network, my lifeline for sending and receiving messages, getting weather updates, and pinpointing my location. Under ideal conditions, messages transmit swiftly, though the rugged terrain can sometimes delay this process. It's through this device that I stay abreast of weather changes, given the absence of cell service or Wi-Fi. In an emergency, a press of the SOS button alerts the Garmin Response team, who can then dispatch the necessary help to my coordinates. Having this technology at hand, a silent guardian in the vast wilderness, is reassuring.

At about eighty miles past the junction with the Alcan Highway, I stopped for the night near Baya Lake at the Beaver Dam rest stop. The temperature was ten degrees, and I anticipate it dropping even further during the night. I took a walk with Dexter, and she had a great time exploring all the trails left by passing animals. I often wonder what she will do if she encounters one. While the past few nights have been clear and cold, there haven't been any Northern Lights, which has been frustrating. However, the scenery is breathtaking, so I am more than content with that.

I've noticed that my walks are becoming more challenging due to the pain in my legs, with the right leg being a bit worse. I am also suffering from shortness of breath on these walks and attribute it to being out of shape. Sitting for extended periods while driving can't be helpful, from an overall health perspective. While I try not to dwell on it, I can't help but wonder if it's a symptom of the cancer returning. Fortunately, I don't have cell service, so I can't delve into the untiring jaws of the internet that are looking to consume me as I research the cause and effect of these pains. In any case, it forces me to maintain a slower yet manageable pace.

I am still worried, though, that the cancer is still having its way with me and progressing further into the recesses of my body. My last blood work was in November 2021, when the PSA levels were still undetectable. So that is a good thing. It's been this way since the radiation and hormonal treatments of 2020. I am overdue to update the PSA levels. I will need to make it a to-do when I get back home.

After the walk with Dexter, I entered the camper and was immediately hit with the chill of the wilderness that I had enveloped the camper. It did not take too long before I transformed it into a warm and cozy haven. The evening's task at hand was preparing dinner, a welcome activity after the day's demanding drive. My modest kitchen, equipped with a trusty two-burner stove, became the heart of my temporary home.

I should mention my prized possession in the world of cookware: a sturdy cast-iron skillet. It's perfect for searing steaks to just the right degree of caramelization. As the steak sizzled in the pan, its hearty aroma filled the camper, mingling with the earthy scent of potatoes roasting in the pot. To accompany this, I prepared a crisp, fresh salad, refreshingly contrasting the warm, rich flavors.

Settling down to eat, I uncorked a bottle of Australian Shiraz, a robust selection from the Barossa Valley. Each sip was a symphony of flavors, beautifully complementing the rustic meal. The wine's bold notes were a fitting reward for navigating the day's challenging weather.

Dinner concluded with a crucial task. Recalling the day's thoughts about emergency preparedness, I realized the importance of updating loved ones on my journey. Utilizing my InReach communicator, I sent out messages to my friend Mike and my daughters. It wasn't just about informing them of my whereabouts; it was also a test of my faith in this vital piece of technology.

The following day, responses from Mike and Alex chimed in, a comforting reminder of the world beyond my solitary adventure. Their words, beamed across satellites from the vast expanse of wilderness, were more than mere updates; they were lifelines to my familiar existence, a connection to those who matter most.

In that moment, as I reflected on the day's journey and savored the last notes of my Shiraz, I felt a profound sense of gratitude. The challenges of the road, the simplicity of my meal, and the connection to my loved ones, despite the distance, all culminated in a deep, satisfying contentment. Out here, amidst the untamed beauty of nature, life's complexities seemed to fade, leaving only the purest joys of existence.

On my second day on the Cassiar Highway, the desolation of the surroundings became even more apparent. I had concerns about finding an open service station, but fortunately, the station at Dease Lake was open, allowing me to refuel and replenish my propane supply. I'm pleased to report that the Alde heater is back in working order, and last night's sleep was comfortable, with no chilly thirty-two-degree mornings. The Buddy propane heater I brought along has proven to be a valuable addition, saving me from freezing on several occasions during the trip.

My rest stop for the day was at Blue Lake. This place must be a gem in the summer, with its stocked lakes. However, the sight of fallen trees gave the area an almost war-torn appearance. It seemed like every tree had been chopped down and left behind, leaving me wondering if they were all diseased. I made a stop at a brake check rest area, and to my surprise, it was quite active (yeah, one other truck there—a bit of an overstatement). It's incredible to think about truck drivers navigating steep grades in the dead of night during a snowstorm, but I guess the demand for shipping goods knows no time constraints.

As I waited for the morning light, Dexter seeking attention by laying on me, I found myself contemplating my journey again. While I may not engage in strenuous activities like hiking long distances or cross-country skiing daily, I'm deeply aware of my environment. The scenic vistas are simply breathtaking. I worry about potential mishaps while out and about and prefer not to deal with such uncertainties. This might be a unique time in my life when I can embark on something as unconventional as this journey. With no spouse, grown children leading their own lives, no grandchildren, no work commitments, and no compelling reason to remain tied to the Cape House, I have the freedom to wander the earth and simply experience life.

I relish being on the road. The idea that I rest my head in a place different from the last energizes me every night. I often wonder about those who've been before me, the events they encountered, and their challenges. It's undeniably desolate, but there are people out here. Take Dease Lake, for example—hundreds of miles from anywhere, yet it's a sizable community. Gold mining appears to have played a role in its development, and the First Nation community seems to thrive here.

The road can get incredibly narrow at times, making it nerve-wracking for passing trucks, not to mention the occasional close calls that leave me fearing a head-on collision. The road seems endless, but the surrounding mountains, lakes, and forests are undeniably beautiful. This place would be a fantastic destination in the summer or fall. The remoteness would likely deter most people, I imagine. The only individuals I encounter on these roads are workers and those who call this place home. Not many are daring enough to navigate these routes in a camper. So, I feel a bit special—a special kind of crazy, perhaps.

Today, I embarked on a new literary journey, diving into a book titled "The Anatomy of Spirituality." Curiously, I'm not entirely sure why I decided to purchase it, but I've found its contents to be deeply intriguing. The author, whether by intention or not, appears to be constructing a roadmap that suggests that all religions share fundamental similarities at their core. Essentially, they are not primarily about a deity or eternal life but serve as guides for individuals to coexist civilly within society. This perspective has captivated my interest. Each religion, it seems, imparts a common message on how this harmonious coexistence is to be achieved. Some, like Judaism, offer detailed step-by-step guidance, while others, like Christianity, establish premises and leave the "how" to the discretion of the individual.

Reading this book has prompted me to contemplate my spirituality and what it truly means. Here's what I've come to realize: despite my upbringing in Catholicism, including a six-year stint as an altar boy, I find it challenging to place my faith in Catholicism, Judaism, Islam, or any organized religion, for that matter. Instead, I tend to view them as tools designed to guide humanity toward treating one another with kindness and respect. My belief centers around the notion that we are all manifestations of energy forces and that our existence extends beyond our fleeting earthly lives. Our time on Earth is but a transitory phase.

Each religion introduces the concept of an ethereal force that binds us and governs our actions. I believe there is indeed something more, but the lack of memories of any prior existence before our earthly sojourn troubles me. Infinity cannot exist if there is a beginning, and I don't subscribe to the notion that our origins coincide solely with our earthly birth. There must be a purpose we're meant to fulfill during our time here, a key to unlocking the doors to other existences, although I remain uncertain as to what that purpose might entail.

Some have alluded to the concept of a "journey to consciousness," a point in our lives where we come to grasp the means to unlock these metaphorical doors—using my own terminology, as no one has precisely defined it. In my perspective, our time on Earth serves as a platform for us to encounter a rich spectrum of sensations, encompassing the tactile, emotional, and intellectual realms. However, I'm concerned that as our society progresses and becomes increasingly civilized, we might unintentionally drift away from the authentic experiences that shape our emotional landscapes.

Our growing reliance on technology and our relentless pursuit of financial success and upward mobility could lead us further from the tangible facets of life that are instrumental in shaping our experiences. This, in turn, has a profound influence on our emotional states. The range of emotions we encounter is extensive, spanning from the depths of pain and sorrow to the heights of love and happiness. It includes feelings of acceptance and isolation, the sting of rejection, and the profound experiences of heartbreak, understanding, accomplishment, success, and the humbling acceptance of failure.

For me personally, embarking on journeys along the less-traveled paths of the Americas offers a unique opportunity to reconnect with and gain a deeper understanding of what it truly means to be connected to Mother Nature. These ventures into the wilderness allow me to rediscover the essence of our natural world and the profound interconnectedness that it embodies.

The journey along the Cassiar continues, treating me to its consistently awe-inspiring vistas. While there have been the occasional snow squalls, the drive has been mostly uneventful. Along the way, I happened upon a heli-skiing lodge, which, though gearing up for the ski season that was opening in December, was closed. However, after making an inquiry about access to the gas pumps, they graciously provided access to its fuel pumps and a much-needed coffee. Behind the counter, I encountered a friendly young lady, and our conversation drifted to the topic of hot springs.

I shared my experiences with a few in the Lower 48, and she reciprocated by telling me about one on the way to Prince Rupert. I'm looking forward to checking it out, even though it will add an extra three hours to my journey. Fortunately, I've allowed myself the flexibility to indulge in these kinds of side trips.

Despite the miles still stretching ahead of me, I find myself already reminiscing about the open road. It's a truly liberating experience. As the miles pass by and the landscapes unfold, I have the luxury of uninterrupted contemplation. I reflect on the path I've traveled and what lies ahead. I recall the '80s and '90s as a time of focus, marked by raising a family, advancing in my career, and embarking on the adventures of the world, all on my own terms. These memories hold a special place in my heart.

I fondly remember the times in Vermont with my two girls and wife—those leisurely walks, exhilarating ski outings, and the simple joys of spending time in the ski house. Likewise, the moments spent in Nantucket come rushing back—lazy days on the beach, adventurous four-wheeling on the beaches, the crackling bonfires, thrilling body surfing, and idyllic bike rides along Milepost Road. It was a time of cherished moments, simply relishing the sights and sounds while watching and playing with my girls.

I've been fortunate to lead a rich and diverse life with few regrets. Yet, there's still so much more I aspire to see and experience. The road ahead beckons with the promise of new adventures and horizons yet to be explored.

Terrace, BC

Date: November 14, 2022
Weather: 23°F Fair
Location: Ferry Island, BC

Today was a day filled with the simple yet essential tasks of life on the road—ensuring I had enough fuel, propane, clean clothes, and provisions to keep me and Dexter going. Amid this practicality, I found a moment of connection and discovery that made the day feel much richer.

My first stop was at the visitor's center in Terrace, BC, where I had the pleasure of meeting Morgan, a knowledgeable young lady who was a wealth of information about the area. She generously shared insights on hiking trails, dispersed camping sites, and something that piqued my interest—the Nass Valley Hot Springs. This particular hot spring had been mentioned by a young woman I encountered back at the heli-ski lodge, and now it felt like a serendipitous piece of my journey.

Compelled by a sense of duty to Dexter, my loyal canine companion who had been missing lengthy walks, I chose to venture out to Ferry Island, a tranquil spot just a five-minute drive from town. The walk there was peaceful and picturesque, a much-needed break from the continuous travel. During the stroll, I enjoyed engaging in conversations with other hikers, a pleasant reminder of the personal connections that travel often fosters.

One interaction particularly resonated with me—a woman eagerly discussing her upcoming trip to Morocco, including camping in the Sahara Desert. Her enthusiasm was palpable as she described her plans. Listening to her, I found myself captivated, envisioning the vastness of the Sahara under a starlit sky. Such an experience would undoubtedly offer incredible celestial views, something I could relate to from my time in the Yukon. There, the night skies were a spectacle in themselves, adorned with countless stars and the occasional streak of a shooting star. It was a reminder of the awe-inspiring beauty our world holds.

An unsettling sensation crept over me as I continued along the winding path of my hike. It's a feeling that many can relate to—the inexplicable notion that you are being observed, watched by an unseen presence. To say the least, it was eerie.

Amidst this growing unease, I came upon a quaint bench that invited me to pause and soak in the natural beauty of my surroundings. Yet, as I sat there, the sense of being observed intensified, casting a curious shadow over the serenity of the moment. It was as if unseen eyes followed my every move.

Intrigued, I shifted my focus to the intricate details of the towering trees surrounding me. It was then that I noticed anomalies—subtle yet unmistakably manmade. Carved into the bark of these majestic trees were the unmistakable features of faces and what seemed to be tiny elfin dwellings meticulously etched into the wood. It was a sight both enchanting and surreal, as if the forest itself held secrets waiting to be discovered.

As I left the trail, a weathered wooden sign revealed the mystery behind this extraordinary encounter. It explained that what I had witnessed was the result of twenty-five years of woodcarving by a local artist named Rick Goyette. His shop, known as the Red Raven, was nestled in town, a testament to his unique artistry. Rick was a devoted wood carver, leaving a legacy by carving intricate designs into the bark of trees within the forest, creating hidden treasures for those who took the time to immerse themselves in the natural world.

The idea struck a chord deep within me, resonating with an innate appreciation for artistry in unexpected places. I couldn't help but feel inspired, envisioning the possibility of embarking on a similar venture in my own backyard once I returned home. I was excited at the thought and shared my thinking with my niece, Kira. To my delight, she enthusiastically embraced the idea and expressed a desire to participate in this creative endeavor, carving faces into the trees at my Cape Cod home when she visited next summer.

The day's adventures wound down with a humble night's rest in a Walmart parking lot. It wasn't glamorous, but it offered a practical, no-frills place to recharge. The evening was unexpectedly brightened by a meal at Nija Sushi, an oasis of culinary delight that served as a gentle reminder of the joyous surprises that dot the landscape of a journey marked by simple pleasures. Sushi has long been a favorite cuisine of mine. I have many fond memories of introducing sushi to friends and family. There was one such time, during my early days at Coopers & Lybrand in Boston, where I remember taking a very good friend of mine to lunch. We had gone to Boston College together and now worked at the same firm. Tom had never had sushi but was eager to give it a go.

We ordered the classic sushi lunch special and sake (it was the 80s, and the two-martini lunch was still in vogue). Chopsticks are the go-to utensil for much of the world, and in many restaurants, you might not have other options (Sakura Bana was one of those places). I gave Tom a primer on how to use chopsticks and how to follow proper dining etiquette as you chow down. Now, most people think that the use of chopsticks is straightforward in getting your food from point A (the plate) to point B (your mouth). However, like most things, there are right and wrong ways to do things. Let's talk about the actual chopsticks themselves. Often, at Asian dining tables (whether at home or a restaurant), plates of food are shared among the diners. But don't just dive in with the ends of the chopsticks that you've already put in your mouth. Turn them around, pick up communal food with the unused ends, and place the food on your plate. Then turn your chopsticks around again and eat as usual. If you have ever looked closely at a pair of chopsticks, you will notice that one end is usually thicker than the other. The thinner end is what you use to place the food in your mouth, and the thicker end is for communal settings.

When the food came, Tom was game for using the chopsticks and foregoing the usual fork and knife. I have to admit, watching Tom struggle to get the first piece of sushi into his mouth without just picking up the sushi with his hands was hysterical. At first, I didn't say anything and tried not to laugh, but even the sushi chef was trying to keep from laughing. After what seemed like forever, I helped Tom in using his chopsticks. Tom didn't seem to care about which end was which and commented so. "Imagine trying to eat with a fork for the first time but using the handle instead," I joked, offering a comparison as Tom struggled.

With a mock-serious epiphany, he switched ends—his technique hardly improved, but his spirit was undeterred. "Ah, so this is the sophisticated way," Tom quipped, resorting to a more practical, albeit clumsy, approach. I don't think it actually helped him, but he did get better as the lunch progressed.

This blend of culinary exploration and shared laughter underscored the joy of new experiences and the enduring bond of friendship. It wasn't just about mastering chopsticks or sampling sushi but about the unforgettable memories created alongside friends.

New Aiyansh, BC

Date: November 15, 2022
Weather. 38° Clear
Location: Highway 113

As the night unfolded in this unassuming setting, I was treated to a scene straight out of a nature documentary. Amid gently falling snow and biting cold, a majestic elk stood like a sentinel over a huddle of sixty ducks. The ducks, seemingly too chilled to take flight, nestled together on the snowy ground. The elk, stoic and vigilant, appeared to be their guardian against the harsh elements. This unlikely assembly, playing out in the glow of streetlights against the backdrop of a frigid night, was a moment of pure, unexpected magic—a vivid reminder that the road always has more to reveal, often in the most unexpected of places.

Setting out for the Aiyansh Hot Springs in Nass Valley, I was filled with anticipation but uncertain about the landscape and conditions I would encounter. My expectations were simple: a scenic drive, the allure of natural hot springs, and the cultural richness of the First Nation villages. My journey began on Route 16, then onto Route 113 toward New Aiyansh, traversing a road of mixed gravel and pavement, including single-lane wooden bridges. The drive from Terrace was a mere sixty miles, leading me through the Nisga'a Memorial Lava Bed Provincial Park, a place of both natural beauty and somber history. The aftermath of the Tseax Volcano eruption about 250 years ago, with its lava flow and the destruction it wrought, including forest fires and the tragic loss of approximately two thousand Nisga'a lives, loomed large in the park's narrative.[17]

---

[17] "Nisga'a Knowledge Helps Scientists Create First Detailed Map of Tseax Volcano | CBC News," CBCnews, June 10, 2020, https://www.cbc.ca/news/canada/british-columbia/tseax-volcano-map-1.5605111.

The route to the Aiyansh Hot Springs, nestled amidst Nass Valley's lava fields, was not the best marked. I traveled past the hot springs on my first attempt. Located just five kilometers from a nearby creek, the springs were accessible after a brief, five-minute trek. The path, though slightly steep and potentially slick, particularly after snowfall, was engulfed in a strong sulfur aroma akin to the low tide smell in Cape Cod's marshes. This sulfuric scent, more mineral in nature at the hot springs compared to the organic marine smell of low tide, added to the experience. Naturally heated to 110 to 130 degrees Fahrenheit, the springs' waters required mixing with cooler water to achieve the ideal warm bathing temperature.

I spoke at length at the springs with the individual responsible for managing the hot springs. He returned home after university and now lives there with his wife and daughter. His enthusiasm for his community and the significance of the area were palpable. His wife was employed at the Nisga'a Museum and Visitor Center, and he highly recommended visiting the museum.

My attempts to visit the museum were met with closed doors. I had done my homework on the museum and was disappointed that I would not be able to visit one of the most renowned exhibits at the museum, the Ancestors' Collection, which consists of masks, bentwood boxes, and other artifacts of the Nisga'a tribes. I am an avid collector of boxes and masks and was very interested in seeing them. I was impressed with the design of the museum and found that Nisga'a longhouses and feast dishes inspired the museum's architecture. The design reflected the enduring cultural practices of the Nisga'a people. The longhouse is a traditional communal dwelling, and the intricately carved feast bowls are used in potlatches. The potlatch itself, a ceremony of generosity and prestige derived from the Nootka word meaning "gift," illustrates the deep-rooted traditions of the Indigenous peoples of the Pacific Northwest.

I spent two nights camping at the marina not far from New Aiynash, a serene spot where fishing boats were docked. The scenery was breathtaking, with snow-capped mountains in the backdrop, boats neatly tucked behind a jetty, and the harbor waters beautifully mirroring the vibrant sunset. The few people who came to check on their boats didn't seem to mind my presence.

One morning, I noticed someone loading his boat with substantial supplies from his truck, seemingly facing a dozen trips to complete the task. To show my gratitude for being able to stay in such a picturesque location, I offered to help unload his truck. It was refreshing to engage in some physical activity. We spoke as we carried the supplies to his boat, and I found out he was part of a crew working on a construction project on a nearby island and had come to gather supplies for the month. While I can't recall their project's specifics, it piqued my interest.

Queen Charlotte Strait, Mount Waddington

Date: November 18, 2022
Weather: 30°F Fair
Location: Prince Rupert, BC

Today is the ferry day. I'm heading to Port Hardy on Vancouver Island. It will knock off four days of traveling and worry about snow conditions, cold nights, etc. However, I do not expect that I will be any warmer. The cabins had no room—they were all booked, so that means I will be sleeping on deck. We are not allowed to be in our vehicles while the boat is in motion; otherwise, I would be sleeping with Dexter in the camper. It should be interesting. The good news is that by being forced to stay on the decks, I will be able to see the sights, and hopefully, the evening will be clear and create the opportunity for some Northern Light viewing.

My research revealed that the BC Ferry journey from Prince Rupert through the Inside Passage to Port Hardy is celebrated as one of British Columbia, Canada's most picturesque routes, and it truly lived up to its reputation. The Inside Passage is a series of channels and straits between the mainland and coastal islands, providing a sheltered route with calm waters and stunning vistas.

Seated in the almost exclusive VIP lounge with just three other guests, I enjoyed the panoramic views through the expansive floor-to-ceiling windows. This tranquil setting offered an opportunity to take in the breathtaking maritime and landscape vistas. The voyage, lasting just under twenty-four hours, felt like a serene cruise through a rugged, untouched part of the world, showcasing the awe-inspiring Pacific Northwest coastline. During the trip, I was treated to a magnificent sunset, a striking sunrise, and the imposing beauty of monolithic glaciers. The night sky was clouded, obscuring any chance of seeing the Northern Lights. The ferry made stops at various coastal communities along the way. However, they were done during the night, limiting any ability to catch a glimpse of the villages beyond the loading dock.

During the trip, I met some interesting folks, particularly when they opened the car deck for access to take the dogs for a walk so that they could do their business. Despite Dexter being cooped in the camper for so long, I think she enjoyed the time spent with all the other dogs. It was crazy; they allowed the dogs to roam around the car deck. From Prince Rupert to Bella Bella, there was a lot of room for them to wander and play. Dexter would not do her business— either because she was not comfortable or because she was having so much fun with the other dogs.

One of the VIP lounge travelers was a fellow adventurer who was on his own extraordinary journey in his self-converted campervan. He had been exploring for six months, traversing through Alaska, the Yukon, and the Northwest Territories. Now, he was heading south, seeking warmer climates. His plans included a stint in Baha before shipping his van to Europe to continue his explorations. Accompanying him was his small pet, a practical choice considering the compact size of his living quarters. In comparison, my own camper seemed quite luxurious.

As we neared Vancouver Island, the early morning hours welcomed us with a breathtaking sunrise. The Insular Mountains emerged on the horizon, silhouetted as dark shadows against the sky, illuminated by a stunning orange-red glow. The scene was a striking reminder of the natural beauty this journey offered.

Vancouver Island

Date: November 19, 2022
Weather: 28°F Partly Cloudy
Location: Port Hardy, BC, Canada

Perched at the northeastern edge of Vancouver Island, Port Hardy serves as a gateway to an island realm of stunning diversity. Vancouver Island, cradled by the Pacific just off Canada's coast, is a mosaic of natural wonders. Here, lush rainforests merge into wild coastlines, and unspoiled beaches give way to soaring, snow-draped mountains. Renowned for one of Canada's most temperate climates, this island sanctuary invites year-round outdoor adventures.

The island's western flank is particularly celebrated for its heavy rains, which nourish the vibrant, emerald rainforests. Even in the chill of winter, you'll find the undaunted spirit of adventure in the surfers who dot the waters off Tofino, embracing the icy waves with relentless enthusiasm.

My interest in Vancouver Island was piqued by the desire to delve into the intricacies of the island's logging and lumber industries and to explore the intersection of these industries with the rich indigenous cultures. The logging and lumber sector has been a pivotal force in shaping Vancouver Island's economy and its overall development. However, it also stands at the heart of ongoing dialogues around environmental stewardship and the rights of indigenous communities. These discussions highlight the delicate balance between economic growth and honoring both the natural environment and the ancient cultures that have long called this island home.

My personal connection to the logging and lumber industry is rooted in my pursuits of building kayaks and furniture. The materials I use, Douglas Fir, Sitka Spruce, and Western Red Cedar, are all native to and harvested on Vancouver Island. This link draws me closer to the source of these woods, deepening my interest in the sustainable and cultural aspects of the industry on the island.

Disembarking from the ferry, especially while towing my Jeep, required extra caution, but it was a smooth process overall. Dexter seemed thrilled to be on the move again. She appeared to enjoy being out of the camper, eagerly taking in the bustling surroundings rather than being confined to a dim space. In less than twenty-four hours, I covered what would have otherwise been a four-day journey, enjoying magnificent views of glaciers and landscapes, all while relaxing with a few beers from my comfortable vantage point. The temperature here, a mild forty-five degrees, was a welcome change from the subzero conditions I experienced in Yukon and Alaska, and notably, there was no snow.

I was ready for breakfast, but nothing was open yet. So, I pulled over at a rest stop to brew some coffee in the camper and plan out the next few days. There was no hurry on my agenda, just a desire to explore, absorb, and cherish the diverse experiences Vancouver Island had to offer.

I've visited Vancouver Island twice before; my first trip was as a participant in a National Outdoors Leadership School (NOLS) program in 2012, and the second time was in 2022, exploring the southern part of the island, particularly the Tofino area, in my rig. My stint with NOLS, undertaken after retiring from PwC, was an enlightening journey, sharpening both my outdoor skills and team-playing abilities. The curriculum at NOLS focused on essential wilderness skills like backpacking, hiking, rock climbing, kayaking, sailing, camping, navigation, and first aid. As part of the program in the Pacific Norwest, we spent three weeks on Vancouver Island kayaking and circumnavigating the island of Nootka; two weeks rock climbing at Squamish, BC; four weeks hiking from west to east across the Cascade mountains in Washington state; and three weeks sailing down the Strait of Georgia in BC; and six days at the branch in Washington State to get our Wilderness First Aid certificates, replenish our supplies, and equipment.

The NOLS program appealed to me as a means to acquire a solid foundation for leading my own backcountry expeditions. NOLS is distinguished in the realm of outdoor education for its commitment to developing capable, environmentally ethical leaders who are adept at making sound decisions in wilderness settings. What caught me off-guard was the youthfulness of the cohort; the average age for the semester program was around eighteen, and here I was, a fifty-six-year-old amidst them. I often wonder what my fellow participants, all eight of them, must have thought of seeing me join as a peer rather than an instructor. We spent ninety days together, living either under the stars or in tents. It was an unbelievable experience, one I would recommend to anyone, regardless of age.

While leadership training was a key component, I found myself more drawn to enhancing my skills as a team player. Having been at the helm of teams for over three decades and with plans to volunteer post-retirement, it was important for me to learn and adapt to being an effective team member. Fortunately, the NOLS experience enabled me to achieve both learning how to lead expeditions and be a collaborative team player in varied settings.

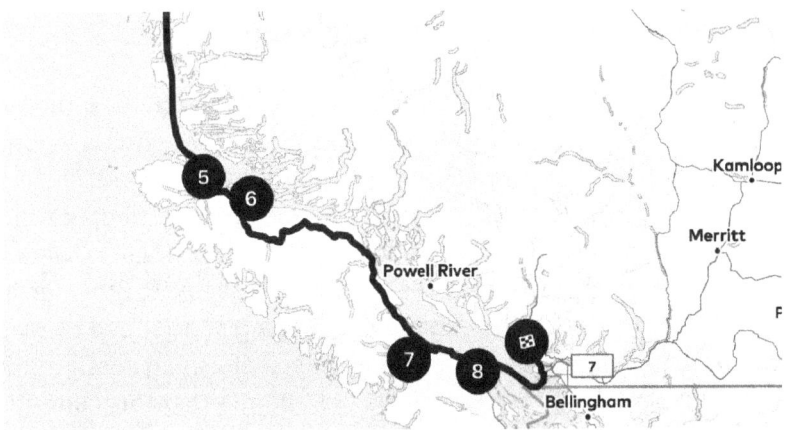

Telegraph Cove

Date: November 21, 2022
Weather: 48°F Overcast
Location: Telegraph Cove, BC

Nestled 130 miles northwest of Campbell River lies a tiny community of just twenty residents. Once a bustling fishing village, it has now transformed into a hub for ecotourism. Sharing the inlet with Beaver Cove, home to a lumber processing facility, this area has become a popular launch point for eco-adventures. Telegraph Cove, a charming and quaint town, is particularly favored by kayakers and those embarking on whale-watching expeditions in Johnstone Strait. Some of my friends have even launched their kayaking adventures from here.

During a leisurely drive through these parts, I stumbled upon a lumber processing site. It wasn't part of my original plan to stop, but the site seemed welcoming. There was a campground back in Telegraph, where I chose to stay. I needed to manage some practicalities with my camper, like waste disposal and refilling water—a much-needed task considering the cost of water, as I mostly boil water for coffee.

The climate here struck me as quite extraordinary. After a month or so of braving subzero temperatures and snow, finding myself in a humid, mid-forties environment without a snowflake in sight was a stark contrast. This "rainforest" creates a unique climate zone, so much so that the local campground remains open in winter, offering water and other services usually unavailable to other locals during these months. The experience of being surrounded by wild trees and inhaling the scent of cedar was a refreshing change. It is amazing to think that across the Strait of Georgia, there are currently snowstorms, with temperatures just below freezing.

My stay at Telegraph Cove Campground was enjoyable. The warmth and hospitality of the hosts at the campground added to the charm of the visit. They have a fascinating side business crafting steel art pieces. I couldn't resist picking up a few to decorate the front of my house back home. (Upon arriving home in 2023 and doing some work remodeling my kitchen, I reached out to them to create a custom piece, which they gladly did, and now it is a focal point in the kitchen, reminding me of my trip to Vancouver Island and, in particular, Telegraph Cove—that land of the Sitka Spruce.)

A few miles outside Telegraph Cove was the WFP Beaver Cove Dryland Sorting site, a lumber processing center that was truly fascinating. It's like a dream for anyone who appreciates heavy machinery in action, both on land and water. This dryland sorting site is where logs from across the island are organized and sorted, a task accomplished by a variety of robust machinery. The site was equipped with front-end loaders, wheel loaders, and knuckleboom loaders, not to mention the dozer boats in the water.

It was captivating to watch the front-end loaders skillfully handle large quantities of logs, their operators demonstrating incredible precision as they navigated the lumber yard. Equally impressive were the knuckleboom loaders with their unique, articulated arms resembling knuckles or fingers. These arms, which can fold compactly and extend for loading, added a certain finesse to the heavy lifting involved.

The spectacle continued as sorted logs were dropped into the water at Beaver Cove. Here, the dozer boats took center stage. The skill of the boat operators was as remarkable as that of the land machinery drivers. These dozer boats, crucial for log management on water, were built to endure the demands of moving heavy logs. Their strong hulls could withstand impacts and abrasions, and uniquely, they were equipped with modified push knees and grapple arms tailored for handling log rafts and barges or manipulating the logs on the water. Another notable feature was their low draft, which greatly enhanced their ability to maneuver through and around the logs and building log rafts for later transport.

After a captivating few hours of observing the operations at the dryland sorting processing site, it was time to continue my journey southward. Returning to the Telegraph Cove campground, I prepared to hitch the Jeep back to the camper. I had forgotten that I lost the cotter pin when I initially decoupled the Jeep. I had assumed there was a spare somewhere and didn't dwell on it at the time. Now I wish I had as I searched high and low for a cotter pin in the truck and camper.

Hoping against the odds that the pin was somewhere near where I had uncoupled the Jeep a few days ago, I retraced my earlier route with the truck. After sifting through the leaves and autumn debris, I quite unexpectedly managed to find the missing cotter pin. It felt like a stroke of luck, akin to finding a needle in a haystack. Discovering the pin saved me a significant detour and time, as otherwise, I would have had to drive for hours in search of a hardware store for a replacement. Finding the pin was a small but helpful victory, allowing me to proceed with my plans without further delay.

Port Alberni

Date: November 23, 2022
Weather: 45°F Cloudy
Location: Sproat Lake Provincial Park, BC

Exploring Vancouver Island has been a truly enriching experience. I've gained a wealth of knowledge from the locals about the multifaceted world of logging. This includes insights into its environmental impact, the intricate dynamics between conservationists, loggers, and First Nations communities, and the efforts made to balance the interests of all parties involved. One evening, over a casual beer with a local logger, I was told about Port Alberni, a significant hub in the lumber processing industry. While my search didn't lead me to any active mills, it did bring me to the doorstep of McLean Mill.

McLean Mill is more than just a historical site; it's a portal to a bygone era. Since its opening to the public on July 1, 2000, it stands as a unique testament to the logging and lumber operations of the early to mid-twentieth century in British Columbia, being the only steam-powered sawmill from that period still in existence.[18] The mill, which operated from 1925 until 1965, was initiated by Robert B. McLean and later managed by his sons Walter, Philip, and Arnold. Its rich history led to its designation as a National Historic Site in 1989.

Visiting McLean Mill in November, an off-season period, I encountered a profound quietness, with the visitor's office, souvenir shop, and food area all closed. The site, once alive with the buzz of industry, now lies in a hushed stillness, offering a sharp contrast to its past vibrancy. The mill, resembling a miniature town, boasts several preserved buildings, including former residences, offices,

---

[18] "McLean Mill History: Mclean Mill National Historic Site," McLean Mill, accessed January 27, 2024, https://mcleanmill.ca/history.

a bunkhouse and cookhouse, a blacksmith area, quartermaster's storage, and other structures.

As I wandered around, the ingenuity and efficiency embedded in the mill's process captivated me. Informational boards dotting the property provided detailed insights into the operations at each station. The mill's lumber production involved three primary stages: slabbing the logs, trimming wood into boards, and cutting these boards to standard lengths. While a mill manager oversees the types of lumber cut for specific orders, a sawyer directs each step, maximizing the wood's value.

Central to the mill's history are the steam donkey and the "spar" tree, which are significant advancements in logging technology. These innovations enabled the harvesting of more timber from challenging terrains, expedited log transport, and reduced the need for manual labor. The mill's workforce comprised various specialized roles, each contributing uniquely to its operations. The steam donkey operator, known as a donkeyman; the dogger, responsible for positioning logs for cutting; the setter, who maximized timber yield; and the edgerman, ensuring the quality and dimensions of the finished boards, all played pivotal roles.

My visit to McLean Mill proved to be both intriguing and informative, providing a comprehensive insight into the various specialized roles and complex operations within a lumber mill. This experience greatly enhanced my appreciation and knowledge of the historical aspects of the lumber industry. Coupled with my time spent in Telegraph Cove, I've gained a deeper and more nuanced understanding of the journey logs undergo to become dimensional lumber. These experiences have offered me a clearer view of the entire process, from the initial logging stages to the final production of lumber.

Nanaimo

Date: November 25, 2022
Weather: 43°F Cloudy
Location: Departure Bay, BC

Last night, I was fortunate to find a parking spot in a residential area that was spacious enough for both my truck and Jeep, and conveniently close to the ferry terminal. Eager to avoid missing tomorrow's ferry, this location was ideal. Intriguingly, there was an Italian restaurant within walking distance, so I decided to head there for dinner. Upon arrival, the restaurant appeared closed, but the door was slightly open, and someone was inside.

Entering, I learned they weren't open for dining in, but I could order takeout. As my meal was being prepared, I engaged in a conversation with the person inside, who turned out to be the restaurant owner. He shared that they were about to have their first opening since the pandemic and that many changes had been made to the establishment.

The owner expressed optimism about the area, which was undergoing gentrification. His former pizza place was transitioning into an upscale, quasi-high-end restaurant with an impressive wine selection. He had even collaborated with the town to enhance the neighborhood's appeal and make it a more desirable destination. With recent road re-routings, the neighborhood would get less auto ferry traffic, which was making walking in the area a bit of a hazard.

The locality was gaining popularity as a commuter hub due to its proximity to the ferry dock, witnessing a significant transformation. During our chat, we enjoyed a glass of exquisite Chianti. The area's evolution and the restaurant's high-quality cuisine made me think that if I were a local, this place would become a regular haunt for me. The experience was delightful, both the conversation and the delicious meal.

The morning ferry journey to Horseshoe Bay in Vancouver was smooth and uneventful. Having become adept at maneuvering my rig on and off ferries amidst the bustling mix of larger vehicles, pedestrians, and commuters, it felt like second nature. Upon arrival, I was immediately struck by the contrast from Vancouver Island; here, the temperatures hovered in the mid-thirties, with snow blanketing the ground.

I planned to head to Whistler, taking the scenic Sea-to-Sky Highway (Route 99) to Squamish, where I intended to spend a few days preparing my rig for a shift in activities, focusing on skiing.

Observations

What stands out for me is the remoteness. The drive along the Cassiar Highway, with its striking views, was impressive, but the feeling of isolation was real. I spent a week traveling that road, and the number of vehicles I passed could be counted on one hand. This same sense of seclusion enveloped me during my travels in the Yukon and parts of Alaska. To live a life in these parts surely instills a level of self-reliance that is uncommon in more urban areas. I could envision having lived an entirely different life.

In these vast expanses, nature dictates the rhythm of life and forces you to master the art of harmony with the elements. The days are interwoven with the land, the rivers, and the endless sky. I imagine that, in summer, the sun barely dips below the horizon, stretching days into endless light, a time when the community comes together for fishing, gathering, and celebration. But as winter approaches, the landscape transforms. The sun becomes a rare guest, and snow blankets the endless forests, turning them into a world of white stillness. It's this time that really pulls at my heart. The quiet that exists after a snowfall, and yet everything seems to be alive as the light dances off the ice crystals.

Here, in the heart of winter's grasp, resilience is not just a trait but a necessity. Traditional knowledge, passed down through generations, becomes a lifeline. They navigate the treacherous terrain not only with physical prowess but with an understanding of the land that is profound and almost spiritual. Despite these challenges—the isolation, the harsh weather, and the distance from modern conveniences—I can feel the sense of community and belonging among the folks who call this home. Living here, far from the bustling cities, one learns the true essence of self-reliance and community.

It's a place where every action and decision is intertwined with the rhythm of the land. And in this dance with nature, there's a deep, unspoken understanding of life's fragility and its beauty, something that those in urban sprawls may never fully comprehend.

Section 6

BC and the Powder Highway

Skiing: A Journey of Freedom

Amidst the mountains' silent call,
Where winter drapes its snowy shawl,
There lies a dance of grace and thrill,
The skier's path, a world to distill.

Gliding over pristine white trails,
Each turn, a story that never pales.
The rush of wind, the world a blur,
In this moment, freedom does occur.

Mountains, vast under azure skies,
Hold secrets where the eagle flies.
Each slope, a journey to unknown,
In the dance of snow, the spirit's shown.

These skis travel far and wide,
Across the slopes, in graceful stride.
A metaphor for life's own quest,
In each descent, we find our zest.

Through valleys deep and peaks so high,
Underneath the winter's sky,
Skiing becomes more than a sport,
It's a traveler's tale of a unique sort.

In the embrace of nature's hand,
We traverse this wondrous land.
The freedom found in skiing's flight,
Illuminates our soul's own light.

British Columbia:
Part 2, Ski Season Is Approaching

The upcoming months promised a thrilling pursuit of snow. December was all about immersing myself in British Columbia's renowned skiing spots, breathtaking vistas, and local breweries. My journey would follow the famed Powder Highway and BC ale trail, one an actual route winding through the Kootenay Rockies, encompassing eight alpine ski resorts and a string of unique, somewhat quirky towns: the other a metaphorical route between breweries in the same area.

The Powder Highway is named for its impressive snow quality in this small corner of British Columbia. What makes it even more appealing is that many of the resorts and towns here offer better value than their larger, more well-known counterparts in North America. Many of the ski resorts are RV-friendly and offer helicopter and cat skiing operations, snowmobile rentals, hot springs, and quirky ski towns; I'm excited about spending a month traveling along the Powder Highway, a trip that many consider a once-in-a-lifetime experience, however for me, this has turned into an annual experience, and one I look forward to each year.

I'm drawn to the champagne powder capital, Kicking Horse, and the breathtaking scenery of Revelstoke Mountain. This journey isn't just about incredible skiing; it's also a chance to visit some of the most authentic ski towns in North America. I planned to spend December traveling the Powder Highway, ideally stopping at five of Canada's best resorts: Revelstoke, Kicking Horse, Panorama, Fernie, and Kimberly.

I looked forward to fresh tracks, steep lines, and exploring some of the world's best powder skiing. I have enjoyed past years skiing the Powder Highway.

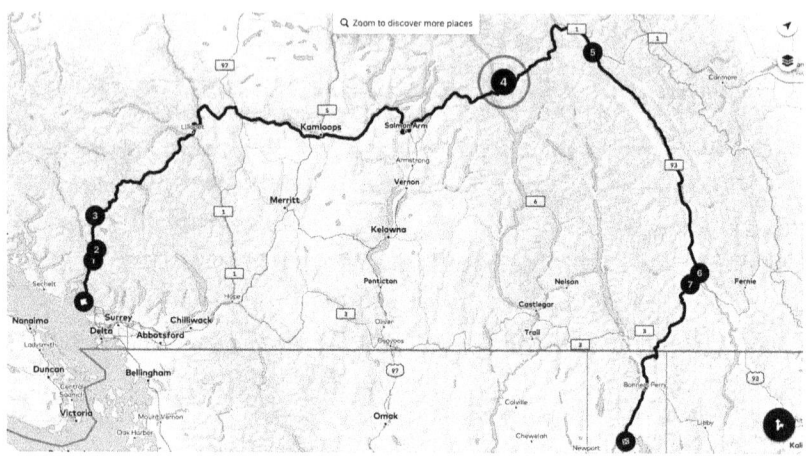

Squamish, BC

Date: December 2, 2022
Weather: 28°F Clear
Location: Howe Sound, BC

Though just about an hour and a half, the drive to Squamish from Vancouver warranted multiple stops simply to marvel at the awe-inspiring scenery. Traversing alongside the Howe Sound, the journey presented breathtaking vistas of the deep fjord, flanked by dramatic mountains. As I journeyed from the coast to higher elevations, the winding roads led me through a transforming landscape, where rugged peaks and dense forests began to unfold. Approaching Squamish, the terrain grew increasingly mountainous, highlighted by the majestic Stawamus Chief, a towering granite monolith that beckons hikers and climbers.

It has been a while since I was last in Squamish. Then, I was participating in a NOLS program learning to rock climb. The program was three weeks in Squamish; however, I don't recall being in the town other than to pass through or to be part of our weekly grocery run. Our routine was mostly being at the campsite and taking the van daily to the various rock-climbing venues, which were many. Squamish is known as a rock climber's mecca. Climbers from around the world are attracted to test their skills in some of the most beautiful and accessible climbing venues, with Howe Sound as the backdrop. My most vivid memory was my first ascent. Most would be surprised that I spent three weeks rock climbing because I have a fear of heights. It seems oxymoronic—someone with a fear of heights willingly rock climbing. My rationale at the time was that I needed to get over it, that if I just looked at the wall and not down, all would be good.

Before I go any further, let me share a few terms regarding rock climbing. Because we were learning to climb, we were using a top-rope method of climbing. Per Wikipedia, "Top rope climbing (or top roping) is a form of rock climbing where the climber is securely attached to a climbing rope that runs through a fixed anchor at the top of the climbing route, and back down to the belayer (or 'second') at the base of the climb. A climber who falls will just hang from the rope at the point of the fall and can then either resume their climb or have the belayer lower them down in a controlled manner to the base of the climb."[19]

Belaying is super important for keeping climbers safe. It's a way for someone (the belayer) to help hold a climber's weight and stop them if they fall. Basically, belaying involves using a rope that connects the climber to the belayer. Nowadays, climbers use special gear like harnesses and belay devices to make this safer and easier. In Appendix N, there is a brief description of the various terms used when rock climbing.

I must be honest; during my first ascent, I was scared. I mean, really scared. As I mentioned before, I am not a small man. The idea of someone not being of equal weight (which were all my climbing mates) serving as my belayer troubled me, and for good reason. My belayer was one of the slighter members of our team. She wanted to be part of my first ascent. As we tied our respective harnesses to the different endpoints of the rope, I looked for the instructor. When we made eye contact, he must have realized the oddity of the match-up and came over to give verbal (and I was hoping physical, when needed) support to our climbing effort.

As I faced the wall about to start, my heart was beyond beating rapidly. It felt as if it was going to pound right out of my chest. My hands were wet from sweat, and I could feel a certain shortness of breath begin. Nonetheless, I began my climb. As I stood there, ready to start the ascent, all the lessons that we covered the past few

---

[19] "Top Rope Climbing," Wikipedia, January 17, 2024, https://en.wikipedia.org/wiki/Top_rope_climbing.

days, like the various grip holds (crimps, jugs, slopers), the position of my body (edging, smearing, flagging), and mastering specific movements (dynos, mantles, laybacks) came into view in my mind's eye. And then, just as quickly, vanished.

I then asked myself, "Wtf am I doing?" But undeterred, I began the ascent. The feel of the rock under my fingers, the texture and cold temperature of its surface, the strain that I was feeling in my arms as they stretched high above my head, searching for a fingerhold, and the shift in weight as my foot found its hold, propelling me further up. Hand over hand, inch by inch, I kept my focus directly in front of me or up, searching for the next opportunity to place my fingers, wondering if I had the strength in my arms to pull me up to the next stage in the climb. I began to feel a rhythm, and with my mates cheering me on, I felt great—until I didn't.

My fingerhold was not as firm as I had thought, and I began to fall from the face of the wall. As my head started to go back, my instinct was to try to grab another handhold, but all I could feel was air, then the sensation of falling. I saw the blue sky swirling above me, and my thought was, "So this is how I die." Just as quickly, I felt a jolt on the rope, feeling the tug of the belayer as they stopped my progression, and a sense of relief, which was brief, as I was beginning to fall again. Now, a certain terror started to penetrate my consciousness. My greatest fear was being realized. "I am falling uncontrollably to my death." Then, just as suddenly, it stopped.

I hung there for a moment, trying to get my breathing under control and my heart rate back to a normal level, not knowing whether to shout with relief or anger. I chose relief and actually laughed aloud. I was so happy that I was just hanging and not spattered on the ground below me. I soon recovered and was back on the wall, continuing my upward path. I soon made it to the top. When I turned around and took in the sight behind me, I felt like something momentous had just occurred, both physically and emotionally. Physically, I conquered my first fall and was able to continue.

Emotionally, I then realized I was not as scared as I thought I would be. Having a near-death experience puts things into perspective. I was so friggin happy to be alive, to have attained the top of this route, and even survived my first fall with only my ego hurt. The rappel down was a breeze, and soon, I found myself high-fiving the other climbers for my first successful ascent. What a feeling.

I did not know this at the time, but my instructor later confided in me what had occurred during my ascent. When I first fell, the jolt was so quick and with such force that even though the belayer responded in time to arrest my falling, she, too, was pulled off the ground. Thus, this is the reason for the initial stop and then falling again. My weight was too much for her to keep herself rooted to the earth. Fortunately for both of us, the instructor was right next to her and caught her as she was ascending, thus the second stop.

Feeling a bit hungry, I was on the lookout for a spot to grab a bite and a drink. Finding parking for my rig in small towns like this can often be challenging. Fortunately, after some searching, I stumbled upon a parking spot near Howe Sound Brewing—talk about serendipity! The brewery was housed in a strikingly beautiful building, and its taproom and bar area were impressively spacious, not to mention the view was quite remarkable too.

I settled in for a comforting soup and sandwich combo while indulging in a tasting of their beers, which were delightfully flavorful. With the place not being too crowded, the bartender had some time to spare, and we struck up a conversation about the local area. He shared insights on the best skiing spots and, for my specific interest, recommended great boondocking areas around Squamish. He mentioned Lake Alice, a popular spot among the boondocking community.

Lake Alice Provincial Park

Date: December 3, 2022
Weather: 40°F Clear
Location: Lake Alice, BC

It turned out to be an excellent recommendation. The presence of other boondockers there meant I could spend a few nights without the worry of being disturbed or asked to move by the Royal Canadian Mounted Police. It was just the kind of spot I was looking for.

The following morning, I noticed that my parking spot was adjacent to a rather sizable RV undergoing what looked like a major renovation. Not one to hold back, I wandered over to introduce myself and offered to help. The RV belonged to a delightful young Australian couple, Claire and Jake, who were gearing up for an ambitious ski tour of their own within Canada and the USA. They planned to visit forty ski areas and ten states/provinces during the winter with their dog, Maya.

In our conversation, it became clear that "road" life was not new to them. Back in Australia, their home country, they had already experienced extensive travel. They had bought the RV in Calgary, Alberta, and had spent the fall season refurbishing its interior to suit the winter conditions better. This entailed a complete overhaul.

Inspecting their progress, I was impressed by the high quality of their work. They had skillfully installed a wood fireplace and cleverly designed a storage space under the RV floor for firewood. They reconfigured the bathroom and bedroom and even created a "wet room" for drying skis, snowboards, and wet gear after a day on the slopes. They had also replaced all the cabinetry and flooring.

Their RV felt like a cozy little cabin with the added advantage of being on wheels. Throughout my travels, we stayed connected through Instagram. Although we hoped to meet again, our paths didn't cross another time. Their story and the transformation of their RV were truly inspiring, a testament to their adventure. After the winter, they set their sights on Europe, put the RV into storage, and continued their world travels.

Winter is here; I awoke to twenty-five degrees in the camper this morning. Not a good start. Problems with the Alde heater will once again be a theme on this trip. This morning, it was a quick fix, though. I had run out of propane, so it was a matter of getting out of the camper and switching over to the other tank. I'm so happy that I have two, but I need to figure out if there is a way to do the switchover from inside (it would be optimum to be able to do it from the comfort of my sleeping bag—haha).

There are a few things I need to pick up while in Squamish. I think I will add a Buddy heater to get the interior warm without having to go outside. That will do for this season, as opposed to trying to find a way to MacGyver the propane tanks on/off switch to the interior. The changeover from one propane tank to the other is a manual process, and I suspect it may be more difficult than I envisioned to automate it.

I cleaned up the skis as best I could; they were in rough shape from being outdoors these past three months. The edges were pretty rusted up, and the bottoms were in terrible shape as well. I am thinking of putting a Thule container on the Jeep to store the skis once I get them tuned; I am worried that the weather is going to continue to beat the heck out of them. I found a place in town that has great reviews and took them down to get tuned up.

I dropped off the rock skis, backcountry, and powder skis. It didn't take long before I received a text from the ski shop that the rock skis that I had dropped off (Dynastar) were ruined by water damage. It's amazing how quick a ski shop can be when nothing is happening. I am glad that I am doing this now and not waiting until I get to

Whistler. The damage was under the binding and could blow out at any moment. The tuning guy won't tune for fear of doing exactly that. So, I went back and purchased a new pair of all-terrain skis. Pretty simple. I suspect this could very well be the last pair of skis I buy. They said that I could pick up the skis in the morning.

The following morning, I made sure to pick up the skis before setting off for Whistler. Additionally, I acquired a storage container and mounted it atop the Jeep. In hindsight, installing this storage solution at the start of the trip would have spared my skis from potential damage. However, I saw this as a serendipitous excuse to indulge in new skis, so it wasn't all bad. Once I had the storage rack assembled and the skis securely stowed, I noticed the new skis were Head skis, matching my existing powder skis.

As I ran through my mental checklist, I realized I had covered most essentials, with the only item left being the Epic pass, which I will get when I get to Whistler Mountain. I had already obtained the IKON pass before leaving home in September. I also made a mental note to check my supply of ski socks once I arrived in Whistler.

Whistler

Date: December 5, 2022
Weather: 25°F Clear
Location: Whistler, BC

The drive to Whistler was only about an hour, and despite the cold, the clarity of the day made for a perfect journey, with the ever-impressive scenery unfolding along the way. Approaching Whistler, memories of my last visit during the final months of Covid restrictions surfaced, leading me to wonder if masks or vaccine records would be necessary this time and whether ski reservations were required.

I checked into the Whistler RV Park and Campground, a spot that was familiar to me from my stay last year. It is conveniently located about a ten-minute drive from Whistler Village. The drive to the park necessitated the use of 4WD to navigate the snowy incline. I recalled the brochure's advice for winter travel: "Four-wheel drive and chains are recommended due to the steep and sometimes unmaintained roads leading to the park." The park itself, perched high, offers stunning views of the surrounding mountains, including Whistler Mountain, Mount Wedge, the Armchair Glacier, and the iconic Black Tusk. I was able to secure a spot where the backdoor of the camper looked out over these stunning mountains when opened. What a great way to start each day, with a cup of coffee in hand and these stunning views.

Close by is Brandywine Falls, which is particularly enchanting amidst the snow. I also remembered there being walking trails, likely used for snowmobiling, right off the RV park—perfect for Dexter's morning and evening strolls.

Once I had the camper set up and the Jeep unhooked, I ventured into Whistler Village. My first order of business was securing my Epic Pass, after which I headed to Function Junction for some food and drinks. I stopped at Coast Mountain Brewery, a place I had enjoyed last year for its unique vibe and great selection of beers. There, I met a fascinating local couple who had lived in the area for a few years. Engaging in a conversation that spanned a wide range of topics was refreshing, especially with people around my age.

On my way back to the RV park, snow began to fall. According to the weather forecast, we were expecting about twelve inches in the next twelve hours. Waking up to continuous snowfall and about six inches of fresh snow, Dexter was ecstatic, playfully jumping and running around in it. Given the poor visibility and my preference to avoid skiing in whiteout conditions, I decided to postpone my first day of lift skiing. I wasn't too disappointed with a clear, sunny day predicted for the following day.

Now hooked up to the RV park's shore power, I planned to use a ceramic heater for additional warmth and to conserve propane. However, I discovered that the camper's outlets weren't working. Initially concerned about a major issue, I decided to check the breaker first and found that a circuit had simply tripped—a quick and easy fix. With the heater running, the camper became comfortably warm.

The camper modifications I made over the summer, like the new captain chairs and moveable table, were proving their worth. I also permanently installed the LED lights I had previously taped to the ceiling, preparing for future boondocking adventures, possibly at the Fernie ski area. The ones in the kitchen area provide much-needed light, and the ones near the cab-over provide a bit of ambiance.

As I sat in the camper, watching the snowfall with Dexter playing nearby, music playing softly, and a freshly brewed coffee in hand, I felt a sense of contentment. Despite a few hiccups, it was turning out to be quite a pleasant afternoon. I worked on my journal, catching up on the past few days. These kinds of days are my favorite: a storm brewing outside, and inside, we are cozy and comfortable.

The next morning was a bluebird day, but friggin cold. I took Dexter out for her morning walk, amazed at how much snow had fallen. My skiing experience on the mountain was quite intriguing, even though only about 30 percent of the trails were open. The fresh snow from the last twenty-four hours certainly improved conditions. Being unfamiliar with the terrain, cautious of the limited snow cover, and feeling my legs weren't in peak skiing shape, it seemed the safest choice to stick to the green runs. Despite these limitations, it was a satisfying first day on the slopes. I was able to get a great view of Blackcomb, the sister peak to Whistler, Decker Mountain, and Mount Currie.

When I arrived back at the camper, Dexter's joy was unmistakable. It was as if we hadn't seen each other in ages. There's something comforting about being missed, and Dexter certainly made her feelings known. We headed out for her walk, and she immediately made a beeline for the wooded forest. Keeping up with her was a challenge. I was supposed to keep her leashed, and consequently, I didn't want to stray too far in case someone came by. Despite the abundance of RVs, the area was eerily quiet. They must be owned by weekend warriors from Vancouver seeking a brief escape. Not a bad setup, if you ask me. A short drive from the city, and you've got your own little retreat.

The next day, I began my journey toward Revelstoke, planning to break the trip into a couple of days. Driving for four or five hours through snowy mountain roads didn't seem wise, so I opted for shorter, two or three-hour drives. This strategy would also allow me to enjoy the scenery along this impressive stretch of road, find a camping spot in daylight, and settle in comfortably. My next destination was Juniper Beach Provincial Park, which looked like an ideal place for an overnight stay. I wish my research was a bit more thorough, though.

The drive was nothing short of enchanting. On this sunny day, the horizon seemed endless, each curve of the road revealing another breathtaking vista. As I headed north from Whistler, the stunning landscape unfolded before me. Compelled by the sheer beauty of the day, I took my time along the Sea to Sky Highway (Highway 99), a route renowned for its spectacular views, especially in summer. I imagined how it would transform under a blanket of winter snow, albeit with more challenging roads.

My first stop was at Nairn Falls. Here, I was greeted by the roar of the waterfall, a wild and untamed beauty that cascaded chaotically into the depths below. The viewing platform offered a safe vantage point, allowing me to be enveloped by the sheer power of nature from above.

Continuing my journey, I reached Duffy Lake, cradled in the embrace of the Coastal Mountains. The scene was a tapestry of contrasts: the clear blue sky, the mountains crowned in white, and the lake itself, with delicate wisps of mist dancing across its surface. I lingered here, savoring my coffee and pastry, lost in the tranquility of the moment. Each sip and bite seemed to enhance the lake's serene beauty, making it a memory not just seen but deeply felt.

Driving through Lilloet and D'Arcy, I was struck by the road's steepness, winding like a snake through the rugged landscape. I felt a wave of gratitude that the skies were clear. On a day like this, the challenge of the road was an exhilarating adventure, with each sharp bend presenting a new vista, each steep grade offering a different perspective of the stunning scenery.

However, I couldn't help but imagine how different this experience could be under a blanket of snow or a sheet of ice. In such conditions, this very road would transform into a very difficult path; each turn a potential pitfall, every descent a nerve-wracking ordeal. Rather than a leisurely drive, it would become a test of nerves, a battle against my own rising anxiety. The thought alone made me grip the steering wheel a bit tighter, even as I admired the beauty of the clear, open road ahead.

Arriving at the provincial park, I was greeted by an unexpected tranquility. There were no other campers there. I was fortunate to have the park, it seemed, to myself, and was looking forward to the solitude. However, this newfound peace was short-lived. Around 10 p.m., a piercing shriek tore through the silence: a train. In a dawning realization, I understood that my campsite lay perilously close to train tracks. The rumbling echoes of trains passing through the valley throughout the night fractured the once-serene atmosphere.

If I had been more thorough in my research, I would have discovered that not one, but two train tracks skirted the park—an attraction for train buffs, as one review put it. Unfortunately, I didn't share this enthusiasm despite the park offering stunning vistas.

The intrusion of the train wasn't my only concern. The heater in my camper, which had been a recurrent issue, malfunctioned yet again. I was thankful for the backup Buddy and electric heater from Whistler, but they were mere stopgaps. The Buddy heater's four-hour limit meant a constant need for propane tanks, and the electric heater was only viable with an electricity supply, like at the Whistler RV Park.

Dealing with the camper's Alde heater turned into a saga of its own. It kept purging its fluid, and my supply to refill it was depleted. At Lake Alice, I had optimistically used the last of it, hoping I had resolved the issue. My attempts to seek help from Alde, Nucamp, and various dealerships led nowhere. Either the fluid was classified as a dangerous good and couldn't be shipped, or it was out of stock with no restock date in sight. The fact that it was a dangerous good seemed oxymoronic. How did they get the shipments in the first place? Did they make the fluid? I doubt it.

As I lay awake, listening to the distant rumble of trains and feeling the chill creep in, I couldn't help but reflect on the unexpected challenges of what I had thought would be a peaceful escape.

Resorting to Amazon, I placed an order for the fluid, hoping it would be delivered to my next booked campsite in Golden, BC. Meanwhile, I needed to figure out the cause of the fluid purging. A quick search of the internet and checking out the FB page for NuCamp campers found that others had experienced the same issue. One solution was just to plug the purge line, which I did with a shaved cork from a fallen soldier. The fix worked, and I was back in business. Another MacGyver effort in the books.

Despite these setbacks, I found some solace in the simple joys of camping, even amidst the unexpected cacophony of trains and the challenges of keeping warm.

Revelstoke

Date: December 6, 2022
Weather: 21°F Light Snow
Location: Highway 1, Columbia Shuswap, BC

I arrived last night at the Boulder Mountain Resort. This is my third year staying here. Each time, the place continues to improve. This year, it seems they have expanded the number of geo domes, as well as cabins. The geo domes look interesting; I wonder, though, how warm they are in winter. This morning, I awoke to six inches of new snow, and it is still snowing. I took Dexter out for her walk, and she was going crazy in the snow. I can't begin to tell you how much she loves the snow. And when we returned to the camper, she jumped up to her perch in the cab-over and watched the snowfall. Soon, I could hear her snoring—quite the content individual.

She is right. It's a beautiful day out. Snow is falling, temps are in the twenties, and the camper is toasty warm. The electric heater is doing its job; the Alde is not functioning because it does not have the necessary fluid, which I don't expect to get until I get to Golden, BC, in a few days' time. What I am worried about is the basement of the camper and what damage is being done there due to the cold temps. It seems like the water is frozen—because the pump is not working. I am worried about this but am unable to do anything about it. I am hoping that since we are stationary at the campground and that the camper is on the truck bed and above ground, whatever little warmth reaches it will be enough to thwart any issues, like busted pipes.

Each day on this journey brings new realizations for me. Recently, I've been contemplating the distinct differences between being alone and feeling lonely. These walkabouts have been instrumental in helping me navigate through personal challenges (like cancer) and understand where I stand in life. I've come to recognize that being alone and feeling lonely evoke vastly different emotions, a distinction often blurred by common misconceptions.

For me, "being alone" refers to the physical state of solitude, not being in the company of others, while "feeling lonely" is an emotional state marked by feelings of isolation or disconnection. Interestingly, I've found that one can feel lonely even amidst a crowd or during various activities. Conversely, being alone can be incredibly fulfilling and serene. On this trip, while I'm mostly alone, my faithful companion, Dexter, is always by my side. Her gestures and expressions convey so much, even in the absence of words.

Traveling solo has endowed me with a liberating sense of freedom. It's an opportunity for positive, peaceful self-reflection, relaxation, and focused engagement in my interests. Being alone is about the lack of physical company but doesn't necessarily imply a lack of connections or relationships. Loneliness, however, is characterized by a sense of emptiness or a yearning for deeper connections, often felt even when surrounded by people. It's linked more to the quality of one's relationships and emotional well-being than to the mere physical presence of others.

I genuinely enjoy being alone, finding solace in solitude. However, loneliness for me sets in when there's been an extended period without contact with my family and loved ones. This feeling of disconnection can happen whether I'm physically by myself or in the company of others. While traveling on my trips, I sometimes ponder whether my preference for solitude is selfish. After much thought, I've come to understand that it's not about selfishness; rather, it's a vital part of my self-care.

Considering my battle with cancer and other health challenges, I could choose to stay home, immersed in endless tests and treatments, wallowing in self-pity. Instead, I opt to travel, explore the world, meet new people, and embrace life. I've discovered that taking care of my mental and emotional well-being makes me more present and supportive in my relationships. It has enhanced my ability to empathize, listen, and connect with others. This mental and emotional rejuvenation is crucial, especially as I confront cancer.

I'm aware that a time may come when my energy wanes or pain intensifies, necessitating a change in my lifestyle. Until then, I am committed to continuing these journeys. The benefits of this lifestyle—the experiences, the joy, the growth—are too significant to forego. These walkabouts aren't just trips; they're an essential part of how I choose to face life's challenges.

The temperatures at Revelstoke Mountain have been extremely cold, hovering between -15°F and -20°F. I've managed a few ski runs but find myself frequently retreating to the lodge for warmth. This is probably the coldest weather I've ever experienced while skiing. Fortunately, the investment I made last year in a super warm, puffy jacket is proving its worth, keeping me mostly comfortable despite the frigid conditions. However, my hands and ears aren't faring as well; I really wish my gloves matched the quality of my jacket.

The intense cold is somewhat hampering my ability to ski safely, which is disappointing. The slopes themselves are fantastic, and the clear, sunny skies make for stunning bluebird days. It's the kind of cold where inhaling through your nose freezes all the hairs in your nostrils. Additionally, my long beard turns into a frozen mass, making me resemble a Yeti—large, with long, gray hair and my beard and hair crusted with snow.

I've developed a real fondness for Revelstoke, not just for its mountain but also for its town and people. There's a genuinely pleasant atmosphere here, and it feels very much like a town geared toward younger folks. What I've particularly appreciated is how inclusive the younger crowd is; they don't overlook me, as happens in some other ski areas. The places I've visited here aren't typically frequented by many older folks, which I find refreshing. My interactions in Revelstoke have led to several memorable experiences.

Throughout the week, I dined and had drinks at various spots. The Village Idiot Bar and Grill stood out with its basic pub vibe, but with some unique culinary twists. The tuna tartare there was exceptional. I struck up a conversation with the bartender, a young woman who had spent the last five years traveling the world, living in China, Europe, and various places across Canada, including working in a heli-skiing outfit. She was quite laid back, and I thoroughly enjoyed our chat. It was quiet, so she spent time talking with me between serving other patrons and waitstaff. During my time there, I met David, 77, mourning the recent loss of his wife and on his way to relocate. He had stopped due to the bad road conditions. We shared a few beers and a good conversation, and I later sent him a text offering my condolences, to which he responded kindly.

When settling my bill, I left the bartender a $100 tip. She approached me at the end of her shift to verify it wasn't a mistake, thinking I might have intended only $10. I assured her it was intentional. She was speechless at first, but eventually asked for a hug, which I happily gave. It was a heartwarming moment; her appreciation and the unexpected hug felt like a small but meaningful connection in both our lives.

Another night at Big Eddy's, over wings and beer, I chatted with a young man who had been living off-grid for several years. He was now moving into the frontcountry with his family and was new to the area. It was interesting to hear how he and his family existed off-grid. Our conversation turned emotional when he mentioned his father, who was going through tough times. We discussed the challenges of helping someone who isn't ready to accept it. When he left, he gave me a kiss on the top of my head, perhaps seeing a reflection of his father in me.

These interactions in Revelstoke have been profoundly touching, adding a rich layer to my experience in this vibrant town.

Kicking Horse Mountain

Date: December 12, 2022
Weather: 27°F Mostly Cloudy
Location: Golden, BC

The drive from Revelstoke to Golden, BC, is nothing short of spectacular, a true feast for the eyes, especially for those who appreciate the majesty of nature. It's a short trip, by my standards, just under two hours, traveling through Glacier National Park (BC, not to be confused with the one in Montana).

As I left Revelstoke, heading eastward on the Trans-Canada Highway (Highway 1), I reflected on the folks I had encountered and what was becoming a familial feel of the town, noting the bonds I had made with the people here. I truly look forward to my next return.

The road took me into the heart of the Selkirk Mountains. This section of the drive was characterized by winding roads, steep grades, dense forests, and occasional glimpses of the Columbia River as it meanders through the valley. The Selkirks give way to the impressive peaks of the Monashee Mountains. Here, the landscape opened to reveal expansive views of towering mountains capped with snow.

The drive took us through Rogers Pass in Glacier National Park, which is unlike any other section of the Trans-Canada Highway. Mountains rise steeply on either side as you traverse the second highest point along the Trans-Canada Highway at almost four thousand feet. In years past, I had spent time backcountry skiing in this area.

Approaching Golden, this small town nestled in the Rocky Mountain Trench, the drive becomes even more dramatic. The Kicking Horse Canyon section near Golden is renowned for its engineering marvels, including bridges and tunnels that navigate through steep cliffs and tight corners. This part of the drive demanded careful attention, but the rewards were breathtaking views of the canyon and the Kicking Horse River below.

What I didn't realize then, and learned while researching for this book, is that the mountain range where Revelstoke exists differs from the one where Kicking Horse exists, despite being only a hundred miles distant. Revelstoke is in the Monashee Mountain range, while Kicking Horse is in the Canadian Rocky Mountain trench. I hadn't realized I was traveling between two different mountain ranges. "Why is that important?" you ask. For those interested in geology, this provides an opportunity to observe and learn about different geological formations and processes. The Canadian Rockies are part of the North American Cordillera, formed by tectonic processes, while the Monashee Mountains are known for their unique mineral deposits and formations. From a visual perspective, these two mountain ranges encompass a variety of landscapes. The Canadian Rockies, known for their rugged, towering peaks, are part of a major mountain system that extends well into the United States; the Monashee Mountains, part of the Columbia Mountains, offer a different kind of beauty with their less rugged but heavily forested slopes.

(The Columbia Mountains include ranges like the Monashee, Selkirk, Purcell, and Cariboo mountains, which are confined to the Canadian side of the border.)

As in the past years, I was staying at the Golden Golf Club and RV park. My purpose for being in Golden was to ski at Kicking Horse Mountain, a place I usually rank just behind Revelstoke in my list of favorites. Unfortunately, my time here turned out to be somewhat disappointing. The lack of fresh snow and reports of icy conditions on the mountain led me to opt out of skiing. I took a trip to the mountain to confirm things and spoke with the ambassador, and they were honest in their appraisal of the conditions. Instead, I spent my time around town and in the camper and taking Dexter for multiple daily walks, which turned out to be beneficial for both of us. I've noticed an improvement in leg strength and a reduction in hip pain.

I regret not having my cross-country skis with me; there was ample snow around the camping area, which was situated on the golf course and had its own Nordic trails. This was my second year staying at the Golden Golf Club RV Park, conveniently located just minutes west of Golden and about twenty minutes from the ski area. I enjoy its simplicity, the fact that there is plenty of space to walk with Dexter, the showers are warm and have a ton of hot water, and that each campsite is secluded, giving the impression that you are the only one about (which was true for the most part).

During one of our daily walks, I decided to make my own trail (actually, there weren't any trails, given that everything was snow-covered). Even though the day was overcast, it was pleasant out, and the walk was invigorating. I was hoping to get a bit of a workout, and the post-holing in places was certainly making it a challenge. After a while, I realized I didn't have a clue where I was. Thinking that this was just going to be a walk with the dog, I didn't bring anything with me, such as my phone, my InReach communicator, or my backpack (which is always packed and ready to go with the ten essentials for backcountry excursions).

Not being familiar with the area or the golf course layout, I couldn't tell if I was still on the golf course or had wandered into a nearby pasture. I started to look for other signs of life by way of any type of footprint in the snow (human or other). I figured that if I was still on the golf course, the best thing was to keep to the edge of the fairway/pasture by walking along the forest's edge. After doing this for a while, I could not see any break in the forest edge, so I opted to change direction and head back over my tracks in the opposite direction.

Dexter was having a blast running in the snow and checking out the rodents or whatever was under the snow that she kept digging for. It's weird; I wasn't the least bit concerned. I was enjoying trying to figure out where the heck I was. It was overcast. Not that it mattered because, even if I knew where the sun was, it wouldn't have made a difference because of my lack of familiarity with the area.

You are going to chuckle over this. After a while, I did find another set of tracks that were, in fact, human with what looked to be a dog. So, I followed these for a while, only to realize that they were my own tracks, and I now was walking in a circle. At this point, my enthusiasm started to wane. It wasn't a game any longer. I needed to figure something out. I tried to find higher ground so that I could have a better vantage point, but I was on a flat golf course. I even thought about climbing a tree, but at my age, that would have been foolhardy. With my luck, I would have fallen out of the tree. Not only would I have been lost but injured as well.

So, I decided to chill where I was, playing with Dexter, but hoping that I would hear a vehicle or see something that could give me a direction to pursue. Murphy's law was coming into being. If I had wanted a nice quiet walk, I suspect that there would have been ATVs or trucks zooming about, but now that I was looking for such a noise—nothing but silence.

In *Alice in Wonderland,* Lewis Carroll said, "When you are lost, any road will get you there," but I felt that if I could find any kind of roadway, it would be better than being in the woods or pasture. So, I kept walking until I did see a break in the woods. It seemed to be a dirt road (I was hoping it was a maintenance road for the golf course); however, there were no tire tracks. After walking a bit, I saw ski tracks coming out of the woods onto the road. Good sign. Now the question is, do I follow the tracks on the road or head back into the woods to follow the tracks? I decided to stay on the road, hoping that the tracks would lead back to the individual car or that another activity would present itself. At least walking on the road was easier than making my own trail, so the positive side of things was that I was not expending as much energy now.

After a half-hour or so, my luck started to change for the better. I came upon an intersection. Now I had to decide. The ski tracks were still heading straight. Should I continue to follow the ski tracks or alter my course?

For some reason, my gut was telling me that the tracks were leading me away from where I wanted to be. My head was telling me to stay the course, rationalizing that you know that there is a human on those skis, and wherever they go, you will eventually find somebody. The question was, for how long did I want to follow these tracks? I decided to go with my gut and changed course, taking a left at the intersection. After a while, I could see a building, which turned out to be one of the maintenance garages for the country club. There were now tire tracks going in the direction I was walking, and soon, I was in familiar territory. I could not understand how I had ended up where I did, but glad that I was where I was, and that was not too far from my campsite.

After another twenty minutes or so, I was walking up to my camper, feeling like I had just accomplished some huge effort and was so happy to be back home. The lesson I learned is that no matter what kind of walk I think I am taking, prepare for the worst and expect the best. Take the darn backpack; that is why it's loaded with essential items, especially when you are alone in unfamiliar territory. And put that InReach back on your hip.

Regarding the town of Golden itself, my latest experience there had a somewhat somber feel. I don't know if it's the aftermath of Covid, but I suspect that it is. The streets were quiet, buildings closed, and the folks I met were a bit more somber this time around. I stopped by the bar/grille on the mountain and found it quite satisfactory. It was lively; folks were hanging out and engaging in discussions. What I liked about Golden in the past was that it isn't just a ski town; it's predominantly a working-class town, characterized by its numerous industrial facilities and the regular, lengthy trains that often result in extended waits at railroad crossings. They have their own brewery in town, the White Tooth Brewery, which I took advantage of during the week.

White Tooth Brewery is known for its crafting of small-batch Belgian-inspired and West Coast-influenced beers. It showcases a diverse range of beers, which I like. I particularly enjoyed the "Blower Pow India Pale Ale," which was characterized by its robust Pacific Northwest style. I tried the "Speed Metal Foreign Extra Stout" just because of the name. According to the menu, the foreign extra stout "salutes the old-school chromoly steel hardtails that started our love affair with mountain biking and beer." And here I thought it was a reference to the '70s heavy metal bands. I thought it was delicious, the chocolaty malts making the difference. While in Golden, I did defer to my go-to restaurant, one that my daughter Caroline introduced me to when we did a ski holiday together with her beau Eric a few years ago.

This restaurant consistently impresses me, though it's on the higher end in terms of price. It's the Cedar House. This place has garnered praise from numerous sources. The secret to their success? Exceptional food quality. The focus here is on local and fresh ingredients, all expertly prepared in their open kitchen, where you can watch the culinary magic unfold. The other reason for their success is the ambiance. As I step into the Cedar House Restaurant, I'm immediately enveloped by the rustic charm that celebrates our mountain surroundings. The decor is a thoughtful blend of wood trim and heavy timbers, perfectly capturing the essence of our alpine setting. Adding to this cozy atmosphere is the cracking fireplace, which truly enhances the après-ski ambiance, making it an ideal retreat after a day on the slopes.

When I went there with my daughter, the chef, Corey Fraser, came out and talked with us about that night's dinner options, how they were prepared, and provided us insights into which wines paired with that night's dishes. And if you're looking for a personal recommendation, try the butternut squash tart and the Duck au Vin. It's an experience you won't forget.

Panorama Mountain Ski Resort

Date: December 17, 2022
Weather: -20°F Cold
Location: Bruce Creek FSR, East Kootenay

At the moment, I'm at Panorama Mountain, though this visit may not be as eventful as I had anticipated. I was hoping to reunite with some acquaintances from last year, Gordon and Denise, whom I met in Sechelt, BC, while exploring the Sunshine Coast north of Vancouver. Gordon and Denise have an approach to life that I deeply admire. My first encounter with Gordon was at Creekside Campground in Sechelt, where he joined me for a campfire chat, and we instantly hit it off. Gordon, an outdoor enthusiast like me, is a fascinating individual with a zest for life. He shared with me a great book about the history of Canada called *A History of Canada in Ten Rivers* by Adam Schoalts. In this book, the author explores the history of Canada through the lens of ten significant rivers, each of which has played a vital role in shaping the country's development and identity. The book examines how these rivers influenced exploration, settlement, trade, and cultural interactions throughout Canada's history.

Ten Rivers provides a unique perspective on Canada's past by focusing on its geographical features and their impact on the nation's history. It is a well-regarded work that offers readers a compelling narrative of Canada's evolution from its early Indigenous peoples to the modern nation it is today.

Gordon and Denise's journey to the Sunshine Coast was a result of her career as a traveling nurse. Embracing a nomadic life, they traverse between the US and Canada, making their home in an RV. Their lifestyle allows them flexibility in duration at each location, ranging from a minimum of three months to potentially a year.

Following their stint in Sechelt, they had set their sights on spending the summer of 2022 at Yellowstone National Park in the US, where Denise was scheduled to work in the park's clinic.

Recently, Gordon reached out after noticing my skiing adventures along the Powder Highway on Instagram. Unfortunately, our paths didn't intersect this time around, but I'm eagerly looking forward to when they do. It's always a pleasure to meet people who share similar passions and who have embraced such an adventurous and fulfilling way of life.

The cold weather has been relentless, far beyond just chilly; it's been seriously freezing, even for someone like me. Enduring temperatures below -20°F, day after day, is a challenge. This experience has given me a newfound respect for those who live and work in such extreme conditions. Thankfully, my mobile home offers warmth, at least for the most part, and a cozy spot to sit back, watch the snowfall, and immerse myself in a good book. I can't really grumble; the views are spectacular, even if I'm not out and about on the mountains themselves. My stay at Panorama Mountain was brief since the ski resort had to close due to the severe cold. Hoping for slightly milder temperatures, I decided to head south to the Kimberley Ski Resort.

Kimberley Ski Resort

Date: December 21, 2022
Weather: -15°F Still Cold
Location: Kimberley, BC

I must admit I underestimated just how cold it would be at Kimberley Ski Resort. In the two nights I've been here, I've battled with the heat going out in various ways, be it gas, electrical, or fan issues, with temperatures lingering around -20°F. Despite these challenges, I've managed to keep the camper at a bearable sixty-five degrees, so I'm holding up alright.

Today promises clear skies, but Kimberley is closed again due to the extreme cold. I spent the entirety of yesterday sorting out my Epic Pass. It turns out I mistakenly purchased an Epic Local Pass instead of the full Epic Pass, despite what's indicated on my lift ticket. Aaron and Danielle at Kimberley were incredibly patient and helpful as I navigated this confusion, though it meant an additional $300 outlay, which feels somewhat wasteful given the circumstances. The ski area had a limited opening yesterday, and today seems no better—opening late and closing early. I opted out of skiing both days, prioritizing safety in this intense cold.

This visit marks my third ski resort stop that I haven't been able to ski due to extreme cold. Kicking Horse had a snow shortage, while both Panorama and Kimberley were unbearably cold, and it seems Fernie might follow suit, if not be even colder. The cold front is affecting a wide area, including the Lower 48 states, with severe weather alerts in places like Montana and Wyoming. Heading further south doesn't promise much respite from the cold.

Right now, my priority is finding warmth for the camper, truck, Jeep, and especially for Dexter. I'm searching for RV parks with electrical hookups so I can stay close to the camper in case any more issues arise. Dexter is also struggling with the cold. She seems uncomfortable on her paws during our walks, and I haven't been able to find the booties I bought for her last year. I'll have to search the Jeep thoroughly to see if they're there.

On my last night at Kimberley Ski Resort, the camper lock froze, and the key broke inside it. I had to punch out the lock, leaving a sizable hole that let in a lot of cold air. Luckily, I had my propane heater and a good sleeping bag to get through the night. The next morning, I managed a makeshift fix to cover the hole and keep the door shut.

In Cranbrook, I visited a few hardware stores and found some helpful folks. We brainstormed ideas for a more permanent fix for the door. Given the cold, I'll wait for warmer weather before attempting further repairs. I've also added a door drape, which surprisingly helps retain heat. The blackout shades are up all the time now, as they're effective in blocking out the cold.

I feel bad for Dexter; she's been cooped up in the camper for a week. Our walks are short due to the cold affecting her paws, and we only stay out long enough for her to do her business.

During my stay in Kimberley, I met some wonderful people working at the hotel/condo complex at the mountain base. One of them, Lachlan, originally from Australia's Gold Coast, now lives in Ontario during the summer and spends winters in Kimberley. Another bartender, a First Nation native, shared familiar stories about the places I've visited, especially the reservations in Alaska, Yukon, and BC.

Though I indulged in too much food and drink, it was just a short walk back to the camper. Despite being stuck in the parking lot for four days without skiing, Kimberley was undeniably beautiful, with some lovely sunsets and sunrises to admire.

8

Cranbrook

Date: December 23, 2022
Weather: -10°F Warming Up
Location: Cranbrook, BC

Last night, I found a picturesque spot for an overnight stop, with beautiful views and the mesmerizing sight of steam rising from the river in the -15°F cold. However, throughout the night, I was unsettled by the sound of traffic on a nearby dirt road, even though I was quite far from Cranbrook. The snowy conditions heightened my worry about a potential accident, with a vehicle possibly skidding off the road and into my camper. This left me half-awake most of the night, a reminder to be more cautious about my roadside camping spots in the future. Fortunately, nothing untoward happened, and I woke up to another frosty morning.

The main reason for my stay near Cranbrook was to pick up some packages: Alex's Christmas gift and a Starlink satellite dish I had ordered. I was tired of not being able to connect to the internet because of the terrible cell service I was having with Verizon. Not being able to gather data about the area, from weather to road closings or ski resort closings, was frustrating. I could have saved myself some unnecessary travel, but then I wouldn't have the kind of adventure that I was having. Unfortunately, both deliveries were delayed due to bad weather. Surprise, surprise—it wasn't just me. The delivery companies were also having a difficult time in this cold weather.

At the UPS point, the staff was incredibly helpful, managing to locate Alex's package and redirect it to Utah, where I planned to stay later. The situation with the Starlink dish was less promising. My efforts to redirect it were unsuccessful, leading me to cancel the order. Disappointingly, I'd already paid for it and now have little hope of receiving the device. Starlink's customer service, or rather the lack thereof, was frustratingly inadequate.

Another reason for my stay was that Fernie Ski Resort was also closed. Checking their Facebook page, I saw for the first time an explanation for the closure; they were waiting for temperatures to rise to -13°F before reopening. That's definitely not within my comfort zone. So, I made the decision not to go to Fernie and instead began planning my return to the USA.

Fort Steele Resort and Park

Date: December 24, 2022
Weather: 1°F Cold and Snowy
Location: Fort Steele, BC

I recently opted to leave the wilderness boondocking and stay at an RV park in Fort Steele, BC, primarily for the much-needed electricity. The cold weather was depleting my camper's batteries rapidly, complicating efforts to maintain warmth. Although I had been using my Buddy propane heater, it was insufficient for the camper's basement area, which houses the water and plumbing systems. I'm worried they might have frozen.

The first night at the park was a significant improvement. Not having to wake up in the middle of the night to manage propane or battery issues was a huge relief. I could comfortably enjoy my time with Dexter, immersed in reading and warmth. I did not want to get up in the morning, but I knew I had a few things I needed to contend with before making the trip back to the States.

The weather is slowly getting better, now at two degrees. I plan to travel tomorrow, hoping for less traffic with people at home for Christmas. My destination is Idaho, slightly warmer, as I gradually make my way to Salt Lake City by January 8th, where I have reservations at an RV park in North Salt Lake.

It was an interesting realization when I checked in at the RV park this morning that it was the same place I stayed last year while leaving Canada. I hadn't recognized it when I arrived late the previous night and directly headed to my reserved spot.

Last year, I encountered a young couple there who had recently made the RV park their home. Since I was planning to cross back into the States the next day and wanted to avoid any complications at customs, I decided to give them my remaining pot. Despite marijuana being legal in both Canada and my destination state, carrying it across the US federal border is illegal, a fact I learned the hard way on my way into Canada. Getting caught could be troublesome, and I preferred simply to purchase more once in Montana.

The couple was quite grateful for the gesture. In return, and to my surprise, they gave me homemade fly-fishing flies. I hadn't expected anything in exchange, but this turned out to be a memorable trade for me. Those flies became a symbol of that encounter, reminding me of that day every time I used them.

With the temperature now more bearable at ten degrees, I focused on fixing the door lock. The cold had previously hampered my efforts to drill out the door for the new lock. After a few hours of work, I successfully secured the door, eliminating the persistent draft.

Since it was Christmas, most places were closed. Instead of a traditional festive dinner at a restaurant, I indulged in a steak and wine, with my trusty companion Dexter eagerly watching and drooling in anticipation of morsels of food that would eventually fall on the floor. She knows I am a messy eater. While I felt a bit guilty about having such a lovely Christmas dinner while she sat and watched, it was still a moment of enjoyment and satisfaction.

Observations

My December in British Columbia was a dance with extremes, marked by a cold so piercing it rewrote my definition of winter. Day after day, the thermometer stubbornly hovered at zero or plunged below, a relentless chill that even stilled the ski slopes. Waking up to thirty degrees in the camper took getting used to. Thankfully, my sleeping bag is good to -30°F. It's that time between getting up in the cold and getting dressed that was the real challenge. Discovering that one of the closed ski areas was awaiting a "warm-up" to -13°F left me incredulous yet in agreement.

Amidst this frostbitten backdrop, my Buddy heater emerged as a true hero, especially during those nights of boondocking, where the icy grip of the wilderness encroached upon my camper. I had envisioned this leg of my journey as a skiing paradise, a dream somewhat dashed as I found myself skiing only for merely eight days, surrendering to the unyielding cold.

Yet, it was not the sting of the cold that would linger in my memory, but rather the beauty of British Columbia in the heart of winter. I recall the trees, cloaked in a heavy mantle of snow, bowing as if in reverence to the weight of winter. The steep grades and mountain passes offered both a challenge and a thrill; it seemed that their treacherous beauty turned every drive into a white-knuckled adventure.

But more than the natural splendor, it was the warmth of the people that truly defined my experience. Their hospitality, kindness, and camaraderie shone brighter than any winter sun, offering a comforting contrast to the frigid air. My time in BC, despite its icy veneer, was profoundly enjoyable and memorable, a testament to the enduring warmth of human connection against the backdrop of nature's stark winter canvas.

Section 7

The Western States

Winter Cowboy: Today's Trail

In lands where winter whispers white,
A cowboy rides as day meets night.
Not of old, with lasso and steed,
But a modern soul, where old paths lead.

His hat, snow-dusted, shades his eyes,
Against the glare of vast, cold skies.
His horse, a pickup, rugged, strong,
Carries him where the days are long.

The prairies vast, now fields of frost,
Echo the tales of the lost.
Yet in his heart, the fire burns bright,
Guiding through the longest night.

Through snowflakes that dance in the chill,
He upholds the cowboy's timeless will.
A symbol of grit in the modern age,
A living chapter, not confined to a page.

His journey under the winter moon,
Sings a tune of a resilient croon.
The spirit of the West, forever alive,
As the winter cowboy continues to thrive.

Back to the States

Now, back on U.S. soil, my journey enters a new chapter, filled with anticipation for skiing adventures across Idaho, Utah, Colorado, Montana, and Wyoming. A February detour to Moab for rock crawling promises a thrilling change of pace. I'm hopeful for milder weather, a stark contrast to British Columbia's chill, and that my recent inactivity hasn't diminished my strength too greatly. Despite the constant companions of shortness of breath and occasional chest pain, my spirit remains undeterred.

Crossing customs was smooth; it was a simple exchange before being welcomed back. Idaho beckons with a promise of exploration and skiing, offering a deeper dive than last year's fleeting visit. Two uncharted ski areas await, igniting excitement for new slopes and challenges.

The coming months are dotted with eagerly awaited reunions: catching up with my college roommate Mike, his sons, my daughter Caroline, and Eric, who will carve through Big Sky's expansive runs, and exploring Utah state parks with Alex will be a highlight.

Caroline, Eric, and I will be nestled in Gallatin Canyon in our cabin at the 320 Guest Ranch, which promises a serene retreat. Hopefully, there may even be a jaunt to Yellowstone, where we can witness Old Faithful's snowy spectacle—an enchanting blend of nature's power and tranquility.

Amidst these adventures, I'm mindful of my health, navigating each day with caution yet unwavering determination. These experiences, shared with loved ones, are not just escapades but affirmations of life's beauty and the richness of human connection set against the backdrop of America's vast wilderness.

Chasing My Northern Lights

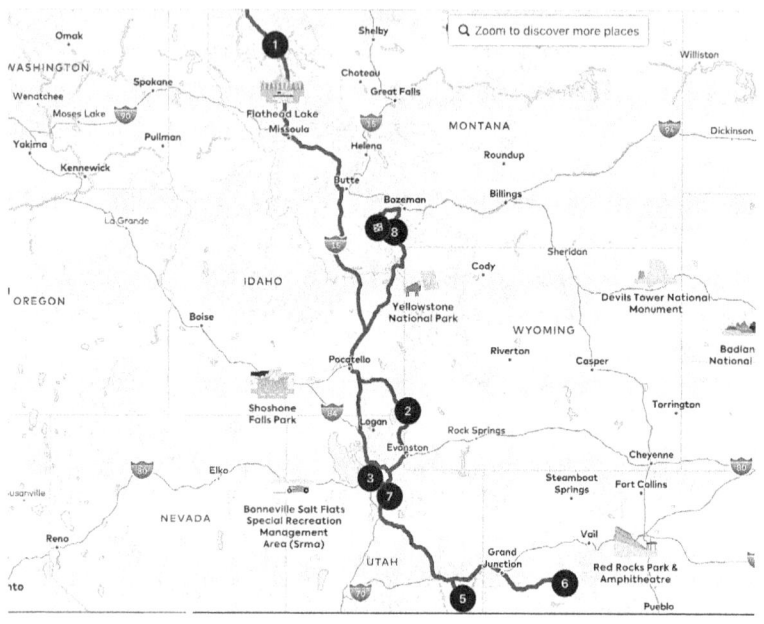

Sandpoint, ID and Whitefish, MT

Date: December 27, 2022
Weather: 37°F Light Rain
Location: Ponderay, ID, USA

When I returned to the USA, I was pleasantly surprised by the smooth customs process, perhaps due to the quiet of Christmas Day. My plan to ski at Schweitzer was thwarted by persistent rain, even at the mountain's summit, which I confirmed on a visit. The area wasn't RV-friendly (or so I thought), leading me to spend nights in a Walmart parking lot, only to later discover a suitable RV parking area for three-night stays right on the mountain. This missed opportunity for camaraderie with fellow travelers and insights into the local skiing scene was a bit of an oversight on my part.

The weather changes have been stark: from -15°F in Cranbrook to a rainy forty degrees in Sandpoint, all within a two-hundred-mile drive south. This has added Schweitzer to the list of mountains, including Kicking Horse, Panorama, Kimberley, and Fernie, where skiing wasn't possible due to various reasons, such as too cold, non-working chair-lifts, no snow, and now rain.

Feeling cooped up in the camper, Dexter and I are eager for more outdoor time. The cold and now rain has limited our walks. Despite this, I remain optimistic about resuming our adventures.

Now moving to Whitefish, MT, the journey involved a stop in Thompson Falls, where I stayed in the parking lot of a church. It looked like there was some function occurring because around 10 p.m., everyone was leaving the parking lot, and I was waiting for that dreaded knock to appear, telling me I had to move on. Nothing happened, and I was able to enjoy a night's sleep and, in the morning, brewed some coffee before folks came back to church and headed on to Whitefish Mountain.

The fog is quite dense here at the mountain. Whitefish Ski Resort allows RVers to park in their RV lot for a few nights, but it's necessary to check in and obtain a pass for this. My intention was to stay in the lot, hoping for a break in the weather and an end to the rain. Whitefish isn't included in either the Epic or IKON ski passes, but I've skied here before and enjoyed it. The day lift ticket is quite affordable at $72, which is impressive for a top-tier resort. The village was bustling when I went to secure my RV parking pass, and I noticed that there were several dining options available. I planned to settle in, take care of Dexter, and then head back for a meal.

When I received the parking pass, I wasn't informed that the RV spots were on a first-come, first-served basis. Given the limited spaces, I assumed they were tracking the number of passes issued. However, upon arrival, all spots were occupied. I had to park my rig and explore other options. Luckily, I found an alternate lot nearby as skiers were leaving, and I discreetly positioned my RV there, hoping to avoid any issues despite having the parking pass displayed.

Before settling in and taking Dexter for a walk, I wanted to grab some beer and food. Roaming the upper village and chatting with locals, I was directed to the "Stube," officially known as The Bierstube. This establishment, a favorite for over fifty years, captivated me with its rough-sawn rafters, cathedral ceiling, and communal tables, evoking a sense of stepping back in time. I half-expected to see a character like William Campbell, aka "the Kid" from the old tales, enter with a six-shooter. Despite the poor weather, the après-ski crowd was lively, adding to the ambiance of this historic spot.

After dinner, I headed back to the rig, sat outside with a beer, and watched the groomers embarking on their nightly journey. It is a mesmerizing sight. As darkness envelops the slopes, these massive machines light up, their powerful headlights piercing through the night like beacons. The groomers are robust, tank-like vehicles equipped with large articulated treads designed to navigate the steep and snowy terrain. Their metal bodies gleam under the artificial light, and their headlights reflect off the pristine snow. At the front of each groomer, a large, blade-like mechanism is visible, used for pushing and sculpting the snow. Behind, they often tow specialized equipment that meticulously churns and smooths the snow's surface, erasing the day's ski tracks and imperfections. This creates the corduroy-like pattern seen on freshly groomed trails, a signature look that skiers and snowboarders adore.

As these groomers methodically traverse the slopes, they move with a sense of purpose and precision. The engines rumble softly, a comforting sound in the stillness of the mountain night. Their lights create dynamic, moving patterns on the snow, casting long shadows and illuminating the otherwise darkened ski runs. The scene is quiet and serene, with only the occasional sound of snow being pushed and compacted.

The nightly voyage of the groomers is akin to a graceful interplay of light and shadows, unfolding like a ballet in the dark. This enchanting process seamlessly converts the day's rugged and disheveled ski runs into smooth, welcoming trails for the following morning. This nightly transformation, a routine yet magical occurrence, illustrates the power of these formidable machines in preparing the mountain for another day of winter sports. Witnessing this serene spectacle unfold is a peaceful and captivating experience.

Waking up to a clear day with the fog lifted and the rain ceased, I felt a surge of excitement about skiing. Despite concerns that the recent cold might have turned the slopes icy, I trusted the groomers had done their job well. My first run was a bit challenging, as it had been a while since I last skied at Revelstoke, but the thrill of being back on the slopes was undeniable.

While queuing for the chairlift, I engaged in conversations with fellow skiers about the day's conditions, seeking advice on the best trails and those to avoid. Engrossed in these discussions, I suddenly realized that the line hadn't moved in some time. A sense of unease rippled through the crowd, accompanied by whispers of a problem with the chairlift. Indeed, the chairs themselves hadn't budged for a while. Eventually, a ski patrol member announced the closure of the lift, with no indication of when it might reopen.

I headed to the lodge for a coffee and more information. I discovered that the lift had broken down and it would be hours before it could be repaired. Ski patrol and others were sending snowmobiles up the mountain. Later, I learned that every skier on the chairlift had to be rescued, a process that took over four hours.

Reflecting on this, I realized the irony of my initial frustration in line. Had I been on the lift, I would have been stuck for hours in the cold, far more frustrated than simply missing another run. It was a stark reminder of how quickly circumstances can change and the importance of patience and perspective in such situations.

After calling it a day and taking Dexter for a walk, I settled back into the camper and spent some time reading the news. This quiet moment led me to ponder the state of current news reporting and its apparent lack of unbiased perspectives. Perhaps it's the luxury of having time to think about such issues, or maybe it's a growing skepticism toward the news I read and the difficulty in finding unbiased, factual coverage on national and global events.

I acknowledge that major broadcast TV networks strive for a centrist approach in their reporting, aiming for neutrality and balance. Yet, I can't help but notice a liberal slant in their coverage. I guess this can be attributed to several factors: the liberal arts and humanities backgrounds of many journalists, which might subtly influence their viewpoints; the urban locations of these media outlets, often in more culturally liberal areas, which could affect story selection and presentation; and the economic imperative to attract viewers in a competitive market. These considerations raise questions about how true independence and unbiased reporting can be ensured, especially when educational backgrounds, audience demographics, and advertiser interests might influence reporting.

My preference leans toward written journalism over TV for news consumption. It's not necessarily because it's better, but because it is usually more in-depth and allows me to corroborate what I read with multiple sources more easily. It's disheartening that I feel the need to fact-check news sources constantly; this doesn't seem like truly independent or factual reporting. I'm not looking for someone to present their opinions as facts; I want to form my opinions based on solid facts, although I may consider their views in shaping my own if they're clearly identified as opinions.

The Founding Fathers placed great emphasis on the role of the press in a democratic society, though they didn't use the term "Fourth Estate." They saw the press as a vital mechanism for checks and balances, with figures like Thomas Jefferson fiercely advocating for press freedom. A free press was deemed essential for transparency, accountability, and an informed public, crucial for facilitating public discourse and healthy debate. Yet today, I find myself having to be vigilant about the biases of TV news stations, missing the straightforward journalism exemplified by figures like Walter Cronkite, Peter Jennings, and Tim Russert. The prevalence of "gotcha" journalism and the challenge of finding truly unbiased reporters are concerning. What happened to the Fourth Estate fulfilling its foundational role?

The advent of the internet, social media, and round-the-clock news cycles has significantly altered the landscape of news production and consumption, affecting the ways journalism is practiced and influencing how the public views media credibility. Various individuals and organizations are putting effort into navigating these complexities. These efforts include advocating for enhanced journalistic standards, bolstering independent media platforms, and implementing media literacy initiatives to assist the public in critically assessing news sources. It's my hope that these efforts will lead us to effective solutions.

Artificial intelligence (AI) presents a potential solution for fostering more unbiased news reporting. AI can automate tasks such as fact-checking, delve into large datasets for investigative journalism, minimize human bias in reporting, customize content for balanced viewpoints, and facilitate the processing of global news in numerous languages. However, it's important to recognize that the impartiality of AI is contingent on the objectivity of the data and algorithms it utilizes.

AI's capabilities in verifying facts, revealing hidden data patterns, and providing unbiased perspectives are counterbalanced by several challenges. These include the possibility of AI reinforcing existing biases in its training data, the absence of human editorial discernment, dependence on the quality of source material, and emerging ethical dilemmas in news production. I understand there isn't a universal solution, and AI is not a standalone remedy. It should be used in conjunction with traditional journalistic practices and ethical guidelines to enhance the quality and fairness of news reporting.

The ultimate objective is to establish a balance that respects press freedom, ensures accurate and unbiased reporting, and maintains the public's trust in media—goals that are currently falling short.

Pine Creek Ski Resort

Date: January 7, 2023
Weather: 24°F Partly Cloudy
Location: Cokeville, WY

Unexpectedly, last night's search for a place to stay led me to some BLM-dispersed camping found on Campendium, located along a forest service road. While I was driving down this dirt road, and at first a desolate road, the amount of traffic coming toward me was surprisingly high, more than what you'd expect from hunters, hikers, or snowmobilers. About five miles in, I stumbled upon the answer: a quaint ski area hidden among the trees, Pine Creek Ski Resort. It had a single chairlift and a small parking area, big enough for about thirty cars. I came to learn that the ski area, while owned by Lincoln County, is family-operated.

Opting for a simple plan, I parked on the roadside to camp. Around 7 p.m., as I was settling in for some reading and sleep, I heard the dreaded knock on the door. To my surprise, it was a ski patrol guy, Nate, checking if I was waiting for anyone on the mountain after their final sweep. I explained I was camping and planning to ski the next day. He warmly invited me to stop by the lodge and say hello, mentioning that he was not just ski patrol but also the groomer, cook, and general bon vivant while his wife handled the ticketing.

The following day, two aspects stood out to me: the affordable lift ticket price of $55 and the quaint charm of the old chairlift and narrow trails, evoking memories of skiing in Vermont back in the day: the picturesque scenery and well-groomed trails with a decent amount of powder made for an enjoyable skiing experience. The lift line was minimal, and I found myself skiing on runs entirely by myself. It was truly enjoyable.

During one run, I took a fall and struggled to get back up. Surprisingly, a young woman appeared and offered help. Even though I initially declined, she insisted and helped me get up, adjust my ski, and even fit my boot into the binding. While I felt a bit like a child receiving help, I was genuinely grateful for her assistance. By the time I gathered my gloves and poles and turned to thank her, she had already left. This incident brought back memories of the community spirit in Vermont during the '80s, where people looked out for each other on the slopes without expecting anything in return. It seemed this mountain in Wyoming shared that familial, caring atmosphere, reflective of a community, where looking out for one another is a way of life—a way of life I have come to miss.

This experience sparked my curiosity about other small ski resorts I had encountered on my travels. For someone of my age and skiing ability, these smaller venues offer a delightful, stress-free experience without the fear of inadvertently taking on a challenging trail. That evening, under a full moon, the temperature was a relatively warm twenty-five degrees. I lay with the moonroof open, lulled by the tranquil sounds of a nearby creek, enveloped in peace. Dexter, too, was delighted with the area, enjoying both the snow and the warmth of the local people. Our walk along the forest road was a serene end to a beautiful day.

Snowbird, UT

Date: January 13, 2023
Weather: 44°F Mostly Cloudy
Location: North Salt Lake, UT

This is my second year coming to the Sun Outdoors RV Park. I chose this RV resort because of its location with respect to the ski areas that I want to visit: Snowbird, Solitude, and Snowbasin. None of these ski areas are RV-friendly; thus, there is a need to be here in North Salt Lake. My previous adventures at Alta left fond memories, and I was eager to experience its sister resort, Snowbird, which is renowned for its breathtaking terrain and exceptional snow conditions. Snowbird averages about 500 inches of snow annually, making it one of the snowiest areas in the U.S. The resort's diverse terrain ranges from wide, groomed runs to challenging off-piste areas.

The Aerial Tram at Snowbird, lifting off from the base to the peak of Hidden Peak at 11,000 feet, offers more than just access to various runs; it presents panoramic views that are nothing short of breathtaking. I remember the days at Snowbird as "bluebird days." Skiing down those frost-kissed slopes, I felt in sync with the serene beauty around me. Bassackwards offered playful twists and turns against the backdrop of the towering American Fork Twin Peaks, while Chip's Run provided a longer, sweeping descent that thrilled with its expansive vistas across the Wasatch Range.

However, not every moment was spent on the slopes. Back at the RV park, life was a mixed bag. I spent a significant chunk of time dealing with the wear and tear on my truck and Jeep—thanks to the rough dirt roads and harsh weather. Being in this maintenance mindset, I realized that my camper needed attention, too, for a variety of issues. Eleven areas of repair were noted, most beyond my DIY skills. I scheduled a service appointment with the manufacturer, who is based in Ohio. Figured I would do this on my way back home. I am anticipating considerable expense, but it is necessary to ensure the camper's reliability for future travels.

In trying to protect my Jeep from further road damage, I purchased a "Tow Defender"—a protective mesh screen designed to shield against flying debris. Though touted as easy to install, my experience proved otherwise, though I hoped that practice might ease the process.

Amid these technical frustrations, the social warmth of RV life glowed. I was looking forward to hanging with Bob and his dog Millie, whom I had met and spent a fair bit of time with last year. I learned that he had moved back to Wyoming. I was disappointed at not being able to see him, as was Dexter, who had grown fond of his dog, Millie. They would play tug-of-war for what seemed like hours.

There is a couple I met last year, Dennis and Melissa, who were still living at the RV resort. We had been keeping in touch via Facebook, and I was looking forward to catching up with them and learning about new bookdocking sites they had stayed in the past year. We went out and had drinks and dinner at their favorite sushi restaurant. It was great to reconnect with them, and the sushi was very good. I learned they continued to take their trips with the RV, boondocking and exploring the western states. We shared our favorite places to boondock.

The conversation eventually turned to the challenges of living the RV life, especially when I told them of the repairs I was working through. "It's the price we pay," Dennis said, clapping me on the back. "But look at what we gain—the mountains, the open road. It's worth it, right?".

Despite the day-to-day frustrations, nothing rivals the sense of freedom that comes with this lifestyle. Strapping on my skis for another glide down Chip's Run, I gaze up at the towering peaks.

The mountain seems to echo Dennis's earlier words, affirming why I return year after year. Despite everything, this life is irreplaceable.

Freedom. Flexibility. Two words that perfectly encapsulate my existence. Here, the world opens, bound only by the horizon and my readiness to explore. Whether it's the serene views that greet me each morning or the soothing sounds of nature that lull me to sleep, this life allows me to shift my scenery with the same ease as shifting thoughts.

Living minimally doesn't just reduce physical clutter—it clears my mind, making space for experiences over possessions. Settling into remote, nature-kissed nooks perfect for outdoor enthusiasts, I find more than solitude; I find community. The nomadic lifestyle might paint a picture of isolation, but in truth, it's a vibrant network of friendships, shared tips, and collective stories continuously woven into a rich tapestry of adventurous living.

Here, in the vastness of the open road, the mountains, and the endless sky, I am free. And I wouldn't trade it for the world.

Deer Valley, Canyons, and Brighton

Date: January 22, 2023
Weather: 12°F Light Snow
Location: Heber City, UT

Currently, I am now staying at the Mountain Valley RV Resort in Heber City, a quaint and intriguing little town. It is only an hour's drive from my last RV resort. My last visit here didn't leave a strong impression of the town itself, but its proximity to several ski areas, including Deer Valley and Canyons Resort, both within a thirty-minute drive, drew me back. The RV Park itself is exceptional. It offers plenty of space for walking Dexter, including a couple of dog parks where she can freely run and play. In Heber City, there's a particularly large dog park where Dexter really enjoys herself.

On my first day here, I went to the Deer Valley Resort, which is beautifully situated in Park City, Utah. It is a prominent skiing destination and one of two major resorts in the area. Despite their proximity, Deer Valley and its neighboring resort are distinctly separated, with a mere stretch of trees between them. This physical closeness does not translate into accessibility, as traversing directly from one resort to the other is strictly off-limits. It's interesting to note that each ski area is on a different pass system; one is IKON, and the other is Epic. One is skier only, and the other allows both. Thankfully, I have both, but I did not venture into the Park City Ski area while skiing Deer Valley.

Among the unique features of Deer Valley, notable is its policy against snowboarding, a distinction it shares with Alta in Utah and Mad River Glen in Vermont. The resort encompasses six diverse skiing areas: Little Baldy Peak, offering short but enjoyable trails; Bald Eagle Mountain, the location of the Snow Park base area with trails suited for beginners and intermediates; Bald Mountain, the largest area known for its more challenging terrain; Flagstaff Mountain, ideal for beginners with its gentle slopes; Empire, the loftiest part of the resort, with trails that have a distinctly western feel; and Lady Morgan, a recent addition featuring advanced trails as well as beginner-friendly slopes.

During my visit to Deer Valley, I focused on exploring Bald and Flagstaff Mountains. I started my day with Hawkeye, an intermediate trail on Flagstaff Mountain, which offered a smooth descent that was perfect for warming up. For me, easing into skiing is just as effective as stretching. The day, cloud-covered and mild with temperatures just above freezing, felt surprisingly warm. Skiing down Hawkeye, Hidden Treasure, and Nabob, I was brimming with confidence, which led me to venture onto Tycoon, a more challenging double-blue run. While I'm capable of handling such terrain, my preference nowadays leans toward a more relaxed skiing style. My current objectives are straightforward: relish each moment, avoid falls (as standing back up is a challenge), and immerse myself in the stunning scenery.

On Tycoon, the bumps at the beginning were a bit daunting, not because they were enormous moguls, but due to the strain they placed on the knees and the lurking fear of a fall. This wasn't exactly the experience I was looking for, so I swiftly navigated through the bumpy section and enjoyed the smoother part of the run.

On the next day, as I reached the summit of Bald Mountain, the skies had cleared, revealing an endless expanse of breathtaking vistas. The panoramic views from atop the mountain, now bathed in bright sunlight, were awe-inspiring. Gazing out over the vast landscape under the clear blue sky, I was struck by the sheer beauty of it all. This magnificent spectacle etched an image in my memory and reminded me why I love to ski the west.

During the evenings, I decided to explore more and was pleasantly surprised by the dining scene in Heber and the nearby town of

Midway. The array of fine restaurants was unexpectedly delightful. One evening at the Back 40 Roadhouse, a chance encounter unfolded while I was at the bar. A group of lively ladies sat next to me, their laughter and jokes filling the air. Soon, I struck up a conversation with one of them. She turned out to be an accountant with her own CPA firm, a lover of the outdoors, snowboarding, and horse riding. It was refreshing to talk to someone who understood my professional background. Her name was Carol, and she had a great sense of humor.

Although I usually keep to myself when I travel, Carol intrigued me. I invited her to dinner the next night, not fully expecting her to accept. But, as they say, you never know unless you ask. To my surprise, she said, "Yes." Our dinner was thoroughly enjoyable. Over the following weeks, Carol became my personal guide, showing me around her town, Park City, and her local ski area, Canyons Resort. It was a wonderful and unexpected addition to my stay in Heber City. We had an enjoyable dinner the next night and found that we had a lot more in common. She was a recent transplant to Heber and had set up shop here because of family ties. In fact, she lived in the same cul-de-sac as her sister and her family; her other sister was not too far away either.

The next ski area I visited was Canyons Resort. Before merging with Park City Mountain, Canyons Resort was an impressive ski area covering nine mountain peaks, with its highest point soaring to 9,990 feet at Peak 9990. The terrain was remarkably varied, featuring 182 trails, five expansive bowls, six natural halfpipes, and three creative terrain parks. The resort also catered to those looking for more daring adventures, offering side-mountain and backcountry skiing accessible through gates on various peaks leading into the National Forest land.

However, during this visit, I chose not to explore these more adventurous options, a decision influenced by the wisdom of age. In the past, I might have eagerly embraced such challenges, but time has taught me the value of "staying in my lane." Now, my approach to skiing is more about savoring the experience rather than seeking the adrenaline rush of my younger days. It's a different kind of enjoyment, one that comes with its own rewards and a more relaxed pace.

The skiing excursion I had planned for today held a special promise, as I was joined by Carol, whose company I've increasingly enjoyed. With Deer Valley not being an option for snowboarders like Carol, we set our sights on Canyons Resort. This choice introduced me to new terrain, adding an extra layer of excitement to our outing. Fortuitously, the day was blessed with the quintessential bluebird sky, creating ideal conditions for our adventure on the slopes.

We started with some gentle descents, easing into the rhythm of the day. As time passed, it became evident that Carol was playfully upping the ante with each run. This nudged the more adventurous side of me to the forefront, and soon enough, the "old" Thom was back in action, eagerly embracing every challenge with gusto. The day turned out to be fantastic, marked by exhilarating runs, no spills, and the mesmerizing beauty of the landscape. Skiing with Carol transformed the experience into something truly memorable.

Our day on the slopes culminated in après-ski drinks at the High West Distillery & Saloon in Park City, a renowned spot known for its unique position as the world's only ski-in/ski-out gastro distillery. The place was bustling, thanks to the ongoing Sundance Film Festival, making parking a challenge. Fortunately, I found a spot close to the Saloon.

Upon arrival, I was greeted by a long line, but luck seemed to be on my side. Often mistaken for Jeff Bridges due to my beard, long hair, and sizable presence, I nonchalantly made my way through the line and went directly to the bar and secured two seats, texting Carol my location. The bartender didn't mind, and soon, we were settled in, enjoying the vibrant atmosphere.

The High West Distillery & Saloon, celebrated as both a tourist landmark and a cherished local haunt, seamlessly marries historical allure with contemporary style. Nestled within a Victorian-style house and an elegantly restored historic stable, it exudes a warm, Western charm. The culinary offerings, curated by Chef James Dumas, include delights like whiskey cider short ribs and the signature High West burger, all showcasing the finest local ingredients. Carol and I savored inventive cocktails, notably the "Huck Yeah," an exquisite blend of double rye, mezcal, blood orange, passionfruit, lime, and jalapeno that masterfully intertwined sweet and spicy notes.

Amidst our conversation, a topic arose that prompted an unexpected reaction from the bartender. I was discussing the challenges of managing my notably long hair, particularly how it had transformed my shower routine from a quick rinse to a ten to fifteen-minute affair. I mused to Carol, "Now I understand why my daughters took so long in the shower."

Overhearing our conversation, the female bartender interjected with a knowing comment, "Finally, a guy who gets it." Her remark, both humorous and affirming, added a layer of camaraderie to the already enjoyable atmosphere at the saloon.

The saloon not only serves up a delectable array of foods and spirits, including on-site crafted whiskeys and vodkas, but also offers a peek into the distilling process. The Western ambiance, combined with Chef Dumas' culinary artistry, creates an unforgettable dining experience. Whether it's for the savory bites, the desserts like s'mores bread pudding, or the unique cocktails, High West Distillery & Saloon epitomizes the spirit of the West with its blend of culinary expertise and spirituous craftsmanship.

While in Heber City, I had the good fortune of reconnecting with my friend Sean and his companion, Brittany, for some skiing. Sean, the son of my close friend Mike, has been a part of my life since his birth. Over the years, we've formed a unique bond. Sean, a nurse like his mother, has been my reliable source for medical advice during my health journey. His insights and candid guidance have often grounded me, especially when I've strayed into the maze of internet information not pertinent to my situation. Brittany, who shares the same profession as a traveling nurse, met Sean on one of their nursing assignments. Their shared career path has not only brought them together, but also added an interesting dynamic to their relationship.

Our rendezvous at Brighton happened on an idyllic bluebird day, with temperatures in the low thirties, setting the stage for a perfect day on the slopes. The ample snowfall meant all trails were open, a prospect that always excites me. Despite its modest size, Brighton impressed me with its four distinct ski areas, each offering a unique skiing experience.

Brighton, perched in Big Cottonwood Canyon just above Salt Lake City, is one of the two ski resorts in this idyllic spot. It has a fantastic advantage for snowfall in Utah, thanks to the lake-effect snow from the Great Salt Lake. This consistently makes it an excellent choice for me when I'm after top-notch snow conditions. The resort, while modestly sized at 1,050 acres, has a vibrant and passionate local community, much like the ones I've encountered at Stowe or Mad River Glen in Vermont.

The Snake Creek lift guided us to the Thor run, a spectacularly twisty trail through dense forests, which I now regard as the highlight of Brighton. The area's superb tree skiing further enriched our experience. Our day was filled with great skiing, shared laughter, and camaraderie.

The day took an unexpected turn when I returned to my vehicle and found a parking violation ticket. I had paid for parking, following the system that required checking in at a kiosk with your parking spot and license plate number. Unfortunately, I mixed up the plate numbers of my two vehicles, leading to the issuance of the ticket. Initially frustrated, believing it to be an error, I contacted the parking system's company and explained the situation, including the registration details of both my vehicles. To my surprise and relief, the company was incredibly understanding and promptly canceled the ticket, much to my amazement and gratitude.

As my stay in Heber City neared its end, I found myself grappling with persistent health issues. Shortness of breath and leg pain had become frequent concerns, leading me to suspect that the high altitude might be affecting me. These symptoms, coupled with occasional chest pain and dizziness, had been a worry for some time. I reasoned that a change to a lower elevation might offer some relief. I chose Moab as my next destination. Sitting at approximately 4,026 feet, I hoped that Moab's lower altitude would help ease my breathing difficulties and other symptoms while also offering a delightful setting for a new adventure. If I had done my homework, I would have realized that Heber City was at about 5,600 feet. But a thousand feet is a thousand feet. I was hoping the difference would help.

I shared my plans with Carol, and, to my delight, she agreed to join me, though she would follow a few days later in her truck. My intention was to spend ample time in Moab, allowing myself to acclimatize to the lower elevation gradually. I was optimistic that this change would not only provide a reprieve from my current health challenges but also allow me to continue enjoying my travels in a vibrant and exciting new environment (and to spend some meaningful time rock crawling in the Jeep).

Off-roading in Moab, UT

Date: February 5, 2024
Weather: 36°F
Location: Horsethief Campground, UT

Five months into my journey on the road, I'm constantly amazed by the incredible places and stunning vistas I've come across. I consider myself immensely fortunate to be living this experience. Each night, as I watch the sunset, I'm filled with a sense of excitement and profound gratitude. Now, I've returned to Moab, a place that has charmingly ensnared a part of my soul. This might be my fourth time here, and I've chosen to stay at the same campsite as last year, Horsethief Campgrounds. It's on BLM land and provides the most basic of services—a vault toilet. This is also the third time I have come in the winter, and it is the time I most enjoy here. While some trails are closed due to weather, the open ones do present an additional layer of challenge, ones where I can utilize my East Coast winter driving skills.

Horsethief Campground is nestled in the pygmy pinyon-juniper forest atop the mesas overlooking Moab and offers spectacular views. My reasons for returning extend beyond the scenic landscapes; its proximity to Canyonlands National Park and Dead Horse Point State Park, the abundance of nearby off-road trails, and its seclusion, particularly in winter, make it an ideal spot. The tranquility here is unmatched, shared only with Dexter and the serene, snow-blanketed surroundings. At just $10 a night, it's an absolute bargain.

Before Carol joined me, I planned to revisit Arches National Park to take in the sight of the snow-covered formations and assess other trails to make sure they were manageable, given that there was snow and ice on the trails. As I settle into this peaceful haven,

I eagerly anticipate embarking on rock-crawling excursions and venturing down unexplored off-roading trails.

Here are a few of the trails that I sampled in preparation for her arrival:

- Potash Road and Shafer Switchbacks
- Long Canyon Trail
- Mineral Bottom Trail
- Gemini Bridges Trail
- Willow Springs Trail

The following sections of this book will provide more details of each trail.

Potash Road and Shafer Switchbacks

One trail that Dexter and I first checked to see was open is the Potash Road and the Shafer switchbacks, also known as the Shafer Trail. This trail, situated in the Island in the Sky district of Canyonlands National Park, has been closed the past few times I have been here due to excessive snow and ice. The Shafer Trail is an impressive route that descends about 1,500 feet through a vast sandstone cliff, displaying a stunning array of colors. It connects with the rugged Potash Road, a path that winds through elaborate canyons and distinctive hoodoos alongside the serene Colorado River, creating an idyllic setting for relaxation and reflection.

The Shafer section of this trek is a demanding dirt road with steep switchbacks, providing a raw and authentic off-road experience. Unfortunately, during our visit to the Island in the Sky Rangers' Station, we found that, once again, the route was closed due to snow and ice. The ranger explained that the trail often becomes treacherously icy, especially in areas that remain shaded, and the proximity to the cliffs poses safety risks. She recommended revisiting the trail after a sustained period of warm weather, which would likely make conditions safer and more navigable. (It's important to distinguish this trail from the Utah 279 Potash Road that connects with Highway 191 in Moab and is fully paved.)

Hopefully, on future visits, I will finally be able to experience this trail and all its glory.

Long Canyon Trail

The Long Canyon Trail has been an unforgettable part of my off-road journey. Spanning 7.5 miles between Canyonlands National Park and Moab, it transforms into a mesmerizing winter landscape, with snow adding a layer of challenge to the trail's moderate difficulty. As I descended, the route offered stunning views of the Colorado River, bordered by snow-covered sandstone fins and the backdrop of the La Sal Mountains. Yet, the trail's steepness, its narrowness, and the daunting two-thousand-foot drops contributed to some pulse-pounding moments, particularly when my Jeep began skidding toward the cliff's edge.

During our off-road adventure, we encountered a particularly daunting moment at a switchback turn. I noticed Carol gripping the handhold tightly, her apprehension clear. The path ahead was not only steep but, much to my concern, also slick with ice. As I navigated the turn, the Jeep lost traction, and we began sliding perilously close to the edge of the trail. For a brief second, I contemplated reversing to regain control, but fortunately, the vehicle came to a stop just in time. Peering down from the driver's side, the sheer drop into the canyon below was both breathtaking and frightening. There was hardly a moment to catch our breaths before we faced the next daunting part of the trail.

This new challenge involved maneuvering around a colossal boulder that had tumbled down onto our path. Initially, I doubted whether the Jeep could squeeze through. Yet, knowing that others had presumably traversed this route, I proceeded with caution. My relief was palpable when we successfully cleared the obstruction without incident. Past this point, the landscape opened magnificently, showcasing the early formation of arches in this remote and less frequented part of the region.

This journey, blending moments of apprehension with wonder, stands out as one of the region's most secluded and picturesque routes, at least for this trip. Once I hit Route 279 and trailed the path along the Colorado River, we paused at various remarkable landmarks, including the Jug Handle Arch and the Potash Rock Art Panel. We also took time to observe rock climbers as they skillfully ascended the cliff faces, adding another layer of admiration to our adventure.

Mineral Bottom Trail

Mineral Bottom Trail is a 4WD route that descends from the upper reaches of Mineral Canyon, leading down to the canyon floor along the Green River. The route offers a visually captivating descent, with switchbacks etched into a shelf road that provides dramatic views of steep drop-offs and towering canyon walls. On our journey down these switchbacks, we had a unique encounter that required careful navigation: a herd of cattle being driven up from the valley by actual cowboys. We had to edge close to the cliffside to let them pass, greeted by the cows' insistent stares, while the cowboys appreciated our efforts to turn off our Jeep's engine to avoid startling the cattle.

For those with a fear of heights, Mineral Bottom Road can be quite an adrenaline-inducing experience. Once at the canyon's base, the environment evokes the feel of an old Western movie, the kind of setting one dreams of when imagining an off-road adventure.

The trail itself started out level and wide, like a typical country road. As it begins its descent into Mineral Canyon via the switchbacks, it narrows but remains passable for vehicles. Deeper in the canyon, near Hell Roaring Canyon and the Green River, Mineral Bottom Road tapers off.

In winter, like during our visit, Mineral Bottom Road's difficulty significantly increases, particularly after a fresh snowfall. The typically straightforward flat sections become challenging to navigate in the absence of previous tire tracks. Being the first to venture out that day, I found no such tracks to guide me. The shadowed and icy switchbacks presented a considerable hazard, necessitating a reduced speed of just five miles per hour to ensure safety.

After reaching the canyon floor, I thought the hardest part was behind us. I took a break for a picnic and a walk with Carol and Dexter. However, the drive back proved to be equally demanding. Fortunately, our earlier passage had left a trail in the snow, offering some guidance on the way out. Navigating Mineral Bottom Road in these conditions was an exhilarating and unforgettable experience.

Gemini Bridges Trail

Moab's landscape is celebrated for its vast and remarkable rock formations, with the Gemini Bridges being the particularly notable highlight on this trail. Accessible via a short hike from the Jeep Road, these twin natural bridges are a prominent attraction. Although many visit specifically for the bridges, my objective was to navigate the Gemini Bridges trail as a scenic detour back to my campsite, connecting Highway 191 and Highway 313.

Setting out on this adventure, the initial drive up the shelf section was both awe-inspiring and challenging. The narrow path, hugging the side of the valley, offered stunning views but demanded cautious navigation due to the steep drop-offs. It was a delicate balance of savoring the breathtaking scenery while staying vigilant of the route's dangers. Looking out over the valley, one could see the road into the town of Moab.

A particular concern on this trail was its combination of steepness and tightness, especially around blind turns, which heightened the risk of unexpected encounters with oncoming traffic. To address this, I honked my horn at these critical points as a precautionary signal to others. The journey became more relaxed as we descended; the path widened, leading us to "Gooney Bird Rock," a fascinating rock formation. Pausing for photos, I was captivated by the spectacular views of the La Sal Mountains and the striking petrified sand spires in the distance. The trail turned into a mixed surface of smooth dirt to slickrock, with minor ledges being present. The slickrock presented a challenge with the snow covering we had.

Further along, I came across a section that resembled stairs. Staying close to the edge, I navigated up these "stairs" with a sense of awe and excitement. The remainder of the trail was relatively straightforward, though I noted numerous branching paths that piqued my curiosity for future exploration.

Willow Springs Trail

Willow Springs Road is a great way to experience the Arches backcountry without the crowds. Willow Springs Road is one of two roads that take you in and out of Arches National Park on dirt and not pavement. The road consists of sand, protruding rocks, and a few areas of slickrock. I took the trail out of the park toward Route 191. It was an enjoyable ride, with some difficult parts due to the snow and ice. The park side is a lot of sand and flats, the middle is rocky, and the highway side is just a gravel road.

Arches National Park

I find myself captivated by the more than two thousand naturally formed sandstone arches at Arches National Park, shaped over millions of years by wind and water erosion. It is home to the largest concentration of natural sandstone arches in the world. As a photographer's dream, it offers forty-three miles of stunningly scenic paved roads, leading to more than seventeen named arches accessible by hiking. Beyond the arches, the park unfolds into a magnificent 76,518-acre landscape dotted with towering sandstone fins, majestic balanced rocks, and soaring pinnacles and spires, each formation leaving visitors like me in complete awe.

Navigating the park's well-maintained roads, I appreciate the ease of accessing these breathtaking viewpoints. But what truly sets Arches apart is its variety of rock formations that capture the imagination of visitors, young and old. As I grow older, I find joy in the accessibility of the park, where I can easily step out of my car and embark on gentle trails that bring me face-to-face with these natural wonders.

For a hiker like me, where mobility can be an issue, Arches National Park is a treasure trove of trails catering to all abilities. Whether it's a leisurely twenty-minute walk to marvel at some of the park's largest arches (which is my usual go-to) or an adventurous excursion into more secluded areas, the park accommodates every type of hiker. Each step through Arches feels like a stroll through an extraordinary outdoor art gallery showcasing the most splendid works of natural geology.

People often ask me why I prefer to visit national parks during the winter. The answer is simple: winter provides a host of unique advantages beyond just avoiding the crowds. The season casts a magical transformation over the landscapes, revealing a different kind of beauty. Imagine snow-capped mountains, ice-glazed lakes, and forests blanketed in frost; it's a photographer's paradise, offering scenes and moments that are utterly distinct from any other time of year.

The wildlife viewing in winter is another aspect I cherish. Animals stand out against the snow, and with fewer people around, they tend to be less shy. It's an ideal time for birdwatching and observing wildlife in their natural settings. The tranquility of a national park in winter lends itself to a more reflective and leisurely experience. As someone who loves boondocking or finding budget-friendly camping spots, winter is perfect since there's less competition for spaces. Like my solitary stays at places like Horsethief Campgrounds, I often find myself as the only camper, which is something I deeply enjoy.

Winter outdoor activities not only boost my physical health but also do wonders for my mental well-being. There's something about the crisp, cold air and the physical exertion that's incredibly rejuvenating. The unique quality of winter light, often softer and at a lower angle, creates extraordinary photographic conditions, particularly in the early mornings and late afternoons.

Each park, when draped in its winter cloak, feels like an entirely different world compared to other seasons. Even familiar parks offer new perspectives and experiences, making each winter visit a novel and exciting adventure.

Crested Butte Ski Resort

Date: February 16, 2023
Weather: -10°F Clear
Location: Crested Butte RV Resort, CO

After leaving Moab, I set my sights on Crested Butte for some skiing. This place has always been one of my favorites in Colorado, not just for the skiing but also for the unique atmosphere of the town and its welcoming inhabitants. I believe this was my fifth visit. Crested Butte has a way of capturing the hearts of everyone who visits. It's often regarded as Colorado's best-kept secret, a sentiment shared by those who understand its charm.

In the local lingo, Crested Butte is affectionately referred to as "CB," a laid-back and enchanting town that appeals to people of all ages and interests. Situated about five hours from Denver and just thirty minutes north of Gunnison, it sits at an elevation of 8,909 feet in Gunnison County.[20] Known as both "the last great Colorado ski town" and the "wildflower capital of Colorado," its population was around 1,335 in 2020.

The mountain at Crested Butte is a paradise for skiers, renowned for its sparsely crowded slopes and its steep, challenging terrain. The town's history, originating as a coal mining town in the 1870s, is as rich as its landscapes. It's intriguing to think that Elk Avenue, the main street, wasn't paved until 1976. By the early '90s, the mountain started hosting extreme skiing competitions, one of the first in the US, marking the birth of its unique ski culture.

---

[20] "Blog," Free Colorado Travel Guide Vacations Travel and Tourism, accessed January 29, 2024, https://www.uncovercolorado.com/towns/crested-butte/.

My first trip to Crested Butte was back in 2000, during my ski mountaineering phase. That year, along with a good friend, I took on a ski mountaineering trip from Crested Butte to Aspen, CO, under the guidance of Jean Pavillard, an internationally certified mountain guide. Jean, who had led us on the Haute Route adventure in 1998, is renowned for his expertise and his role in numerous international rescues. Having him guide us to Aspen was a real honor.

Our journey, which lasted seven days from Crested Butte to Aspen, involved stays in various huts, including Adventure to the Edge's own yurt, as well as the Friends, Taggert, Markley, and Fritz huts. This mode of travel was ideal; we only had to carry the necessary food and equipment, while each hut supplied the rest, like cookware and utensils. Each hut had a distinct character and style, adding to the allure of the adventure. We were fortunate to experience mostly clear, sunny "bluebird" days, which made our trek even more enjoyable.

On that trip, there was one incident that was both a bit embarrassing but also quite thrilling. While my friend was an excellent skier, I was only moderately skilled at the time. We were skiing through a grove coated in fresh snow, and it was absolutely exhilarating until, suddenly, it wasn't. The guide and my friend had moved ahead, and I, preferring to ski cautiously to maintain control, ended up losing sight of them. In a moment of overexcitement, I inadvertently skied off a fifteen-foot cliff. Miraculously, I landed safely in a deep, soft snowdrift, feeling briefly like an X Games champion.

However, the moment of triumph quickly turned comical as my 65 lb. backpack, still in motion, pushed my face awkwardly between my skis. There I was, stuck in a bizarre position. I could hear laughter from above, which only added to my embarrassment. My face flushed with a mix of humiliation and annoyance at my blunder, as if my red cheeks could melt the surrounding snow. My friends skied down swiftly and helped me out of my pack and the awkward position.

As the journey continued, this incident turned into a running joke among us. It's true what they say: an adventure isn't really an adventure until something unexpected happens. What started as a lovely skiing trip quickly escalated into a thrilling adventure. I always try to make the best out of every situation, ensuring enjoyment for everyone, even if it means becoming the butt of the joke!

This time around, the skiing in Crested Butte was quite enjoyable, though it was bitterly cold, with temperatures hovering between 0° and 15°F. The heavy snowfall had transformed the landscape significantly. I spent most of my time enjoying the intermediate runs that offered wide, sweeping turns while providing incredible views of the surrounding Elk Mountains, like Paradise Bowl, East River Express. and Painters Boy. Finding powder stashes and enjoying the corduroy-groomed trails were stunning. The legs were certainly burning. I had one bluebird day, and the cold, fresh air was rather invigorating between the lungs full of crisp air and the stunning views.

I didn't stay on the mountain for après drinks but rather headed into town to enjoy a hearty dose of local color and cowboy charm. My favorite spot is the Eldo Brewery and Taproom, a "sunny place for shady people," is how I recalled how they described themselves. They are the only brewery in town and had an outside deck, which, on a bluebird day, is a great place to hang out, with views of the main street. The Eldo IPA is a good New England IPA and my favorite. It has changed owners, and the "dirt" bar is now moving up in the respectability column. The food, which is Himalayan, is very good. I have enjoyed the tikka marsala and lamb vindaloo.

The other restaurant that I love is the Wooden Nickel. The Wooden Nickel captures the essence of a traditional American steakhouse. The bar maintains a rustic and charming Western decor that echoes the town's mining-era past. The interior is lined with historic photographs and memorabilia that give diners a glimpse into Crested Butte's rich history. It specializes in high-quality, traditional American steakhouse fare. It is particularly renowned for its selection of steaks, ranging from prime rib to New York strips, all cooked to perfection.

I struggled to find a spot for boondocking due to the snow and ended up staying at the Crested Butte RV Park, which, despite offering only electricity and no other amenities like bathrooms or showers, turned out to be the most expensive stay of my journey. In previous years, I managed to find boondocking spots, but that was later in the season.

Carol arrived in Crested Butte a few days after I had begun my solo adventure. Together, we immersed ourselves in the powdery slopes and the quaint charm of the town, creating memories wrapped in the crisp mountain air. It was bliss, until it wasn't.

On Sunday, our joy was abruptly replaced by a chilling sense of déjà vu. While relaxing with après-ski drinks, I started feeling ominously familiar symptoms: shortness of breath, a tightening chest, dizzy spells, and my hands turning clammy and numb, echoing the harrowing emergency of 2017 when I had three stents placed in my arteries at Mount Auburn Hospital.

Staggering towards the Jeep, I barely caught myself, gripping it hard to avoid collapsing. Gasping for air, I felt the edges of my vision begin to blur. "Carol, I need an ER—now," I managed to say. Without hesitation, she helped me into the Jeep and sped towards the mountain clinic, her quick actions cutting through my mounting panic.

As the ambulance sirens wailed, cutting through the thin mountain air, all I could think about was, "Where is the oxygen?" Anxiety and an attempt to stay composed wrestled within me. The shortness of breath and dizziness weren't new; they had haunted me since my days skiing in Utah. I had assumed it was just Acute Mountain Sickness from the high altitudes—how wrong I was.

When the ER doors swung open in Gunnison, a nurse swiftly escorted me to a bay. "Not again," I thought as they hooked me up to monitors and IVs, a flurry of activity around me. The dread of repetition weighed heavily—another heart issue, another battle.

The next two days blurred into a series of tests and consultations. I was surprised to find out the cardiologist had access to my entire medical history from an angioplasty I underwent in 2017. "Has technology really come this far?" I wondered, a nagging doubt about privacy laws lingering in the back of my mind.

During our discussion, something felt off. The questions seemed disconnected from my current symptoms. After reconfirming my identity, it was revealed they were confusing my records with someone else's. "You have to be kidding me," I muttered under my breath when we discovered the mix-up. Correct records in hand, the cardiologist suggested an angioplasty to inspect for blockages.

But there was a hitch—the local hospital lacked a Catheter Lab. I would have to travel to another facility in Montrose. Concerned about my deteriorating condition and dubious luck, I joked grimly to myself, "Really? What next?" At least Montrose had a helicopter pad if things turned dire.

Following the cardiologist's advice, I embarked on what felt like a never-ending journey to Montrose Hospital. During the angioplasty, they discovered and worked to remove a tricky thrombosis, adding two more stents to my weary heart. Despite their efforts, the symptoms persisted—dizziness, shortness of breath, the works. Lying in the hospital bed, I couldn't help but think, "Great, I probably do have AMS and still no oxygen."

I left the hospital as battered and breathless as when I had entered. Retreating to my camper, I spent a day simply trying to breathe, both physically and emotionally. Unlike my quick recovery in 2017, this time, my progress was painfully slow, a constant reminder of my vulnerability. Opting against my initial plan to visit Steamboat Springs, I decided to return to Utah, craving the comfort of familiar surroundings. Surrounded by friends, I found not just comfort but also a mirror reflecting my new reality—one where each breath was a gift and every day a negotiation with my own mortality. This episode wasn't just another medical scare; it was a profound confrontation with my limits and a stark reminder to cherish the mundane miracles of everyday life.

Antelope Island State Park

Date: February 27, 2023
Weather: 34°F Cloudy
Location: Heber City, UT

Once I decided to leave Crested Butte, preparing the camper for the journey to Heber City was quick work. Fortunately, there was no need to fret over the Jeep, as Carol had already driven it back to her hometown. As I set off westward, Crested Butte shrinking in my rearview mirror, I pondered the whirlwind of the past week—from exhilarating ski runs in pristine conditions to an unexpected hospital stay that forced me to face my mortality yet again. It was a sobering chain of events. On the one hand, I felt grateful that the outcome was only the placement of stents rather than open-heart surgery—or something worse. On the other, I grappled with the question of my recovery. There was still so much I yearned to achieve. Strangely, throughout this ordeal, the specter of cancer, which loomed in the background, hadn't crossed my mind.

Continuing west on U.S. Highway 50, I passed Gunnison and headed towards Montrose. Ordinarily, I would stop to admire the breathtaking views of the Gunnison River and the enveloping national forests and seize every chance to absorb Colorado's rugged terrain and unspoiled wilderness. This time, however, my mind was preoccupied with doubts about whether the doctors had prioritized their wants over my needs. My symptoms persisted, and frankly, I felt awful.

Crossing into Utah, the scenery shifted dramatically from mountainous terrain to the high desert plains of eastern Utah. The stark contrast of red rock formations and expansive open spaces defined the new landscape.

I was returning to the same RV resort I had visited before. Driving into Heber City, nestled in the Heber Valley, the environment transformed once again. This quaint town, encircled by the Wasatch Mountains, offered a tranquil end to my journey. Pulling into the RV resort felt like a small victory—a familiar place amidst so much change. With nothing pressing except a planned visit to see my daughter Caroline in Big Sky in ten days, I could take a breath. Exhausted, I looked forward to settling in with Dexter and surrendering to a long, deep slumber.

During this recovery period, I was joined by my eldest daughter, Alex. She came to visit, bringing a welcome presence. Carol, embracing the role of a travel guide, took us on a series of sightseeing trips. Among these excursions was a memorable visit to Antelope Island, allowing us to explore and enjoy the beauty of Utah together. This period of rest and the company of loved ones helped significantly in my recovery journey.

Antelope Island is an amazing spot for observing wildlife. The island, which had been missing its namesake pronghorns for many years, saw their reintroduction in 1993, and now they are a common sight throughout the park.[21] The island is also home to deer, bobcats, coyotes, various birds, and waterfowl. But it's most famous for its American bison population, which was introduced in 1893. Now numbering around 600, these bison thrive in the dry, native grassland of the island and are vital to conservation efforts because of their important genetic contribution.

After a two-week recovery period in SLC, the urge to resume my travels was growing stronger. While my symptoms persisted, they had diminished in intensity, leading me to believe I was ready to reengage with the nomadic lifestyle. In just three days since hitting the road again, I've encountered a series of adventures: crashing

---

[21] "Antelope Island State Park," Utah State Parks, accessed January 29, 2024, https://stateparks.utah.gov/parks/antelope-island/.

into a snowdrift during a whiteout, discovering three campsites completely blocked by snow, and roaming aimlessly in search of a viable camping spot.

The location I've settled in now is stunning yet incredibly remote, situated beside a frozen river. I was seeking a campsite when I accidentally drove into the snowdrift. A logging truck was rapidly approaching from behind, and in my haste to give them room, I misjudged the edge of the road and ended up in the snowbank. My truck's hood was engulfed in snow, but thankfully, it wasn't a solid block of ice. I squeezed out of the door to assess the situation and realized I needed to dig out the front to access the truck's winch. The Jeep was stuck as well, but its winch was within reach.

Each of my vehicles is equipped with a shovel and axe, but the truck's shovel, mounted on the hood, was inaccessible. Fortunately, the Jeep's tools were inside and within easy reach. Just as I was preparing to start digging, a snowplow appeared. The driver, restricted by company policy, couldn't assist directly, but I persuaded him to let me attach my winch to his plow. When I first attempted to pull the Jeep out, the plow started sliding, prompting the driver to quickly stabilize his vehicle. Eventually, I was able to free the Jeep.

The situation with the truck and camper was more complicated due to their combined weight of approximately 2.5 tons, significantly more than the Jeep. I was relying heavily on the Jeep's winch, hoping it would be able to handle the task without causing the Jeep to slide into the truck, as had happened with the snowplow. I used a tow rope from the Jeep, creating a link between the Jeep and the snowplow, and then connected the winch to the truck. At first, both the Jeep and the plow began to slide, but the plow driver managed to halt their movement, allowing me to move the truck gradually. It was a huge relief to finally free it.

I was immensely grateful to the plow driver. As we shook hands, I offered him some money as a token of my gratitude, which he initially laughed off. He remarked that this was a novel experience for him, watching an East Coaster figuring out how to extricate himself from a snow trap. He even confessed that he thought he'd end up taking me to a service station. If that snowplow hadn't shown up, I'm not sure what I would have done. Luckily, the back of the camper was accessible, so in the worst-case scenario, I could have spent the night there, waiting for daylight and the storm to pass.

This entire ordeal served as a stark reminder of the unpredictability and adventure inherent in life on the road.

Big Sky, MT

Date: March 9, 2023
Weather: 16°F Some Clouds
Location: Big Sky Ski Resort

There's something almost magical about Big Sky Resort, a gem nestled in the southwestern cradle of Montana, close to Yellowstone National Park and just south of Bozeman. This will be my seventh season returning to its sprawling slopes. The resort spans three impressive mountains—Lone, Andesite, and Flat Iron—each offering unique skiing experiences that contribute to Big Sky's reputation as one of the largest ski resorts in the U.S. by acreage.

Unlike more renowned resorts like Vail or Aspen, Big Sky often feels like my own private winter wonderland. There are moments on the trails when I find myself alone, surrounded by silence, except for the crunch of snow underfoot. On weekdays, I can find lifts without lines, a rare luxury in the skiing world.

The view from any point is breathtaking. From the top of Lone Mountain, standing tall at 11,166 feet with its distinctive pyramid shape, the panorama of the Rocky Mountains unfolds—a vista so vast, you feel on top of the world. The cold, crisp air fills your lungs, refreshing the body and soothing the soul amidst the stunning landscapes. With an average snowfall of 400 inches, the conditions remain ideal throughout the season, from my early visits in January to spring skiing in March.

Of course, age and health have shifted my skiing preferences. Where I once tackled Challenger's steep chutes and deep powder, now I find joy in the gentle sweeps of Elk Park Ridge, with its impeccably groomed corduroy paths. My first visit to Big Sky was somewhat accidental, originally aimed at Moonlight Basin, but since the

2013 merger that brought both areas under Big Sky's umbrella, my routine has included wearing my old Moonlight Basin ski vest, sparking conversations, and reminiscing about the old days.

Big Sky's rich history adds another layer to its charm. Founded in 1973 by Chet Huntley, it echoes with stories of past and present, blending tradition with modernity. Over the years, Big Sky has become a staple in my skiing itinerary, cherished for its lengthy trails and diverse terrain.

This year, though, brought a change. After meeting Mike and his boys on past road trips, we planned to include Caroline and Eric. Yet, facing a recent health scare, I opted out of skiing. Instead, I booked a cabin at the 320 Ranch, perfectly positioned between Big Sky and Yellowstone. While the others skied, I found solace in the serene, snowy walks with Dexter, turning our strolls into daily meditations. Each evening, as they returned with tales of mountain adventures, I soaked in the joy of their experiences, connecting over the day's escapades.

While we were at 320 Ranch, it was not just about skiing. One day, we decided to visit Yellowstone National Park and organized a snowcat tour of Old Faithful and other sights in the park. Traveling to Yellowstone in the winter transforms the park into a serene wonderland, a stark contrast to its bustling summer days. The roads, once teeming with tourists, now serve as quiet trails for snow coaches and snowmobiles—the essential vehicles for navigating the thick blanket of snow. From the cozy confines of our snow coach, we admired the park's snowy landscapes as we journeyed to Old Faithful, making several stops along the way to fully experience the sights beyond our frosty windows.

Before this trip, my knowledge of geysers was minimal, but the insights shared by our knowledgeable guide were enlightening. From learning the differences between a fumarole and a mud pot to discovering the variety of elements that the earth emits, the experience was nothing short of educational. Fumaroles, appearing as small vents, release steam, and gases, while mud pots bubble in hues ranging from gray to vibrant red, colored by the minerals they contain.

As we traveled, it became apparent that Yellowstone's thermal fields are unique. Resting atop a volcanic hotspot, the park's geothermal features owe their characteristics to the underlying rhyolite—a silica-rich volcanic rock. This composition means that instead of sulfur, the steam from Yellowstone's geysers carries silica, creating glistening deposits around their openings.

I learned that there are two types of geysers: cone and fountain. Cone geysers, like the iconic Old Faithful, offer predictable and spectacular eruptions through their narrow openings, shooting water high into the air. In contrast, fountain geysers, such as the Great Fountain Geyser, burst energetically from pools, sending water cascading in dramatic, unpredictable patterns.

Our route also afforded us encounters with the local wildlife—bison and elk grazed on the sparse winter vegetation, using the geothermal heat to endure the biting cold. We even spotted Trumpeter Swans in the warm waters, which serve as vital refuges where they can find food and shelter from the winter chill.

The most dramatic natural performances, however, came from the geysers like Castle, Grand, and Riverside. These geysers erupted against a backdrop of snow-dusted trees and ice-bound rivers, their boiling waters soaring into the frosty air and returning as a shimmering mist under the sunlit sky. The climax of our adventure was at Old Faithful. Standing with Caroline and Eric in the hushed, wintry silence, we watched in awe as it erupted—a spectacular display of nature's power, the steaming water a brilliant contrast against the serene, snowy expanse.

Amid the awe, I found myself pondering the delicate balance of nature and our place within it. The eruption, a timely reminder of the earth's latent energy, brought forth reflections on the smallness of our concerns against the backdrop of such grandeur. Caroline, Eric, and I exchanged looks of wonder, words unnecessary to convey our mutual appreciation. I learned much on that trip.

Observations

The skiing in the USA did not pan out the way I had hoped. And this was one remarkable winter, marked with record-breaking snowfalls and bluebird days. Each day, the tallies of the previous night's snowfall were unbelievable, measured not in inches but feet. I had never witnessed this kind of continued snowfall. After enjoying a few of these remarkable days, the pain in my legs, the shortness of breath, the chest pains, and the dizziness became too much to ignore. My health was taking its toll on me. What I thought was altitude sickness was more than that.

I made the most of things while in a debilitated state. But when I almost passed out while in Crested Butte, I realized that something was off. Heading to the hospital was something I should have done sooner, like when I was in Salt Lake City, given the quality of the hospitals there. I ended up in Montrose, CO, where I had an angioplasty performed and stents implanted. From that point forward, there was to be no more strenuous activity. No skiing with my daughter and my friends. No spring skiing. And no fly-fishing in Montana or Wyoming.

Nonetheless, I must admit that I had an enjoyable time visiting Montana and Wyoming with my daughter and friends and seeing the sights. I just wish I was more ambulatory.

Section 8

All Good Things Must Come to an End

The Last Trail: Homeward from Montana and Wyoming

In the land where mountains kiss the sky,
And prairies stretch far and wide,
Our journey finds its closing pages,
In the heart of Montana and Wyoming's stages.

Through valleys where rivers run free,
Under the vast, starlit canopy,
Each step, each trail, an untold story,
Moments of grace, fleeting glory.

Now, as the sun dips low,
Casting on the peaks a golden glow,
We face the end of our wandering route,
In this land where eagles soar and trout.

The drive home, long and silent,
Filled with memories, vivid, vibrant.
The road stretches, endless, ahead,
Lined with thoughts of days that sped.

In the rearview, horizons fade,
Of the wild, unbridled escapade.
Yet, in farewell, there's a subtle grace,
In the beauty of this tranquil space.

Each mile, a step from what was known,
Into a future, yet unshown.
A journey not just of miles, but heart,
From which we never truly part.

So, as we drive into the night,
Heading home, from peaks to city light,
We carry a piece of the mountain's song,
And the feeling of where we truly belong.

The Push Home

My journey wound down in a rather subdued way. I had grand plans to spend March and April spring skiing, followed by fly-fishing in Montana and Wyoming. Even after the heart procedure, I had thought that the healing power of nature would have a positive effect and that I could still pursue my passions despite physical limitations. Even if I couldn't enjoy the physical aspects, then maybe just appreciate and take in the simple joys of this solitary adventure.

After my time with Caroline in Big Sky, I intended to fish the Madison, Yellowstone, and Missouri Rivers in Montana, followed by a trip to Wyoming's Green River and the areas around Dutch John and Flaming Gorge. I was looking forward to standing in the streams, rod in hand, and being amazed by the beauty around me. (I was also looking forward to grilling a few trout over an open fire and savoring every bite.)

Montana, a paradise for fishermen, offers plenty of boat landings and parking spots perfect for trailers, which I often used for short-term camping in my camper during winter. I found some spots around Ennis, MT, and chose to start at Chutes Landing near Ennis Lake. Ennis was ideal due to its proximity to the Madison River and its well-known fishing guides. I picked the Madison River Fishing Company and teamed up with guide Jimmy Morrison for some drift fishing, given the cold water temperatures.

One chilly morning, Jimmy and I set out, loading gear into his Jeep and towing the drift boat to the river. However, we encountered frazil ice in the river, making fly fishing quite challenging for a novice like me. Frazil ice is a unique form of ice that forms in flowing water. In rivers and streams, frazil ice can accumulate to form a slushy mixture on the surface. This phenomenon can pose challenges for activities like fishing or boating, as it can clog water intakes. After checking other ramps and facing similar issues, Jimmy and I postponed our fishing to Sunday, hoping for warmer weather.

Yet, after talking with my friend Mike, who firmly urged me to prioritize my health, I began to reassess my plans. Despite the angioplasty and stents, I was still dealing with chest pain and shortness of breath, showing no improvement four weeks after the procedure, unlike my first angioplasty.

Mike, aware of my cancer and other health issues, questioned why I was still on the road instead of getting medical attention in Boston. His concern made me realize I might be jeopardizing my health by being stubborn. Reflecting on his advice, I acknowledged he was right. Despite the allure of this magical place and my love for the road, I was struggling not only to enjoy it but also to cope with the fear of worsening my condition. With a heavy heart, I decided to head back home to Marstons Mills, embarking on a 2500-mile journey. I canceled my fishing plans with Jimmy and began the long drive, planning to see my cardiologist and develop a health plan upon returning.

On my journey, I paused in Livingston, MT, to dine at Neptune's Taphouse and Eatery. I savored sashimi and seaweed, opting out of beer. Later, as hunger resurfaced, I regretted not eating more.

The following day involved a hefty drive of 350 miles to Gillette, Wyoming. I contemplated visiting Devil's Tower but decided to press on. The drive itself offered a sort of momentum, helping me zone out from everything else. A stop at Los Compadres Mexican Restaurant provided a welcome break, where I enjoyed shrimp enchiladas, maintaining my seafood diet.

Accompanied by audiobooks, I stayed focused on the long road ahead. Fortunately, I didn't run into any snowstorms, but leaving the mountainous landscapes for flat, rolling plains was a poignant shift. The mountains slowly disappearing in my rearview mirror marked a transition to more open landscapes.

In Oacoma, SD, I visited AL's Oasis, an establishment that was quite different from what its exterior suggested. Inside, it was more a collection of souvenir shops than the western town facade it portrayed. There, I had an open-faced turkey sandwich with a salad buffet and indulged in a delicious pecan pie. That day, I got off to a late start and managed to cover only 250 miles.

March 21st saw a more determined effort, with me covering 475 miles. I stopped at a county park in Iowa, only to be asked to leave by a ranger, despite no signs indicating closure. I couldn't help but wonder if my Massachusetts license plate influenced his decision. Dinner that evening was at McDonald's, where I opted for a spicy chicken meal.

The next leg took me another 326 miles to Kingsville, OH, and on March 23rd, I drove 333 miles to Waterloo, NY. Breakfast at a truck stop provided decent, plentiful coffee. However, the final stretch was grueling, an exhausting 630 miles.

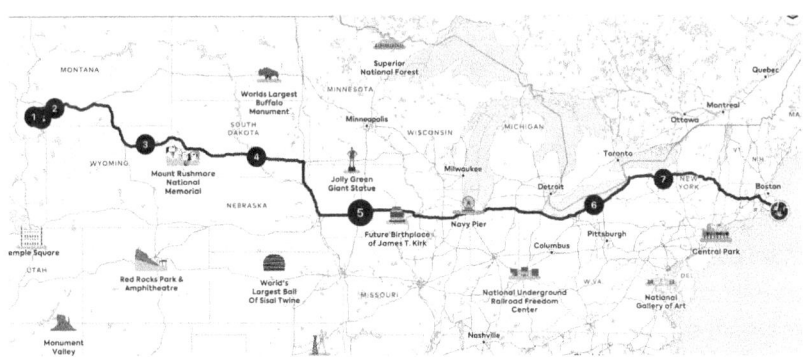

Home Sweet Home

There's a timeless truth that never fades with age: the allure of coming home to your own bed is a source of unparalleled joy. The other night, as I wearily stepped across the familiar threshold of my home, this sentiment resonated more deeply than ever. The very thought of sinking into my own bed was an elixir to my travel-weary soul. I couldn't wait to immerse myself under the comforting embrace of my quilt, rest my head on my well-worn pillow, and feel Dexter, my loyal companion, jump up beside me. Together, we succumbed to a deep, restorative sleep, the kind that only home can bestow.

This morning, cradling my coffee and witnessing the dawn's early light, I sensed the stirrings of spring. It's a magical transformation: the tender green shoots emerging defiantly, the persistent buds inching their way through the earth's crust, the crocuses boldly piercing the ground's surface, heralding the season's change. The air buzzes with birds' chatter and wildlife stirrings, signaling spring's arrival. It's a picturesque canvas of renewal and hope right outside my window.

Yet, amidst this natural reawakening, I'm reminded of the tasks that lay ahead. Beyond addressing my health concerns, there's the matter of tending to the house and its surroundings, neglected by winter's harsh embrace. Spring cleanup looms as a daunting, albeit necessary, challenge. The rejuvenation of nature outside mirrors the renewal I must undertake, both in health and at home—a journey of revival and rejuvenation.

This recent journey of mine stands apart from all my previous travels in ways more profound than I could have anticipated. It unfolded as a journey of self-discovery, revealing layers of my character I hadn't known before. I encountered a myriad of challenges—physical, mechanical, and medical—each presenting a unique hurdle. Yet, in facing each obstacle, I found strength and resilience within myself.

More importantly, I learned the art of being present, of savoring each experience for its intrinsic value, despite the health issues I carry with me.

This trip taught me that while navigating life with my health conditions is far from easy, it's certainly possible. Being out in the world, especially within the embrace of nature's raw and unfiltered beauty, has offered me new perspectives. There's something about the wild, untamed spirit of nature that renews me, that gives me a sense of vitality I find nowhere else.

Hitting the road ignites a sense of invigoration in me. The tranquility and the sheer joy of being immersed in the moment are as compelling as they are addictive. The opportunities to find peace and to live in the here and now are not just therapeutic but deeply transformative. This journey has not just been traveling across landscapes, but a profound exploration of my inner self, teaching me lessons in resilience, presence, and the rejuvenating power of nature. All these lessons will be needed as I march forward on my health odyssey.

Through all this, I've grown to appreciate solitude. While it's wonderful to share experiences with others, there's also something to be said for moving at your own pace and enjoying your own company.

Future Trips

As one adventure ends, the anticipation for another builds. In February 2024, I'm setting off on a four-month sojourn across South America, traversing this vibrant continent by train, plane, and bus. Starting in Buenos Aires, Argentina, this journey promises a rich blend of culture, nature, and adventure.

My itinerary kicks off with the majestic Iguazu Falls, followed by a two-week Antarctic expedition from Ushuaia, the world's southern tip. After navigating the Drake Passage and exploring Antarctica's surreal landscapes, I'll head north along South America's western coastline.

The journey will weave through Chile's diverse landscapes, from the stark Atacama Desert to Easter Island's mystical Moai statues and through the vineyards and urban vibrancy of Santiago. In Peru, the ancient Incan city of Machu Picchu awaits, high in the Andes, followed by the rich cultural tapestry of Ecuador's Quito and the Galapagos Islands, a living showcase of evolution.

My adventure then leads to Colombia, where a mix of colorful culture, lush landscapes, and historic cities like Bogota and Cartagena await. The grand finale will be in Bonaire, a Caribbean paradise, capping off this South American odyssey.

Throughout this journey, I'll immerse myself in the heart and soul of the continent. From Argentina's tango rhythms to the Andean melodies and from Argentine asados to Peruvian ceviche, every step will be an exploration of the diverse cultures, flavors, and warm hospitality of South America.

Join me as I not only journey through these incredible places but also delve deep into the vibrant spirit of this captivating continent.

Observations

As I reflect on this journey and write these words in January 2024, it's important to share the realities that followed my return home. The months between April and November 2023 were a testament to the ongoing challenges life had in store for me.

Firstly, my heart issues persisted, necessitating a complete overhaul of my medications. Then, the pain in my legs, which I attributed to the wear and tear of travel, was diagnosed as osteoarthritis in my hips, leading to a hip replacement in September. More dauntingly, my cancer progressed to stage IV, with tumors now in my pelvis and chest. This period wasn't just about physical rehabilitation; it was also a time of mental and emotional resilience. Each day was a step toward recovery, albeit with its own set of hurdles.

The results of the PMSA PetScan done in January 2024 revealed that the tumors identified in May 2023 had not only grown, but have multiplied and are now in the spinal, heart, and abdomen areas. Not the news that I was hoping to hear. My oncologist and I decided to delay any treatments for another five months so that I can continue with my travel plans to explore South America. As the oncologist noted, "no point in being miserable on your trip." When we do start the treatments, I doubt that I will be coming off them. Regardless of what lies ahead, my resolve to continue exploring, embracing the world, and cherishing each moment remains as strong as ever. It's not just about fighting; it's about living fully and making the most of the time I have.

Reflecting on my seven-month journey, time seems to have blurred into a mosaic of adventures across two countries, six provinces and territories, and seventeen states. While I didn't catch the Northern Lights, this unfulfilled dream now fuels my future travel plans, possibly to distant lands like Iceland or Russia.

This expedition was a magnificent tapestry of seasons, from Ontario's vibrant fall to the stark, frozen beauty of Alaska's winter and the rejuvenating onset of spring. The contrast of landscapes, from the Yukon's golden hues to Vancouver Island's diverse microclimates, underscored nature's variety and resilience.

Along British Columbia's Powder Highway, the cold was more biting than anticipated, a challenge for both me and my faithful companion, Dexter. The diverse terrain, from Manitoba's sprawling grasslands to the rugged wilderness of Alaska, offered a canvas of breathtaking scenes.

The wildlife refuges were sanctuaries of serenity, showcasing nature's balance and resilience, like the unique bison of Yellowstone Park. The wilderness was a living tapestry, filled with creatures from majestic bison and elk to soaring eagles and industrious beavers, each adding to the rich, natural diversity.

Terrace's whimsical wood carvings and British Columbia's Inside Passage, with its glaciers meeting the ocean, were among the many enchanting sights. The First Nations' fishing villages and Vancouver Island's lumber mills illustrated the seamless blend of culture and industry.

My ski adventures varied from Revelstoke's winter wonderland to Deer Valley's peaceful trails and Crested Butte's imposing slopes. Each area, including smaller resorts like Pine Creek, added its own charm to my skiing experiences.

In Moab, I navigated off-road trails revealing Earth's hidden stories, while Yellowstone's geysers were a spectacle of natural wonder. This journey wasn't just about places; it was a deep exploration of nature and humanity's tapestry.

The kindness of strangers was a constant throughout, from shared meals and heartfelt moments to assistance during unexpected challenges. Their generosity enriched my journey immeasurably. However, the trip was also marked by health trials, from Covid to a serious cardiac incident, leading to visits to various emergency rooms. The medical care I received, from ski resort stations to rural outposts, was exceptional. The doctors, nurses, and volunteers provided not just medical assistance but also human kindness and understanding.

This journey, with its blend of beauty, challenge, and human connection, was a testament to the resilience of the human spirit and the bonds that unite us. It was an odyssey of discovery, not just of landscapes and cultures, but of my own resilience and the unyielding kindness of people.

Appendices

Plan Your Own Adventure

Appendix A: Checklists for Travel

When you're planning to be away from your home for a few months, especially during the winter, it's important to ensure that everything is to keep your home safe, secure and well-maintained while you're gone. Here is a checklist of tasks you might consider before departing:

1. **Secure the Home:**
   o   Lock all doors and windows.
   o   If you have an alarm system, ensure it's activated and functioning.
   o   Inform a trusted neighbor or friend that you'll be away and provide them with contact information for emergencies.
   o   Consider motion-detector lights or timed lighting systems to give the appearance that the home is occupied.

2. **Manage Utilities:**
   o   Set the thermostat to a temperature that will prevent pipes from freezing (typically no lower than 55°F/13°C) but low enough to save energy.
   o   Shut off the main water supply if there's no need for water while you're away to prevent flooding from any possible leaks and to prevent drain pipes from freezing.
   o   Unplug all unnecessary appliances to prevent fire hazards and save energy.
   o   Stop or forward your mail and pause any subscription services.

3. **Prepare for Weather:**
   o   Clean gutters and downspouts to prevent ice dams or water buildup.
   o   Check the roof for any damage that might worsen with winter weather.
   o   Arrange for snow removal from your driveway and sidewalks if you'll be away during times of expected snowfall.

4. **Home Maintenance:**
   o   Remove any perishable items from the refrigerator and pantry and dispose of them to prevent odors and pests.
   o   Take out all trash from the home.

o Check that all smoke detectors and carbon monoxide detectors are in working order and replace batteries if necessary.

o Perform any necessary repairs that might worsen while you're away, such as fixing leaks or sealing gaps where pests might enter.

5. Plumbing & HVAC:

o If you're in a region with freezing temperatures, consider adding antifreeze to drains and toilets to prevent water from freezing and cracking the fixtures.

o Have your heating system serviced before you leave to ensure it runs smoothly through the winter.

o Consider shutting off and draining outdoor faucets to prevent freezing and bursting.

6. Garden and Exterior:

o Trim trees or branches that could fall on your home under the weight of snow.

o Store or secure outdoor furniture and any loose items that could be moved by winter storms.

o Cover or store grills and other outdoor cooking appliances.

7. Communication:

o Leave emergency contact information with a neighbor, friend, or family member.

o Ensure someone has a key and knows how to manage any issues that may arise with your home.

o Provide your contact information to the local police department and inform them of your absence, especially if you live in a small community.

8. Financial and Legal Matters:

o Pay any bills that will be due while you're away, or set them up to be paid automatically.

o Notify your bank and credit card companies that you'll be traveling to avoid any fraud alerts on your accounts.

9. Insurance:

o Check with your insurance to ensure coverage continues uninterrupted and is fully comprehensive while you're away.

Know what is required of you to keep your home insured while vacant.

10. **Pest Prevention:**
   o   Ensure all food is sealed and stored properly.
   o   Seal any cracks or holes on the exterior of your home to prevent pests from entering.
   o   Consider setting up pest traps or scheduling a preventative visit from a pest control service.

By following this checklist, you can have peace of mind knowing that your home is secure, energy-efficient, and well-maintained while you're away for an extended period, especially during the demanding winter months.

Must-Have Items

In my experience, I've learned what items I really needed on my boondocking trips.

Vehicle Equipment:
o   Reliable Vehicle: Ensure your vehicle is robust and suitable for off-road conditions.
o   Spare Tires and Repair Kit: Always carry at least one spare tire and tools for vehicle repair.
o   Recovery Gear: Include items like a winch, tow straps, and traction mats.
o   Extra Fuel: Carry extra fuel containers in case there are long stretches without fuel stations.
o   Navigation Tools:
    o   GPS Device and Maps: Have both electronic GPS and physical maps.
    o   Satellite Phone or Communicator: Essential for areas without cell service.

Camping Gear:
o   Quality Tent and Sleeping Bags: Weather-appropriate and durable.
o   Portable Stove and Cooking Supplies: Compact and easy to use.
o   Water Purification System: Vital for ensuring access to safe drinking water.
o   Solar Charger or Portable Generator: For powering electronic devices.

Food and Water Supplies:
o   Non-perishable Food: Enough to last between resupply points.
o   Adequate Water Storage: Large, durable water containers.
o   Cooler or Portable Fridge: To keep perishables fresh.

Clothing and Personal Items:
o   Layered Clothing: Suitable for changing weather conditions.
o   First Aid Kit: Comprehensive and tailored to your group's needs.
o   Personal Hygiene Products: Biodegradable soap, toothpaste, and other necessities.

Emergency and Safety Gear:

o   Fire Extinguisher: Make sure it's suitable for vehicle fires.

o   Emergency Beacon or Locator: Critical for alerting rescue services in an emergency.

Comprehensive Tool Kit: For any necessary repairs or adjustments.

Entertainment and Leisure:

o   Books, Games, and Downloaded Entertainment: For downtime and relaxation.

o   Camera or GoPro: To document your adventures.

Appendix B: Create Your Own Travel Plan

Where do you want to go and why? Write a list of countries, states, cities, highways, resorts, ski areas, or campgrounds you plan to visit. Include specifics, such as dates, and plan to make reservations where needed.

_____

_____

_____

_____

_____

_____

_____

_____

_____

_____

_____

_____

_____

_____

_____

_____

_____

_____

Objectives of Your Trip

What are the primary goals of your trip? Are you looking for adventurous or casual travel? What is important to you on this trip? Write a list here.

_____

_____

_____

_____

_____

_____

_____

_____

_____

_____

_____

_____

_____

_____

_____

_____

Appendix C: Considerations When Traveling in Winter

Heading out on a winter road trip, especially in the mountains, I know I need to prepare carefully to ensure my safety, comfort, and enjoyment. Here are key items I always consider:

1. **Winter-Ready Vehicle:**
    *   **Dual Batteries with Isolator**: Both of my vehicles (truck and Jeep) are equipped with two batteries, separated by a battery isolator. This setup prevents one battery from draining the other, ensuring a backup is always ready for use while keeping both charged during drives.
    *   **Regular Vehicle Service:** I always make sure both my vehicles are serviced and winter-ready.
    *   **Antifreeze Check:** I check and refill antifreeze levels as necessary to prevent freezing.
    *   **Well-Charged Batteries:** Ensuring that both batteries are well-charged and in good condition is crucial for cold starts and electrical reliability.
    *   **Winter Tires and Chains:** I equip my vehicles with winter tires for better traction and carry chains. I've found it's not redundant but essential, particularly for navigating through snowdrifts, ice, or challenging areas like summits or passes.
    *   **Half-Full Gas Tank**: I keep the gas tank at least half-full to avoid gas line freeze-up and use gas line antifreeze for extra protection.

2. **Emergency Roadside Kit:**
    *   Jumper cables.
    *   Flares or reflective triangles.
    *   Ice scraper and brush.
    *   Shovel and ax. Yes, I have these in both vehicles. The ax has proven to be worth its weight in gold, given the number of down trees that I have dealt with when on dirt roads that are not maintained regularly.
    *   Tow rope or chain. I have installed winches on both of my vehicles, and they have proven time and again to be very helpful.

3. **Basic tools:**
    *   **Multi-Tool or Knife**: A good quality multi-tool can serve many purposes, from cutting to screwing or gripping.
    *   **Screwdrivers**: A set of screwdrivers in various sizes, including both flathead and Phillips head. I use a cordless drill and have bits that cover a wide array of screw types.
        1. **Flathead (Slotted)**: This is one of the oldest and simplest types, characterized by a single slot. It's used widely but can be prone to slippage if not aligned properly.
        2. **Phillips**: Recognizable by its cross-shaped slot, the Phillips screw head is designed to cam out under too much torque, preventing over-tightening.
        3. **Posidrive**: Similar to Phillips, but with extra lines between the cross, offering more engagement points. It's less likely to cam out compared to Phillips and is commonly used in Europe.
        4. **Torx (Star)**: This screw head has a six-point star shape. It provides a better grip and torque than Phillips or flathead and is less likely to cam out.
        5. **Hex (Allen)**: This type has a hexagonal recess and requires an Allen key or hex key for driving. It's often used in furniture assembly and bicycles.
        6. **Square (Robertson)**: This screw head has a square recess and provides good torque without slipping. It's very popular in Canada and is gaining popularity in other regions for its ease of use and reliability.
        7. **Tri-Wing**: This type has a triangular slot and is often used in applications where tamper resistance is important.
        8. **Torq-set**: Similar to Phillips, but with the wings offset, this is used in aerospace and applications where more torque is necessary.
    *   **Torque wrench**: A torque wrench is a precision tool used to apply a specific amount of torque to a nut, bolt, or fastener. It is essential in scenarios where the tightness of screws and bolts is crucial. I learned the hard way that the lug nuts on my tires were not adequately torqued, and I lost a tire because of sheared lug bolts because the nuts were not adequately torqued. As part of my daily routine when driving the truck, I now review the torque on the lug nuts.

- **Pliers**: These include standard pliers, needle-nose pliers, and possibly a pair of vice grips.
- **Adjustable Wrench**: An adjustable wrench can be very useful for various nuts and bolts.
- **Socket Set**: A basic socket set can help with more complicated repairs that involve nuts and bolts (both metric and imperial).
- **Hammer**: A small hammer can be useful for minor repairs or breaking ice.
- **Ice Scraper and Snow Brush**: Essential for clearing snow and ice from your vehicle's windows and lights.
- **Jumper Cables**: Not a tool per se, but essential for any vehicle for emergency starts.
- **Tire Pressure Gauge**: Check that your tires are at the right pressure, which is more important in fluctuating winter temperatures.
- **Tow Strap or Rope**: In case you or another vehicle needs pulling out of a ditch or snow.
- **Duct Tape and Cable Ties**: For temporary fixes on hoses or to secure loose parts temporarily.
- **Flashlight and Extra Batteries**: Essential for any nighttime or low-light situation where you may need to work on your vehicle.
- **Shovel**: A compact, foldable shovel can be a lifesaver to dig out of snow.
- **Gloves and Hand Cleaner**: Protect your hands and keep them clean after the job is done.

4. **Winter Survival Kit**: In case I get stranded, I carry a kit with extra winter clothing and blankets, waterproof matches, a whistle, and a compact, high-energy food supply like energy bars. Don't forget extra water, but I keep it insulated to avoid freezing.

5. **Snow Removal Tools**: A good-quality ice scraper and snow brush, plus a small, collapsible shovel, are essential for keeping my vehicle clear of snow and ice.

6. **Traction Aids**: When a vehicle's wheels are stuck, the flat, sturdy surface of the traction pad allows the tires to grip something solid, enabling the vehicle to drive out of a slippery situation.

- **Ease of Use**: Traction pads are straightforward to use. You simply place them under the vehicle's drive wheels. They don't require the physical effort or technical knowledge that other recovery methods might.
- **Safety**: Traction pads can be a safer option than other recovery methods involving heavy, tensioned cables or winches. There's less risk of injury from snapping cables or other mishaps.
- **Portability**: Traction pads are lightweight and designed to be easily stored in your vehicle, taking up minimal space. This makes them an ideal tool to always have on hand.
- **Versatility**: They can be used in a variety of environments — whether you're stuck in sand, mud, snow, or ice, traction pads can provide the necessary grip to get unstuck.
- **Durability**: Most traction pads are made from tough, durable materials designed to withstand the weight of a vehicle and the harshness of various terrains.
- **Cost-Effectiveness**: Compared to other recovery methods like winches or professional recovery services, traction pads are relatively inexpensive and offer good value, given their effectiveness.
- **Timesaving**: Instead of waiting for help or trying multiple methods to free your vehicle, traction pads can offer a quick solution to get you moving again.
- **Multipurpose Use**: In addition to providing traction, some people use these pads as shovels to remove excess sand, snow, or mud from around the tires or under the vehicle. They can also be used as a base for a jack on soft ground.
- **Environmentally Friendly**: Unlike some methods that might involve digging or altering the terrain, traction pads are a less invasive way to recover a vehicle, minimizing impact on the environment.

7. **Flashlight and Extra Batteries**: With winter days being shorter, a reliable light source is crucial if I'm stuck or need to check my vehicle in the dark.

8. **First-Aid Kit**: I ensure it's stocked with items to handle minor injuries or illnesses, including any medications my passengers or I may need. See Appendix E for a recommended list for a wilderness first aid kit. I

keep a separate first aid kit in the vehicles and another in my go-bag for when I hit the trails.

9. **Maps and Navigation Tools**: While I rely on my truck's internal GPS, I also bring physical maps or printed directions as a backup, especially in remote areas where my truck's GPS system may not have been updated to include the detail I need. This frequently happens when traveling along fire or logging roads.

10. **Charged Cell Phone and Charger**: I keep my phone charged and bring along a car charger or portable power bank. I also use a portable solar panel when traveling or parked.

11. **Warm Clothing and Blankets**: I pack extra gloves, hats, scarves, and thermal socks, ensuring there are enough blankets or sleeping bags for everyone in the car.

12. **Sunglasses**: To protect against the harsh snow glare, I never forget my sunglasses.

13. **Water and Snacks**: I keep hydrated and have enough food, especially items that don't need heating, in case I am delayed or stranded.

Before Heading Out:
1. **Check the Weather and Road Conditions**: I always make sure I know what conditions to expect and plan my route accordingly.
2. **Inform Someone of My Plans**: I let a friend or family member know my route and expected arrival time.
3. **Plan for Extra Time**: Knowing winter travel can be slower, I don't rush and allow for frequent breaks.

Remember that the key to a successful winter road trip, particularly in mountainous areas, is thorough preparation. I ensure my vehicle is equipped and maintained for winter conditions, and I pack with both comfort and emergencies in mind. Staying informed about the weather and road conditions is crucial, and I always prioritize safety over sticking to a schedule.

Appendix D: Ten Essentials to Carry When in Backcountry

When venturing into the backcountry, especially in winter, it's crucial to be well-prepared for various conditions and emergencies. Here are ten essential items you should carry:

1. **Navigation Tools**: A topographic map and compass are indispensable for navigation, even if you carry a GPS device. In winter, when trails are covered in snow, navigation can be more challenging, making these tools even more important.
2. **Headlamp/Flashlight**: A reliable light source is essential, especially in the winter when daylight hours are shorter. Make sure to carry extra batteries or a backup light source.
3. **Extra Food and Water**: Always carry extra food in case your trip takes longer than expected. In winter, your body burns more calories to stay warm, so high-energy foods are preferable. Also, bring sufficient water and a way to melt snow for drinking, as dehydration can be a risk in cold weather.
4. **Extra Clothing**: Weather conditions can change rapidly in the backcountry. Carry additional warm, waterproof, and windproof clothing, including an extra layer of insulation, a warm hat, gloves, and thermal underwear.
5. **First Aid Kit**: A comprehensive first aid kit is essential. In winter, your kit should include items to treat hypothermia and frostbite, such as chemical heat packs.
6. **Shelter**: A lightweight tent, bivy sack, or emergency space blanket can be lifesaving if you get stranded or injured. In winter conditions, the shelter is even more critical to protect against the elements.
7. **Fire Starting Kit**: Carry waterproof matches, a lighter, and fire starters. Being able to start a fire is crucial for warmth, cooking, and emergency signaling in winter.
8. **Knife or Multi-tool**: A good knife or multi-tool is incredibly useful for various tasks, from preparing food to making repairs.
9. **Sun Protection**: Sunscreen, sunglasses, and lip balm are important even in winter, as snow reflects sunlight, increasing the risk of sunburn.

10. **Communication Device**: In addition to a cell phone, consider carrying a satellite phone, two-way radio, or a personal locator beacon (PLB), especially in areas with poor cell coverage.

Remember, the key to safe travel in the backcountry, particularly in winter, is preparation and self-sufficiency. Always inform someone about your travel plans and expected return time, and consider the avalanche risks if applicable.

Appendix E: Wilderness First Aid Kit

When assembling a wilderness first aid kit, consider the remoteness, duration, and nature of your trip, as well as the number of people involved. A well-stocked wilderness first aid kit should be tailored to address a wide range of injuries and medical emergencies that might occur in the wild, where immediate professional medical assistance isn't readily available.

I would highly recommend taking a first responder first aid class. A Wilderness First Aid (WFA) class is a course designed to teach individuals how to provide first aid care in remote or wilderness settings, where emergency medical services (EMS) may be delayed or inaccessible. It is a basic level of training aimed at equipping outdoor enthusiasts, guides, rangers, and anyone who spends a significant amount of time in remote areas with the skills necessary to address common injuries and illnesses that may occur in these settings.

The course is typically a weekend. I took my first WFA course through REI. There are several entities like NOLS that provide wilderness first aid courses. Here are critical elements that you should consider for your wilderness first aid kit:

1. **Bandages and Wound Care:**
   - o   Various sizes of adhesive bandages.
   - o   Sterile gauze pads and rolls.
   - o   Adhesive tape for securing gauze.
   - o   Butterfly bandages or wound closure strips.
   - o   Blister treatment patches or moleskin.
   - o   Antiseptic wipes and antibiotic ointment.

2. **Tools and Supplies:**
   - o   Tweezers for splinter or tick removal.
   - o   Scissors or shears for cutting clothing or bandages.
   - o   Safety pins to secure splints or bandages.
   - o   Thermometer.
   - o   Irrigation syringe to clean wounds.

3. **Splinting and Immobilization:**
   - o   Elastic wraps for sprains or strains.

o   Splints for fractures or injured limbs.
o   Triangular bandages for making slings or wraps.

4. **Medications:**
    o   Pain relievers such as ibuprofen or acetaminophen.
    o   Antihistamines for allergic reactions.
    o   Aspirin for heart attacks (where appropriate).
    o   Prescribed medications (if any specific are needed for individuals in the group).
    o   Anti-diarrheal medication.

5. **Infection Control:**
    o   Nitrile gloves to prevent contamination.
    o   Hand sanitizer or alcohol wipes.
    o   Face masks for CPR or if there's a risk of infectious disease.

6. **Emergency Equipment:**
    o   CPR face shield or mask.
    o   A whistle to signal for help.
    o   Emergency blanket for treating shock or hypothermia.

7. **Documentation:**
    o   Notebook and pencil to record vital signs, symptoms, or treatment given.
    o   First aid manual or quick reference guide.

8. **Specialty Items:**
    o   Snake bite kit if in a snake-prone area.
    o   Water purification tablets.
    o   Insect sting treatment.
    o   Sunburn relief gel or cream.
    o   Frostbite and hypothermia prevention supplies.

Remember, the key to an effective wilderness first aid kit is not only having the right supplies but also knowing how to use them. Regularly check and replenish your first aid kit, especially before embarking on any trip, to ensure all items are in good condition and medicines are not expired. Your wilderness first aid kit can be a lifeline in critical situations and is an indispensable part of your outdoor gear.

Appendix F: Types and Components of Travel Insurance

1. **Travel Insurance**: This is the most comprehensive type of insurance for travelers. It can cover trip cancelations, lost luggage, travel delays, and sometimes even lodging in case you're stuck somewhere due to unforeseen circumstances. Make sure to check the specifics of what's covered, as policies vary widely.

2. **Medical Insurance**: Perhaps the most critical insurance for any traveler. Ensure that your policy covers medical expenses for injuries or illnesses that might occur abroad, including medical evacuation if necessary. Not all domestic health insurance plans cover international travel, so you may need to purchase a separate travel health insurance policy.

3. **Emergency Evacuation Insurance**: This covers the costs of transportation to a medical facility in case of an emergency, which is especially vital if you are traveling to remote or underserved areas. It's often included in travel medical insurance but check the specifics of your coverage.

4. **Accidental Death and Dismemberment Insurance (AD&D)**: This insurance pays a benefit if you die or are dismembered in an accident while traveling. It's a grim thing to consider, but it can provide important financial support to your family in the worst-case scenario.

5. **Adventure and Sports Coverage**: If your expedition includes activities like scuba diving, mountain climbing, or other high-risk sports, make sure you get a policy that doesn't exclude these activities. Standard travel insurance might not cover accidents occurring during "adventure activities."

6. **Rental Car Insurance**: If you plan to drive in the country you're visiting, consider rental car insurance to cover any damage to the vehicle. Check first if your regular car insurance or credit card offers any coverage internationally.

7. **Trip Interruption Insurance**: This can reimburse you for pre-paid, non-refundable travel expenses if an emergency happens and you need to return home earlier or interrupt your trip. Scenarios can include an unexpected illness, natural disaster, or other crises.

Before purchasing any insurance, it's important to read the fine print and understand what is and isn't covered. It's also a good idea to purchase your insurance from a reputable company and to carry proof of your insurance and their emergency contact numbers with you during your trip. In addition, consider the stability and healthcare infrastructure of your destination, as this might influence the type and extent of coverage you need. Always plan for the unexpected and make sure you're covered for any eventualities that could occur while you're away from home.

Appendix G: Apps for Backcountry Travel: Hiking, Off-Roading

Traveling in the backcountry requires careful planning and navigation, and fortunately, there are several apps designed specifically for off-road and backcountry travel that can enhance your safety and experience. Here are some apps you might find helpful:

1. **onX Offroad:**
   o **Purpose**: Provides detailed off-road maps.
   o **Features**: Shows trails, public and private land boundaries, 4x4 roads, and more. It's particularly popular for its detailed and accurate GPS mapping, which is crucial for off-road navigation.

2. **GAIA GPS:**
   o **Purpose**: Hiking, hunting, and off-road mapping.
   o **Features**: Offers topographic and satellite maps for offline use, tracking, and route planning. Gaia is well-regarded for its extensive map layers and detailed trail data.

3. **AllTrails:**
   o **Purpose**: Trail discovery and navigation.
   o **Features**: A vast collection of trail maps for hiking, mountain biking, and more. It includes user reviews, trail conditions, and the ability to download maps for offline use.

4. **Avenza Maps:**
   o **Purpose**: PDF mapping.
   o **Features**: Allows you to use geospatial PDFs, GeoPDF, and GeoTIFF maps for offline GPS navigation. Users can download maps from a vast library or import their own.

5. **Cairn:**
   o **Purpose**: Safety and tracking.
   o **Features**: Cairn is unique as it lets you share your location and trip plans with friends and family. It also shows where you might find cell coverage and allows for downloading maps.

6. **The Dyrt:**
   o **Purpose**: Campsite finding.
   o **Features**: Offers a comprehensive database of campsites across the US, including reviews and tips. It's beneficial for planning where to stay overnight in the backcountry.

7. **PeakFinder:**
   o **Purpose**: Mountain identification.
   o **Features**: Uses your phone's camera and GPS to identify mountain peaks in real-time. It's a fun and useful tool for hikers and climbers.

8. **Compass 360 Pro Free:**
   o **Purpose**: Direction finding.
   o **Features**: A simple app that turns your device into a functional compass. While many smartphones have built-in compasses, dedicated apps might offer additional features like declination adjustment.

9. **First Aid—American Red Cross:**
   o **Purpose**: Emergency preparedness.
   o **Features**: Provides step-by-step instructions on first aid procedures for a variety of common situations, which is crucial in the backcountry where medical help is not readily available.

10. **Offline Survival Manual:**
    o **Purpose**: Survival knowledge.
    o **Features**: Contains information on how to make fire, build a shelter, find food, and more. It's a useful resource for worst-case scenarios.

When selecting apps for backcountry travel, consider the following:

- **Offline Capability**: Ensure that the app works offline or allows you to download necessary data, as you will likely be in areas without cellular service.
- **Battery Usage**: Be aware that using GPS and other features can drain your battery quickly. It's wise to bring additional power sources.

- **Accuracy and Reliability**: Look for apps with good reviews regarding their accuracy and reliability, especially for critical tasks like navigation.
- **Personal Needs**: Choose apps that fit your specific activity, whether you're hiking, off-roading, camping, or engaging in any other backcountry activities.

Before relying on any app in a remote or risky situation, familiarize yourself with its functionality and limitations. No app should replace basic survival skills, proper preparation, and the use of physical maps and traditional navigation tools as a backup. Always let someone know your itinerary and expected return, especially when venturing into remote areas.

Appendix H: Off-Roading Trails

When tackling off-roading trails during winter, it's essential to exercise caution and ensure the trails are passable. Here are considerations to prepare before you head out on the trails:

1. Check Weather and Trail Conditions: Weather can be unpredictable in winter, with possible snow and ice. Always check the latest weather forecasts and seek out recent trail reports from reliable sources or local off-roading clubs.

2. Vehicle Preparation: Ensure that vehicles are equipped for winter conditions. This includes having suitable tires (preferably with good tread or chains), a winch, and recovery gear. It's also wise to have your vehicle checked and winterized by a professional.

3. Travel in Groups: Never hit the trails alone in winter. Traveling in groups ensures that help is at hand in case a vehicle gets stuck or encounters mechanical issues.

4. Communicate Clearly: Use radios or other communication devices to stay in touch with your group. Clearly discuss and agree on what signals or messages will be used to indicate different situations, such as needing assistance or turning back.

5. Know Your Limits and Respect the Trail: It's vital to understand the capabilities of your vehicle and your own driving skills. Avoid trails that exceed these limits. Additionally, adhere to the principles of "Leave No Trace" to protect the natural beauty and integrity of the landscape.

6. Emergency Plan: Always have an emergency plan in place. This includes carrying sufficient supplies (water, food, warm clothing), having a first aid kit, and knowing the location of the nearest hospital or emergency service.

Alaska

Several great off-road trails outside Anchorage, Alaska, offer beautiful scenery and exciting off-roading opportunities. Remember that trail conditions can change depending on the season and weather, so checking local information and trail reports before heading out is essential. Here are some popular off-road trails near Anchorage:

1. **Palmer Creek Road:** Palmer Creek Road is near Hope, Alaska, on the Kenai Peninsula. This famous off-road trail provides access to the scenic Palmer Creek area. Palmer Creek Road offers beautiful views of glaciers, mountains, and lush forests. It's known for its mining history, and you may come across old mining relics along the way. It's suitable for most high-clearance 4x4 vehicles and off-road enthusiasts. The trail is relatively mild and suitable for beginners.

   • **Winter Accessibility:** Palmer Creek Road is typically not maintained during the winter months, and access may be restricted due to snow and weather conditions. Visiting in the summer or early fall is best for optimal off-roading experiences.

2. **Purchase Creek:** Purchase Creek is situated near Haines, Alaska, in the state's southeastern part. This trail takes you through the coastal rainforest of the Chilkat Peninsula. Purchase Creek offers a lush and scenic route with opportunities to spot wildlife like bears, eagles, and salmon. It provides access to beautiful viewpoints and the Chilkat State Park. This trail is open to various off-road vehicles and skill levels. It's an excellent option for those seeking a more relaxed off-road experience in a stunning natural setting.

   • **Winter Accessibility:** Purchase Creek is generally inaccessible due to snow and challenging road conditions. It's recommended to visit during the warmer months.

3. **Knik Glacier:** Knik Glacier is in the Matanuska-Susitna Valley, near Palmer, Alaska. The trail takes you through a glacial landscape with views of Knik Glacier and the surrounding mountains. Knik Glacier offers a unique off-road experience with opportunities to explore a glacier's terminus, icebergs, and breathtaking scenery. The area

is known for its impressive ice formations. This trail requires high-clearance 4x4 vehicles and off-road experience. It's not recommended for beginners, as the terrain can be challenging.

- **Winter Accessibility:** The Knik Glacier area is accessible in the winter and is a popular spot for snowmobiling adventures. Be sure to check trail conditions and safety recommendations for winter activities.

4. **Cottonwood Creek:** Cottonwood Creek is found in the Talkeetna Mountains near Willow, Alaska. The trail provides access to the Talkeetna Mountains and Cottonwood Creek area. Cottonwood Creek offers a mix of forested terrain and mountain landscapes. You can explore the Cottonwood Creek Valley, go fishing, and enjoy the tranquility of the wilderness. This trail is generally accessible to off-road vehicles, including ATVs and off-road motorcycles. It's suitable for various skill levels, including beginners.

- **Winter Accessibility:** Cottonwood Creek trails are usually covered in snow during winter, making them inaccessible for off-roading. Plan your visit for the summer or early fall.

5. **Denali Highway:** Denali Highway, also known as Alaska Route 8, stretches from Paxson to Cantwell, parallel to the Alaska Range. This mostly gravel road offers incredible scenic views and plenty of opportunities for dispersed camping. Denali Highway passes through remote wilderness areas with opportunities to spot wildlife and offers access to beautiful lakes and hiking trails. The route is approximately 135 miles long.

- **Winter Accessibility:** Due to heavy snowfall, the Denali Highway is generally closed to vehicle traffic during the winter. Winter access may be limited to snowmobiling or cross-country skiing.

6. **McCarthy Road:** McCarthy Road is in the Wrangell-St. Elias National Park and Preserve, starting from Chitina. This gravel road provides access to the historic town of McCarthy and Kennecott Mines within the park. The McCarthy Road offers a unique off-road experience in a remote and historic area. It passes through

beautiful landscapes, river crossings, and old mining sites. The drive is approximately sixty miles long.

- **Winter Accessibility:** McCarthy Road is typically closed to vehicle traffic during the winter months. Access may be limited to snowmobiles and skis, depending on snow conditions.

7. **Dalton Highway (Haul Road):** The Dalton Highway extends from Fairbanks to Prudhoe Bay, passing through the Arctic wilderness. This gravel highway is known for its challenging terrain and remote locations. The Dalton Highway is famous for its rugged and remote landscapes, including the Brooks Range and Arctic tundra. Travelers can explore the Arctic Circle and the Trans-Alaska Pipeline and witness unique wildlife. The route covers over four hundred miles.

- **Winter Accessibility:** The Dalton Highway is open year-round but can be extremely challenging in winter due to icy and snowy conditions. Winter travelers should be well-prepared and aware of the risks.

8. **Resurrection Pass Trail:** The Resurrection Pass Trail is on the Kenai Peninsula, near Hope. This multi-use trail is open to hiking, biking, and off-roading. The Resurrection Pass Trail offers a scenic and challenging off-road experience in a mountainous, forested environment. The trail crosses streams, passes by lakes, and provides camping and wildlife viewing opportunities.

- **Winter Accessibility:** While the Resurrection Pass Trail is open year-round, it is primarily used for winter recreational activities such as cross-country skiing, snowshoeing, and snowmobiling during the winter months. The trail may be covered in deep snow, making it suitable for winter sports enthusiasts. Check local trail conditions and snow depth before planning your winter visit.

9. **Petersville Road:** Petersville Road is located near Talkeetna in the Susitna Valley. This dirt and gravel road offers access to the foothills of the Alaska Range. Petersville Road is known for its excellent mountain

views and proximity to the Denali (Mount McKinley) area. The road is relatively easy, making it suitable for RVs.

- **Winter Accessibility:** Petersville Road can be covered in snow during the winter, limiting off-roading options. Snowmobiling and winter sports may be possible depending on snow conditions.

10. **Caribou Creek Recreational Mining Area:** Caribou Creek is in the Matanuska Valley, north of Palmer. This area offers recreational mining opportunities, including gold panning and sluicing. Caribou Creek provides a unique off-roading experience and recreational mining activities. It's a family-friendly destination with beautiful surroundings.

- **Winter Accessibility:** Caribou Creek Recreational Mining Area may have limited accessibility in winter due to snow. It's best visited during the warmer months for recreational activities.

11. **Powder Line Pass:** Powder Line Pass is in the Chugach Mountains and offers stunning panoramic views of the surrounding landscapes. The trail provides opportunities for off-roading, including ATV and snowmobile riding. You'll encounter diverse terrain, from alpine meadows to forested areas.

- **Winter Accessibility:** Powder Line Pass is typically accessible in winter, making it a popular destination for snowmobiling and backcountry skiing. However, winter conditions can be extreme, so checking weather and avalanche conditions is essential before heading out.

12. **Peters Creek:** Peters Creek is known for its scenic beauty and varied terrain, making it a favorite spot for off-roading enthusiasts. The trail offers a mix of challenging sections and more leisurely routes, with opportunities for ATV and dirt bike riding.

- **Winter Accessibility:** Peters Creek may be accessible in winter, primarily for snowmobiling. However, the trail conditions can change significantly with snow and ice, so be sure to check for current conditions and safety precautions.

13. **Eklutna Lakeside:** Eklutna Lakeside features picturesque views of Eklutna Lake and the Chugach Mountains. The trail offers opportunities for off-roading, including ATV and dirt bike riding. You can enjoy the pristine beauty of the lake and forests.

   • **Winter Accessibility:** Eklutna Lakeside may be accessible in winter for snowmobiling and cross-country skiing. Like other trails in Alaska, winter conditions can vary, so monitoring weather and trail conditions is crucial.

14. **Jim Creek Recreation Area:** Jim Creek Recreation Area offers various outdoor activities, including off-roading, camping, fishing, and wildlife viewing. The area features numerous trails catering to various off-road vehicles, including ATVs, dirt bikes, and 4x4 vehicles. You can explore forested areas, creeks, and open spaces while enjoying the scenic beauty of the surrounding Chugach Mountains.

   • **Winter Accessibility:** Jim Creek Recreation Area is typically accessible in the summer and early fall. However, it may have seasonal closures or restrictions, so it's essential to check with the managing agency or local authorities for the most up-to-date information.

15. **Matanuska Glacier State Recreation Area:** Matanuska Glacier State Recreation Area is famous for its stunning views of the Matanuska Glacier, one of Alaska's most accessible glaciers. While the primary activity here is glacier hiking and exploration, some off-road trails in the vicinity offer scenic driving experiences. You can enjoy the unique landscape of the glacier and surrounding valleys.

   • **Winter Accessibility:** The accessibility of off-road trails near Matanuska Glacier can vary. It's best to ask local authorities or the managing agency for specific trail conditions and access restrictions. Please note that the main attraction is glacier hiking.

16. **Hatcher Pass:** Hatcher Pass is a popular destination for outdoor enthusiasts. It offers off-road trails that wind through the Talkeetna Mountains, providing opportunities for ATV and dirt bike riding. The

pass is known for its historical gold mining sites, alpine tundra, and breathtaking mountain scenery.

- **Winter Accessibility:** Hatcher Pass is typically accessible during the summer and early fall when the trails are free of snow. However, winter conditions can make some trails inaccessible. Always check for seasonal road closures, trail conditions, and any restrictions before planning your visit.

Yukon

The Yukon Territory in Canada offers a vast and rugged wilderness with plenty of opportunities for off-roading and exploring the great outdoors. Here are some of the best off-roading trails in the Yukon.

1. **Dempster Highway:** The Dempster Highway is one of the most iconic and challenging off-road routes in the Yukon. It starts near Dawson City and runs north to Inuvik in the Northwest Territories, crossing the Arctic Circle. The highway is mostly gravel and offers breathtaking tundra, mountains, and wildlife views. It's a true adventure, but be prepared for remote conditions and limited services.

   • **Winter Accessibility:** The Dempster Highway is not typically recommended for travel during the winter months due to extreme weather conditions, heavy snowfall, and icy roads. It is primarily a summer and early fall route.

2. **Canol Road:** The Canol Road is another historic and challenging off-road route in the Yukon. It was initially built during World War II and stretched from Johnson's Crossing to Norman Wells in the Northwest Territories. The road is rough and remote, but it takes you through stunning wilderness areas.

   • **Winter Accessibility:** Canol Road is not maintained for winter travel and is typically inaccessible due to snow and extreme cold. It is best explored during the summer and early fall.

3. **Silver Trail:** The Silver Trail is a network of gravel roads that connects several Yukon communities, including Mayo, Keno City, and Elsa. It offers a mix of terrain, including mountain passes, forests, and scenic vistas. The road is suitable for off-roading, and it provides access to various outdoor activities like hiking and fishing.

   • **Winter Accessibility:** The Silver Trail may not be accessible in winter due to snow and freezing temperatures. Travel is more suitable during the warmer months.

4. **Top of the World Highway**: Starting in Dawson City, the Top of the World Highway crosses into Alaska, offering spectacular panoramic views of the rugged terrain. While much of the highway is paved, it can be rough and narrow in places, making it suitable for off-road enthusiasts.

    • **Winter Accessibility:** Travel on the Top of the World Highway during winter can be challenging and is not recommended. Snow and weather conditions make it less accessible during the colder months.

5. **Bonnet Plume River Road:** Located in the remote Peel Watershed region of the Yukon, the Bonnet Plume River Road is a challenging route that takes you through pristine wilderness. It's a remote and rugged trail, best suited for experienced off-roaders with well-equipped vehicles.

    • **Winter Accessibility:** These remote roads are typically not maintained or accessible during the winter months. They are best explored in the summer and early fall when conditions are more favorable.

6. **North Canol Road**: The North Canol Road is a historic route built during World War II. It starts near Johnson's Crossing and goes into the Mackenzie Mountains in the Northwest Territories. The road is rough and remote, providing access to incredible backcountry adventures.

    • **Winter Accessibility:** These remote roads are typically not maintained or accessible during winter. They are best explored in the summer and early fall when conditions are more favorable.

British Columbia

British Columbia, Canada, offers many off-roading opportunities with diverse landscapes, from coastal rainforests to rugged mountain terrain. Here are some of the best off-roading trails in British Columbia.

1. **Whipstar Trail:** The Whipstar Trail offers scenic off-roading through forests and rugged terrain. Highlights include challenging trails, beautiful landscapes, and opportunities for outdoor recreation.

   • **Winter Accessibility:** Winter conditions, with deep snow and icy roads, can make the Whipstar Trail inaccessible. It's typically more suitable for off-roading during the warmer months.

2. **Kettle Valley Rail Trail:** The Kettle Valley Rail Trail is a historic rail corridor converted into a multi-use trail in British Columbia. It traverses diverse landscapes, including tunnels, trestles, and scenic vistas. Highlights include the Myra Canyon Trestles and the opportunity for long-distance biking and hiking.

   • **Winter Accessibility:** Some sections of the Kettle Valley Rail Trail may be accessible in winter for snowshoeing and cross-country skiing but not typically for off-roading due to snow and trail conditions.

3. **Vedder Mountain:** Vedder Mountain, near Chilliwack, British Columbia, offers trails suitable for off-roading, mountain biking, and hiking. Highlights include various difficulty levels, forested trails, and beautiful views.

   • **Winter Accessibility:** Winter conditions may limit off-roading access on Vedder Mountain, as snow and icy trails can make travel challenging.

4. **Stave Lake West:** Stave Lake West is an off-roading area near Mission, British Columbia. It offers a variety of trails through forests and scenic terrain, along with opportunities for outdoor recreation.

- **Winter Accessibility:** Like many off-roading areas, Stave Lake West may not be accessible in winter due to snow and trail conditions.

5. **Harrison West Forest:** The Harrison West Forest area provides off-roading enthusiasts access to trails amid a beautiful natural setting. Highlights include forested terrain, wildlife viewing, and potential for exploration.

   - **Winter Accessibility:** Winter conditions can limit access to the Harrison West Forest area, making it more suitable for off-roading during the non-winter months.

6. **Elaborate Valley:** Elaborate Valley offers off-roading adventures in a scenic environment with diverse trails and terrain. Highlights include challenging routes, forested areas, and opportunities for outdoor activities.

   - **Winter Accessibility:** Winter conditions, including snow and icy trails, can affect accessibility for off-roading in Elaborate Valley.

7. **Duffy Lake Road:** Duffy Lake Road is a scenic route in British Columbia known for its beautiful mountain vistas and access to outdoor recreation. Highlights include mountain views, lakes, and potential camping spots.

   - **Winter Accessibility:** Winter conditions, such as snow and road closures, can impact accessibility on Duffy Lake Road. It's important to check road conditions before traveling.

8. **Churn Creek:** Churn Creek is an off-roading area in British Columbia with diverse trails and landscapes. Highlights include challenging routes, desert-like terrain, and the opportunity to explore the region's natural beauty.

   - **Winter Accessibility:** Churn Creek may not be accessible in winter due to snow and weather conditions, making it more suitable for off-roading during other seasons.

9. **Bean Creek Off-Roading Recreation Area:** Bean Creek Off-Roading Recreation Area provides off-roading enthusiasts with designated trails and areas for recreational vehicles. Highlights include off-roading challenges and a designated space for outdoor fun.

   • **Winter Accessibility:** Like most off-roading areas, Bean Creek Off-Roading Recreation Area may not be accessible during the winter months due to snow and trail conditions.

10. **Whipsaw Creek Recreational Area:** Situated near Penticton, this area provides a range of off-roading trails suitable for various vehicles. You'll encounter rocky terrain, creek crossings, and challenging ascents.

   • **Winter Accessibility:** Whipsaw Creek may be accessible in winter due to snow and weather conditions.

Moab

Moab, Utah, is renowned for its spectacular off-road trails that cater to various skill levels, from beginners to experienced off-road enthusiasts. It is advisable to check with the Bureau of Land Management (BLM) to find out the latest regarding trail openings/closures, as well as a good source for maps.

1. **Kane Creek Canyon:** An easy-to-moderate trail with picturesque canyon views, water crossings, and a variety of terrain. It's suitable for a wide range of skill levels, including beginners.

2. **Hurrah Pass:** Another easy-to-moderate trail with views of the Colorado River and Canyonlands, historic mining ruins, and a relatively easy trail. It's suitable for beginners and up.

3. **Hurrah Pass:** Another easy-to-moderate trail with views of the Colorado River and Canyonlands, historic mining ruins, and a relatively easy trail. It's suitable for beginners and up.

4. **Chicken Corners:** A moderate trail with red rock formations, views of the Colorado River, and the "Chicken Corners" overlook. It's suitable for intermediate drivers with high-clearance 4x4 vehicles.

5. **White Rim Trail:** A moderate-to-difficult trail that includes a multi-day, hundred-mile loop through Canyonlands National Park with stunning vistas. It's suitable for experienced off-road enthusiasts with well-equipped vehicles (requires permits).

6. **Fins and Things:** A moderate-to-difficult trail with sandstone fins and challenging obstacles. It's suitable for intermediate to experienced drivers.

7. **Hell's Revenge:** A difficult trail with challenging slickrock sections, steep climbs, and the famous "Hell's Gate" obstacle. It's suitable for experienced drivers with high-clearance 4x4 vehicles.

8. **Poison Spider Mesa:** A difficult trail with technical slickrock sections, steep climbs, and the "Golden Crack" obstacle. It's suitable for experienced drivers with capable off-road vehicles.

9. **Moab Rim:** A difficult trail with stunning views of Moab and the Colorado River, rocky obstacles, and a challenging ascent to the rim. It's suitable for experienced drivers looking for a thrilling experience.

10. **Porcupine Rim:** A difficult trail with scenic views of Castle Valley, technical descents, and the famous "Porcupine Rim Trail." It's suitable for experienced riders and mountain bikers; it's also popular for Jeeps.

11. **Top of the World:** A difficult trail with high-altitude views of Moab and the La Sal Mountains, steep climbs, and challenging terrain. It's suitable for experienced drivers with modified 4x4 vehicles.

12. **Lone Canyon OHV Trail:** Lone Canyon OHV Trail is located near Moab, Utah, and offers a challenging and scenic ride through sandstone canyons, slickrock, and desert terrain. You'll encounter steep ascents, descents, and rocky obstacles.

13. **Potash Road and Shafer Switchbacks:** This trail near Moab provides breathtaking views of the Colorado River and features the famous Shafer Switchbacks, a series of switchback turns that descend from the mesa top to the White Rim below. The trail also passes by petroglyphs and offers diverse landscapes.

14. **Mineral Point OHV Trail:** Mineral Point is located near Ouray, Colorado, and offers a challenging and rocky ride with stunning alpine scenery. You'll navigate through forests and rocky outcroppings and enjoy panoramic views.

15. **Gemini Bridges OHV Trail:** This trail near Moab, Utah, takes you to the iconic Gemini Bridges, two massive natural sandstone arches. You'll traverse scenic desert terrain and enjoy fantastic photo opportunities.

16. **White Rim Trail:** Located in Canyonlands National Park near Moab, the White Rim Trail offers a multi-day adventure through the

breathtaking landscapes of the park. You'll encounter mesas, canyons, and the mighty Colorado River.

17. **Hell Roaring Rim OHV Trail:** Hell Roaring Rim OHV Trail offers riders panoramic views of the mountains and valleys surrounding Hell Roaring Canyon near Ketchum, Idaho. It's a challenging trail with rocky sections and steep climbs.

Always check trail conditions and closures and obtain any necessary permits before embarking off-road. It's essential to be well-prepared, have the appropriate gear, and follow Leave No Trace principles to protect this beautiful desert environment. It's essential to check with local authorities, trail organizations, or park rangers for the most up-to-date information before planning off-roading trips. Consider your vehicle's capabilities and driving skills when choosing a trail.

Appendix I: Highways and Byways

Traveling between the USA, Canada, and Alaska offers a unique opportunity to experience some of the most scenic and treacherous highways in North America. While my travels will need to use major highway systems at some time, my goal is to use the scenic or byways whenever I can. I have learned that this is where adventure awaits, and it is always different. The following is a brief synopsis of the road systems that I hope to conquer and experience.

1. **Trans-Canada Highway**: This highway is not a single route and consists of several different routes that cross Canada. My trip will be on the main Trans-Canada Highway (Highway 1) that passes through Winnipeg, Regina, Calgary, and Banff.

2. **Alaska Highway (Alcan Highway):** Originally built as a military supply road during World War II, this highway starts in Dawson Creek, British Columbia, and stretches to Delta Junction, Alaska. The route provides breathtaking views of mountains, forests, and an array of wildlife.

3. **Cassiar Highway (Highway 37):** This is a less-traveled alternative to the Alaska Highway. It provides a wilder experience, passing through dense forests and near stunning glaciers. I will travel this on my way to Prince Rupert, BC.

4. **Seward Highway:** Recognized for its scenic, natural, historical, and recreational values, the 127-mile Seward Highway holds a triple designation: USDA Forest Service Scenic Byway, Alaska Scenic Byway, and All-American Road. This highway connects Anchorage to the coastal town of Seward. It provides stunning views of the Turnagain Arm, glaciers, waterfalls, and frequent sightings of wildlife like mountain goats, whales, and eagles.

5. **George Parks Highway (Alaska Route 3)**: This road connects Anchorage and Fairbanks, passing by the incredible Denali National Park and offering views of Denali, North America's tallest peak.

6. **Yellowhead Highway (Highway 16):** This transcontinental highway stretches from Manitoba to British Columbia and passes through

Edmonton and Saskatoon. It's a major east-west route in the Northern Prairies and offers a diverse range of landscapes.

7. **The Haines Highway or Haines Cut-Off**: This byway is encompassed by the lush coastal rain forest as it makes its way up the St. Elias Mountains and into Canada, where the forest gives way to alpine tundra, and the Haines Highway connects with Alaska.

8. **Sea to Sky Highway (Highway 99)**: A 120-kilometer stretch of road between Vancouver and Whistler and is one of the most scenic routes I have experienced (the most scenic one between Banff and Lake Louise), especially in winter with the snow-covered mountains, the ocean, forests, waterfalls, and lakes.

9. **Pacific Rim Highway (Highway 4)**: A 150-kilometer drive across Vancouver Island from Parksville in the east to Tofino in the west and travels through ancient forests, mountain ranges, and lakes.

10. **BC Trans-Canada (Highway 1)**: A part of the Trans-Canada Highway, spanning 651 miles from the provincial capital, Victoria, on Vancouver Island to Alberta near Banff National Park.

11. **Richardson's Highway (Highway 4)**: A highway in the US state of Alaska, running 368 miles and connecting Valdez to Fairbanks. I took this Alaska Route 4 from Valdez to Delta Junction. It continues up to Fairbanks as Alaska Route 2.

12. **Scenic Byway 12 (Highway 12)**: A beautiful 122-mile drive that starts in Panguitch, Utah, near Bryce Canyon National Park and ends in Torrey, Utah, near Capitol Reef National Park with towering red rock formations, deep canyons, and lush forests.

13. **Flaming Gorge-Green River basin Byway (Highway 191)**: It has dramatic landscapes surrounding Lake Flaming Gorge and quickly evolves to high desert and open shrub vegetation as it leaves the mountains.

14. **BC Ferry System Prince Rupert to Port Hardy**: Traveling the Inside Passage in BC is truly an unforgettable experience, combining

stunning natural beauty, diverse wildlife, and the serene ambiance of the Pacific Northwest coastal waters.

Idaho

Idaho boasts a variety of scenic byways, each offering unique landscapes and experiences. Some notable ones include:

1. **Northwest Passage Scenic Byway**: This 202-mile route begins in Lewiston and follows US 12 northeast to the Idaho-Montana border. It offers year-round attractions like boating, fishing, and heritage sites. The road conditions can be challenging in winter, with black ice and snow-covered roads at higher elevations.

2. **Panhandle Historic Rivers Passage**: Starting at the Washington border, this byway follows the northern shore of the Pend Oreille River to Oldtown, Priest River, and Sandpoint over 28.5 miles. It's known for its beautiful river scenery and historical significance, dating back to explorer David Thompson's journey in 1809.

3. **Pend Oreille Scenic Byway**: This route along Idaho's largest lake, Lake Pend Oreille, stretches from Sandpoint to the Montana state line, covering forty-eight miles of breathtaking scenery.

4. **Lake Coeur d'Alene Scenic Byway**: Ideal for bird watching, this drive provides stunning views and opportunities to spot bald eagles and osprey.

5. **St. Joe River Scenic Byway**: Traveling along Forest Road 50 between St. Maries and the Montana border, this byway is rich in wildlife, including deer, elk, moose, and bear.

6. **White Pine Scenic Byway**: Discover tranquil lakes and marshlands adjacent to the lower Coeur d'Alene River while traveling through the St. Joe National Forest.

7. **Hells Canyon Scenic Byway**: This twenty-two-mile journey offers a glimpse into North America's deepest river gorge.

8. **Payette River Scenic Byway**: A 111-mile route along the Payette River, passing through Smith's Ferry and by Cascade Lake to McCall.

9. **Wildlife Canyon Scenic Byway**: A route along the turbulent South Fork of the Payette River from Banks through Garden Valley to Lowman, known for wildlife viewing and hot springs.

10. **Ponderosa Pine Scenic Byway**: Wind through 131 miles from the Stanley Basin, along the South Fork of the Payette River, past Lowman, and through historic Idaho City to Boise.

11. **Snake River Canyon Scenic Byway**: This high desert byway stretches over fifty miles through scenic agricultural landscapes along the Snake River.

Utah

Utah is known for its diverse and breathtaking landscapes, and it features several major highways, byways, and scenic drives that allow travelers to explore the state's natural beauty. Here are some of the major highways, byways, and scenic drives in Utah.

1. **Interstate 70 (I-70):** This east-west interstate highway traverses the southern part of the state, offering access to national parks and scenic areas. It's known for its stunning views along the San Rafael Swell and the Spotted Wolf Canyon.

2. **US Route 89 (US-89):** US-89 extends from the Arizona border to the Idaho border, passing through some of Utah's most iconic national parks, including Zion, Bryce Canyon, and Grand Staircase-Escalante National Monument.

3. **Utah Scenic Byway 12 (Scenic Byway 12):** Often referred to as "A Journey Through Time Scenic Byway," this route takes travelers through some of Utah's most picturesque landscapes, including Red Canyon, Bryce Canyon, and Capitol Reef National Park.

4. **Utah Scenic Byway 24 (Scenic Byway 24):** Running from Sigurd to Hanksville, this scenic byway provides access to Capitol Reef National Park and offers views of the Waterpocket Fold and Cathedral Valley.

5. **Utah Scenic Byway 143 (Scenic Byway 143):** Known as the "Patchwork Parkway," this byway takes you through colorful forests and leads to Brian Head Resort and Cedar Breaks National Monument.

6. **Utah Scenic Byway 128 (Scenic Byway 128):** This scenic route follows the Colorado River and offers views of red rock canyons and cliffs. It's often called the "River Road" and is near Moab.

7. **Utah Scenic Byway 279 (Scenic Byway 279):** Also near Moab, this byway is known as "Potash Road" and provides access to petroglyphs and stunning views of the Colorado River.

8. **Mirror Lake Scenic Byway:** Located in the Uinta Mountains, this byway offers access to Mirror Lake and several high-elevation lakes, making it a popular route for outdoor enthusiasts.

9. **Alpine Loop Scenic Byway:** This byway near Provo Canyon takes travelers through alpine meadows and forests and offers views of Mount Timpanogos and Sundance Resort.

10. **Zion-Mount Carmel Highway:** Inside Zion National Park, this scenic drive includes the Zion-Mount Carmel Tunnel and provides access to notable features like Checkerboard Mesa and the East Rim Trail.

Montana

Montana offers a variety of scenic byways that showcase the state's natural beauty and diverse landscapes. Here are some of the scenic byways in Montana and their locations.

1. **Beartooth Highway (US 212):** Located in Southern Montana, near the Wyoming border, it offers breathtaking mountain views, alpine tundra, and access to Yellowstone National Park.

2. **Going-to-the-Sun Road:** Located in Glacier National Park in Northwestern Montana, highlights include glaciers, pristine lakes, mountain vistas, and wildlife.

3. **Chief Joseph Scenic Byway:** Located in North-Central Montana, it offers views of the Absaroka Mountains, Clarks Fork of the Yellowstone River, and history.

4. **Big Sheep Creek Back Country Byway:** Located in Southwestern Montana, near the Idaho border, highlights include remote and rugged terrain and wilderness.

5. **Kings Hill Scenic Byway:** Located in Central Montana, through the Little Belt Mountains, it offers rugged beauty and mountain landscapes.

6. **Pioneer Mountains Scenic Byway:** Located in Southwest Montana, in the Pioneer Mountain Range, highlights include views of the Pioneer Mountains, Beaverhead-Deerlodge, and National Forest.

7. **St. Regis-Paradise Scenic Byway:** Located in Western Montana, along the Clark Fork River, it offers scenic views and the Clark Fork River.

8. **Garnet Back Country Byway:** Located in Western Montana, near Garnet Ghost Town, highlights include access to a historic ghost town and wilderness.

9. **Missouri Breaks Back Country Byway:** Located in Central Montana, through the Missouri River breaks and badlands, it offers rugged terrain and the Missouri River.

10. **Lake Koocanusa Scenic Byway:** Located in Northwestern Montana, along Lake Koocanusa, highlights include views of Lake Koocanusa and mountain scenery.

Wyoming

Wyoming offers several scenic byways that showcase its stunning landscapes and natural beauty. Here are some of the scenic byways in Wyoming and their locations.

1. **Beartooth Highway:** Located in Northeastern Wyoming, near the Montana border, it offers high alpine scenery, Beartooth Pass, and access to Yellowstone National Park.

2. **Chief Joseph Scenic Byway:** Located in Northwestern Wyoming, near Cody, highlights include the Bighorn Mountains, historic and cultural sites, and views of the Absaroka Range.

3. **Wind River Canyon Scenic Byway:** Located in Central Wyoming, near Thermopolis, it offers views of Wind River Canyon, Hot Springs State Park, and Bighorn River.

4. **Big Horn Scenic Byway:** Located in Northern Wyoming, connecting Sheridan and Greybull, highlights include the Bighorn Mountains, scenic views, and opportunities for outdoor activities.

5. **Medicine Wheel Passage:** Located in Northern Wyoming, near Lovell, it offers views of the Bighorn Mountains, Medicine Wheel National Historic Landmark, and outdoor recreation.

6. **Snowy Range Scenic Byway:** Located in Southeastern Wyoming, in the Medicine Bow National Forest, highlights include the Snowy Range Mountains, pristine lakes, and hiking trails.

7. **Wind River Mountains Scenic Byway:** Located in Western Wyoming, connecting Lander and Dubois, it offers views of the Wind River Mountains, Shoshone National Forest, and outdoor adventures.

8. **Flaming Gorge—Green River Basin Scenic Byway:** Located in Southwestern Wyoming, near Flaming Gorge National Recreation Area, highlights include the Flaming Gorge Reservoir, Green River, Red Canyon, and diverse landscapes.

9. **Black Hills Scenic Byway:** Located in Northeastern Wyoming, near Sundance, it offers views of the Black Hills, Devil's Tower National Monument, and historic sites.

10. **Wind River Heritage Center:** Located in Central Wyoming, near Riverton, highlights include cultural and historical sites and the Wind River Indian Reservation.

Colorado

Colorado is known for its stunning landscapes, and it features several scenic byways that showcase the state's natural beauty. Here are some of the scenic byways in Colorado.

1. **Trail Ridge Road—Rocky Mountain National Park**: This iconic byway takes you through Rocky Mountain National Park and offers breathtaking views of the Rocky Mountains, including the opportunity to cross the Continental Divide.

2. **San Juan Skyway**: Located in southwestern Colorado, this byway passes through the historic town of Durango and offers views of the San Juan Mountains. It's particularly stunning during the fall when the aspen trees turn golden.

3. **Peak-to-Peak Scenic Byway**: This byway runs through the Front Range and provides views of the state's high peaks, including Longs Peak. It's known for its recreational opportunities and charming mountain towns.

4. **Silver Thread Scenic Byway**: Passing through the San Juan Mountains, this byway offers views of waterfalls, historic mining towns, and the scenic Lake City area.

5. **Dinosaur Diamond Scenic Byway**: This unique byway crosses the Colorado-Utah border and takes you through areas known for dinosaur fossils. It's an educational and scenic journey.

6. **Kebler Pass**: Located in the West Elk Mountains, Kebler Pass is famous for its expansive aspen groves. It's a must-visit during the fall for colorful foliage.

7. **Independence Pass**: This high-altitude byway crosses the Continental Divide and offers spectacular views of the Sawatch Range. It's typically open only in the summer months due to snow.

8. **Frontier Pathways Scenic and Historic Byway**: Running through southern Colorado, this byway passes by historic sites, including forts and mining towns, and offers views of the Sangre de Cristo Mountains.

9. **Scenic Highway of Legends**: Located in southern Colorado, this byway takes you through the Spanish Peaks region, known for its volcanic dikes. It also passes by Trinidad and Cokedale, two historic towns.

10. **Flat Tops Trail Scenic Byway**: This byway crosses the Flat Tops Wilderness Area and offers opportunities for fishing, hiking, and enjoying the high country scenery.

11. **Top of the Rockies Scenic Byway**: Connecting Leadville and Aspen, this byway provides views of Colorado's two highest peaks, Mount Elbert and Mount Massive.

12. **Cache la Poudre—North Park Scenic Byway**: Running through North Park and along the Cache la Poudre River, this byway offers opportunities for fishing and wildlife viewing.

Appendix J: Ski Areas and Resorts

To make this trip from a skiing perspective as economical as possible, I chose to get two ski passes, the IKON (I) and the EPIC (E). Between the two of these passes, I will have access to over sixty ski areas in the USA and Canada. While that may be the goal for a different year, this year, I plan to visit as many ski areas as possible in British Columbia, Idaho, Utah, Colorado, Wyoming, and Utah. I hope to get a full experience this year: skiing in the early season, the winter, and spring. The areas on my list are as follows:

1. **Whistler (E):** An interesting ski area. I skied here twice before. Like the mountain, not crazy about the town. It seems that if you don't stay in town, it's difficult to get around and find a place to park for free. Lots of interesting small restaurants. Whistler is not RV-friendly. However, there is an RV resort just outside of the town, Whistler RV Park and Campground. The views from the RV park are great; I have stayed here for a few years now.

2. **Revelstoke (I):** One of my favorites. The terrain is steep and wild. It has the longest vertical drop in North America. It's going through a change, however; tons of building. Mostly condos and expansion of the ski area. I hope that it doesn't lose its charm. The resort allows for one complimentary night of camping for fully enclosed RVs; for the past few years, I have stayed at the Boulder Mountain Campground.

3. **Kicking Horse (E):** Known for its advanced and expert terrain. Situated at the summit is Canada's highest restaurant. The food is outstanding, and the view of the Purcell Mountains is breathtaking. For the past few years, I have stayed at the Golden Golf Club RV Park. It's close to both the mountain and the town of Golden.

4. **Fernie (E):** Fernie's has diverse terrain and remarkable views of the Rockies, and it's RV-friendly. Long-term RV parking is available for a fee, but act quickly because space is limited, and the locals are quick to reserve the spots.

5. **Kimberly (E):** Known for consistent snowfall, short lift lines, and abundant sunny days, the staff is very personable. If you speak with the

guest services desk, they may allow a few overnight stays; I was able to stay for a few days during a terrible cold snap.

6. **Schweitzer Mountain Resort (I):** Parking at Schweitzer Mountain costs $20 per night in the Gateway lot; no hookups; maximum stay three consecutive nights.

7. **Deer Valley (I):** A luxurious ski resort known for its upscale amenities, groomed trails, and ski-only slopes. No RV facilities. Overnight RV parking is generally not allowed at the resort.

8. **Canyons Resort (E):** Part of Park City Mountain Resort, it offers extensive terrain with a mix of beginner to expert runs. No RV facilities. Overnight RV parking is generally not allowed at the resort.

9. **Brighton (I):** Popular for its affordability and diverse terrain suitable for all skill levels. No RV facilities, no overnight parking.

10. **Alta (I):** Known for its challenging terrain and powder snow, it's a ski-only resort. Overnight RV parking is not typically allowed at Alta.

11. **Solitude (I):** Offers a variety of terrain for all levels and is known for less crowded slopes. No RV facilities. No overnight parking.

12. **Crested Butte (E):** Renowned for its extreme terrain and quaint, historic mountain town. NO RV facilities, no overnight parking.

13. **Aspen (I):** Famous for its luxury ski experience and four different ski areas. Limited RV parking in Aspen itself, but nearby campgrounds can accommodate RVs.

14. **Steamboat Springs (I):** I consider this my "local ski area" because of how long I have been coming here and the number of times I have skied here (over forty years). The town has undergone a real transformation over the past thirty years. Long gone is the sleepy cowboy ski town; it is one of my favorite places to ski, but it is not RV-friendly. I usually stay at the KOA in Steamboat Springs; the town bus (free) takes you to the ski resort.

15. **Jackson Hole** (**I**)**:** Because I am in a truck camper, I am not too keen on the town itself; it's not at all RV-friendly. I usually camp at the Jackson Hole Campground at the Fireside Resort, drive to the satellite parking lot (free), and take the bus into town to ski. I love the mountain, though.

16. **Whitefish (Independent):** Whitefish allows RVs to park overnight in the Willow Tail lot for a maximum of three days; register at lodging check-in.

17. **Big Sky (I):** Renowned for its vast and impressive skiing terrain, it is one of the largest ski resorts in North America. The resort features the iconic Lone Peak. It's not RV-friendly. I have boondocked in the past when there was not too much snow; when there was too much, I rented a cabin.

Appendix K: National Parks, Provincial Parks, Wildlife Refuges, and BLM Lands

Trans-Canada Route 1

1. **Sleeping Giant Provincial Park**: Located on the Sibley Peninsula in Ontario, Sleeping Giant is famous for its unique rock formations that resemble a sleeping giant when viewed from Thunder Bay. The park offers a variety of recreational activities, including hiking, with over a hundred kilometers of trails, wildlife viewing, and breathtaking views of Lake Superior. The park's highlight is the Top of the Giant Trail, which leads to one of the highest points in Ontario, offering panoramic views.

2. **Lake Superior Provincial Park**: This park, situated along the shore of Lake Superior, is known for its scenic beauty, encompassing rugged shorelines and beaches, dense forests, and numerous rivers and lakes. It's a popular destination for canoeing, kayaking, fishing, and hiking, with the Coastal Trail being a notable hiking route. The park is also rich in cultural history, featuring several Indigenous rock art sites.

3. **Thousand Islands National Park**: Located along the Saint Lawrence River, Thousand Islands National Park consists of several islands and mainland properties. It's famous for its rich biodiversity and scenic beauty. The park offers unique opportunities for boating, kayaking, and exploring diverse wildlife. Camping on one of its many small islands is a unique experience, offering a tranquil escape with stunning river views.

4. **Chutes Provincial Park**: Situated near the town of Massey, Chutes Provincial Park is named for its scenic waterfall on the Aux Sables River. The park is relatively smaller but offers a peaceful nature experience. It's known for its beautiful hiking trails, including the Twin Bridges Trail, which winds along the river and offers views of the waterfall and rapids. The park is a great spot for camping, picnicking, and wildlife observation.

5. **Georgian Bay Islands National Park**: Located in Ontario, Canada, is a unique federal park known for its scenic beauty and diverse landscapes. This park comprises a collection of sixty-three islands in the Georgian Bay, part of Lake Huron, including the largest island, Beausoleil Island.

The Yellowhead Highway (Highway 16)

1. **British Columbia:**
   - **Mount Robson Provincial Park**: This park is home to Mount Robson, the highest peak in the Canadian Rockies. Visitors can explore hiking trails, view glaciers, and enjoy the pristine wilderness.
   - **Jasper National Park (Alberta)**: While not in British Columbia, Jasper National Park is easily accessible from the Yellowhead Highway and is known for its stunning mountain scenery, glaciers, and abundant wildlife.

2. **Alberta:**
   - **Jasper National Park**: As mentioned, Jasper National Park is a major attraction along the Yellowhead Highway in Alberta. It offers outdoor activities like hiking, wildlife viewing, and exploring lakes and canyons.
   - **William A. Switzer Provincial Park**: Located near Hinton, this provincial park features a variety of recreational opportunities, including camping, fishing, boating, and hiking.

3. **Saskatchewan:**
   - **Moose Mountain Provincial Park**: Located near Carlyle, this park offers a mix of forests, lakes, and hills. It's a popular spot for camping, fishing, and water activities.
   - **Duck Mountain Provincial Park**: Situated in the Duck Mountain region, this park provides opportunities for outdoor adventures such as hiking, camping, and birdwatching.

4. **Manitoba:**
   - **Riding Mountain National Park**: Accessible from the Yellowhead Highway, this national park is known for its diverse landscapes, including forests, grasslands, and lakes. It offers hiking, camping, and wildlife viewing.

5. **Ontario:**
   - **Pukaskwa National Park**: Located on Lake Superior's north shore, this national park features a rugged coastline, forests, and hiking trails. It's known for its wilderness and stunning views.

The Alaska Highway

1. **Muncho Lake Provincial Park (British Columbia)**: This park is known for its stunning Muncho Lake, a bright turquoise glacial lake surrounded by mountains. It offers opportunities for wildlife viewing, fishing, and hiking.

2. **Liard River Hot Springs Provincial Park (British Columbia)**: Famous for its natural hot springs, this park provides a unique and relaxing experience in a lush boreal forest setting. It's a great spot for camping and wildlife observation.

3. **Stone Mountain Provincial Park (British Columbia)**: This park features alpine ridges, lush valleys, and diverse wildlife. Hiking and wildlife viewing are popular activities here, with the Summit Lake and Flower Springs Lake trails being particularly noteworthy.

4. **Northern Rocky Mountains Provincial Park (British Columbia)**: Known for its spectacular, unspoiled wilderness, this park offers rugged landscapes with deep valleys, towering peaks, and abundant wildlife. It's a haven for backcountry hiking and camping.

5. **Kluane National Park and Reserve (Yukon Territory)**: Although not directly on the Alaska Highway, it's close enough to be a significant stop for travelers. This UNESCO World Heritage Site is home to Canada's highest peak, Mount Logan, and offers stunning glacial and mountainous landscapes.

The Cassiar Highway

These parks offer a glimpse into the remote and unspoiled landscapes of Northern British Columbia, with opportunities for outdoor activities like fishing, hiking, boating, and wildlife viewing. The Cassiar Highway itself is known for its scenic beauty and is a less crowded alternative to the more famous Alaska Highway.

1. **Boya Lake Provincial Park**: Known for its crystal-clear waters and unique color, Boya Lake is ideal for canoeing, kayaking, and fishing. The park's landscape is characterized by rolling hills, boreal forests, and an abundance of wildlife.

2. **Kinaskan Lake Provincial Park**: This park offers stunning views of the surrounding mountains and is a popular spot for fishing and camping. Kinaskan Lake is known for its tranquil setting and is a great place for wildlife viewing.

3. **Meziadin Lake Provincial Park**: Located near the junction of the Cassiar Highway and the road to Stewart, BC, and Hyder, Alaska, this park is known for its excellent fishing, especially salmon and trout. The park's lush, forested campground is a pleasant stopover for travelers.

4. **Tā Ch'ilā Provincial Park (Boya Lake)**: This park, also known as Boya Lake Provincial Park, is notable for its strikingly clear and turquoise lake, ideal for boating and swimming. The park also has significant cultural value, with many archaeological sites in the area.

5. **Spatsizi Plateau Wilderness Provincial Park**: While not directly on the Cassiar Highway, it's in the general vicinity and is one of the largest and most significant wilderness parks in British Columbia. Known for its vast, unspoiled wilderness, it's a destination for backcountry hiking, camping, and fishing.

Seward Highway

1. **Chugach State Park**: Just outside Anchorage, this is one of the largest state parks in the United States. It offers a variety of recreational activities such as hiking, biking, skiing, and wildlife viewing. The park features rugged mountains, serene lakes, and diverse wildlife.

2. **Chugach National Forest**: Although not a national park, this expansive national forest borders the Seward Highway and is the second-largest national forest in the US. It's known for its breathtaking landscapes, including glaciers, fjords, and rivers. Activities like hiking, fishing, and kayaking are popular here.

3. **Kenai Fjords National Park**: Near the end of the Seward Highway in Seward, this national park is famous for its ice fields and fjords. It's a prime spot for glacier viewing, wildlife watching, and boat tours. The park's centerpiece is the Harding Icefield, from which nearly forty glaciers flow.

4. **Alaska Maritime National Wildlife Refuge**: While not directly on the highway, it includes the waters and coastline near Seward. The refuge is vital for seabird nesting and marine mammals. Boat tours from Seward offer chances to see this rich marine environment.

5. **Kenai National Wildlife Refuge**: This refuge is a bit off the Seward Highway but easily accessible. It's known for its diversity of habitats, from lakes and wetlands to mountains and forests, providing excellent opportunities for fishing, canoeing, and wildlife observation.

The Richardson Highway

1. **Chugach State Park**: While not directly on the Richardson Highway, it's within reach as you approach the southern end near Valdez. It's one of the largest state parks in the US and offers a diverse range of activities, such as hiking, wildlife viewing, and winter sports.

2. **Wrangell-St. Elias National Park and Preserve**: This park is accessible via a connector from the Richardson Highway and is the largest national park in the US. It's known for its massive glaciers, towering peaks, and diverse wildlife. The park provides opportunities for hiking, camping, and scenic drives.

3. **Delta Junction State Recreation Site**: Located near the northern end of the Richardson Highway, this site offers facilities for picnicking and overnight camping. It's a nice stopover for travelers heading to or from Fairbanks.

4. **Donnelly Dome State Recreation Site**: This area provides access to the scenic Donnelly Dome, an interesting geological feature offering hiking opportunities and panoramic views of the Alaska Range.

5. **Fielding Lake State Recreation Area**: Situated at a higher elevation, this park offers cooler temperatures and is a popular spot for fishing, hiking, and wildlife viewing. In the winter, it becomes a destination for snow activities.

6. **Blueberry Lake State Recreation Site**: This site, closer to Valdez, is known for its beautiful setting and offers camping, fishing, and hiking opportunities in a serene environment.

7. **Keystone Canyon and Worthington Glacier State Recreation Site**: Near Valdez, this area is known for its spectacular waterfalls in Keystone Canyon and the easily accessible Worthington Glacier, providing a close-up view of a glacier.

The Denali Highway

1. **Denali National Park and Preserve**: While not directly on the Denali Highway, this world-renowned national park is easily accessible from the highway. It's home to North America's highest peak, Denali (formerly Mount McKinley), and offers a wide range of outdoor activities, including wildlife viewing, hiking, and bus tours.

2. **Denali State Park**: Located along the highway, this state park provides opportunities for camping, hiking, and wildlife observation. It offers scenic views of the Alaska Range and the Susitna River.

3. **Tangle Lakes Archaeological District**: Situated near Mile 21 of the Denali Highway, this area contains numerous archaeological sites and offers camping and fishing opportunities.

4. **Brushkana Creek State Recreation Area**: Located near Mile 30 of the highway, this recreation area provides access to fishing, camping, and hiking, along with scenic views of the Alaska Range.

5. **Alpine Creek Lodge**: A popular stop for travelers along the Denali Highway, the lodge offers accommodations, dining, and a chance to enjoy the wilderness setting.

6. **Maclaren River Lodge**: Another lodging option along the highway, this lodge is known for its remote location and offers cabins, dining, and access to outdoor activities.

7. **Lake Louise State Recreation Area**: Located near Mile 82 of the Denali Highway, this area offers camping, picnicking, and fishing opportunities. Lake Louise is known for its scenic beauty.

8. **Paxson Lake Campground**: Situated near Paxson at the eastern end of the highway, this campground offers lakeside camping, fishing, and boating on Paxson Lake.

9. **Wrangell-St. Elias National Park and Preserve**: While not directly on the Denali Highway, this massive national park is accessible

via the McCarthy Road, which intersects with the Denali Highway. It's the largest national park in the US and offers a wide range of wilderness experiences.

US Route 191

This long north-south highway in the United States passes through several states, including Arizona, Utah, Wyoming, and Montana. Along this route, there are numerous national and state parks, each showcasing the diverse natural beauty of these regions. Here's an overview of some of the key parks along Route 191.

1. **Arizona**
   - **Petrified Forest National Park**: Known for its vast deposits of petrified wood, the park also offers colorful badlands, historic structures, and various fossils.

2. **Utah**
   - **Arches National Park**: Near Moab, this park is famous for its over two thousand natural sandstone arches, including the world-famous Delicate Arch.
   - **Canyonlands National Park**: Also near Moab, Canyonlands is known for its dramatic desert landscape carved by the Colorado River.
   - **Dead Horse Point State Park**: Located near Moab, this park offers spectacular views of the Colorado River and Canyonlands National Park.

3. **Wyoming**
   - **Grand Teton National Park**: Although a bit west of Route 191, this park is known for its stunning mountain landscapes, wildlife, and alpine lakes.
   - **Flaming Gorge National Recreation Area**: Spanning the Wyoming-Utah border, it offers activities like boating, fishing, and hiking.

4. **Montana**
   - **Glacier National Park**: This is a bit northwest of Route 191's terminus, but it's renowned for its glaciers, alpine meadows, and beautiful lakes.

5. **Other Notable Parks and Recreation Areas**
   - **Yellowstone National Park**: Located primarily in Wyoming but also extending into Montana and Idaho, Yellowstone is close to Route 191 and is the first national park in the world, famous for its geysers, hot springs, and diverse wildlife.
   - **Gallatin National Forest**: In Montana, near the northern end of Route 191, offers opportunities for hiking, camping, and fishing.

George Parks Highway: Alaska Route 3

Officially, Alaska Route 3 runs from Anchorage to Fairbanks in Alaska and is named after George Alexander Parks, a former governor of the territory. These parks along the George Parks Highway showcase some of Alaska's most spectacular landscapes and provide a range of outdoor activities. The highway itself offers stunning views and is a popular route for those traveling to and from Denali National Park. Along this scenic route, there are several notable national and state parks.

1. **Denali National Park and Preserve**: Denali is the most famous park along the George Parks Highway. It encompasses North America's highest peak, Denali (formerly Mount McKinley). The park is known for its diverse wildlife, vast wilderness areas, and opportunities for hiking, camping, and sightseeing.

2. **Chugach State Park**: While primarily accessed from Anchorage and not directly on the Parks Highway, it's close enough to be a significant destination for travelers starting their journey from Anchorage. Chugach is one of the largest state parks in the United States, offering a variety of recreational activities, including hiking, skiing, and wildlife viewing.

3. **Nancy Lake State Recreation Area**: Located near Willow, this park offers a tranquil setting with a chain of lakes ideal for canoeing, fishing, and camping. It's a great spot for enjoying Alaska's natural beauty.

4. **Denali State Park**: Situated between Anchorage and Denali National Park, this state park offers stunning views of the Alaska Range and Denali itself. It provides excellent opportunities for hiking, camping, and wildlife observation.

5. **Byers Lake Campground**: Within Denali State Park, this campground near Byers Lake is a popular spot for both day use and overnight stays. It's known for its scenic beauty and is a great location for fishing and kayaking.

The Pacific Rim Highway (British Columbia Vancouver Island Highway 4)

1. **Pacific Rim National Park Reserve (National Park)**: This park reserve consists of three separate units: the Long Beach Unit, the Broken Group Islands Unit, and the West Coast Trail Unit. It offers a combination of rugged coastline, sandy beaches, temperate rainforests, and marine environments. Visitors can explore the coastline, hike the West Coast Trail, go kayaking in the Broken Group Islands, and enjoy various outdoor activities.

2. **Long Beach Unit**: Part of Pacific Rim National Park Reserve, this unit is known for its long sandy beaches along the West coast of Vancouver Island. It's a popular spot for surfing, beachcombing, picnicking, and wildlife viewing.

3. **Broken Group Islands Unit**: This unit, also within the Pacific Rim National Park Reserve, is an archipelago of over a hundred islands and islets. It's a paddler's paradise, offering sea kayaking, camping, and opportunities to explore the coastal rainforest.

4. **Strathcona Provincial Park**: While not directly on the Pacific Rim Highway, it's accessible via a side road and is Vancouver Island's oldest provincial park. Strathcona is known for its rugged mountain landscapes, alpine lakes, and hiking trails, including the popular Della Falls trail.

5. **Sproat Lake Provincial Park**: Located near Port Alberni, this park offers a beautiful lake setting with opportunities for swimming, boating, and picnicking. It's known for its clear waters and petroglyphs.

6. **Englishman River Falls Provincial Park**: Situated near Parksville, this park features a series of waterfalls along the Englishman River, surrounded by lush forests. There are hiking trails and picnic areas for visitors to enjoy.

7. **MacMillan Provincial Park (Cathedral Grove)**: Known for its ancient Douglas fir and red cedar trees, Cathedral Grove is a popular stop for seeing massive old-growth trees. It's a short walk from the highway and offers a glimpse into the region's temperate rainforest.

Idaho: Interstate 15 (I-15) and US Route 95 (US-95)

Idaho passes through various natural and recreational areas, including national and state parks, as well as hot springs. Here are some of the notable parks and hot springs along these highways in Idaho:

Along I-15

1. **Massacre Rocks State Park**: Located near the town of American Falls, this state park offers camping, hiking, and views of the Snake River. It also has historical significance related to the Oregon Trail.
2. **Pocatello**: While not a park, Pocatello offers recreational opportunities along the Portneuf River, including parks and walking trails.
3. **Lava Hot Springs**: This charming town is famous for its natural hot springs. Visitors can enjoy soaking in the hot pools and exploring the surrounding area. It's located off I-15, just south of Pocatello.

Along US-95

1. **Coeur d'Alene**: Coeur d'Alene City Park offers a sandy beach and swimming area along Lake Coeur d'Alene, providing a great place to relax.
2. **Farragut State Park**: Near Athol, this state park is one of Idaho's largest and offers camping, hiking, and water activities on Lake Pend Oreille.
3. **Round Lake State Park**: Located near Sagle, Round Lake State Park is known for its serene Round Lake and forested landscapes, making it suitable for hiking, fishing, and picnicking.
4. **Priest Lake State Park**: Near Priest River, this state park provides access to the pristine Priest Lake, where visitors can enjoy boating, fishing, hiking, and camping in a beautiful mountain setting.
5. **Dworshak State Park**: Although not directly on US-95, it's accessible via a short drive from the highway. The park

surrounds Dworshak Reservoir and provides camping, boating, and hiking opportunities.

6. **Hot springs at Syringa**: Located near the town of Kooskia, Syringa Hot Springs offers natural hot springs for soaking in a beautiful, forested setting. It's not far from US-95.

Utah State Route 30 (SR-30)

1. **Bear Lake State Park (Utah)**: This park encompasses the Utah side of Bear Lake and offers various water-based activities, including boating, fishing, swimming, and picnicking. It's a popular spot for beachgoers and outdoor enthusiasts.

2. **Bear Lake State Park (Idaho)**: Located on the Idaho side of Bear Lake, this state park provides additional access to the lake, offering similar activities such as boating, fishing, and picnicking. The Idaho side also has a marina for boat rentals.

3. **Garden City Park (Utah)**: Situated near the center of Garden City, this park provides access to Bear Lake's shoreline and features a playground, picnic areas, and a pavilion.

Hot Springs

1. **Soda Springs**: While not directly on the Bear Lake Scenic Byway, Soda Springs is a town in Idaho known for its natural mineral springs, including the famous "Soda Springs Geyser." Visitors can enjoy the city's naturally carbonated water and learn about its geological features.

2. **Lava Hot Springs**: Located south of Bear Lake, Lava Hot Springs is known for its natural hot springs and pools. It's a relaxing destination for soaking in hot mineral water and is a popular stop for travelers exploring the region.

Utah Scenic Byway 279 (Also Known as Potash Road or the Lower Colorado Scenic Byway, U-279)

1. **Historic Native American Rock Art**: Utah Scenic Byway 279 is renowned for its collection of historic Native American rock art. These ancient petroglyphs and pictographs can be found on the towering rock walls on the western side of the byway. These rock art sites hold cultural and historical significance and provide a glimpse into the past.

2. **Canyonlands National Park**: While not directly on the byway, Canyonlands National Park is nearby and accessible from the area. The park offers stunning canyon landscapes, hiking trails, and opportunities for outdoor exploration. Island in the Sky, one of the park's districts, is relatively close to the byway.

3. **Dead Horse Point State Park**: Located near the entrance to Canyonlands National Park, Dead Horse Point State Park offers panoramic views of the Colorado River and Canyonlands. It features hiking trails and overlooks with breathtaking vistas.

4. **Colorado River Scenic Views**: As you drive along Utah Scenic Byway 279, you'll enjoy scenic views of the Colorado River and its red rock canyons. The winding road provides opportunities for photography and taking in the beauty of the river.

Appendix L: Mountain Passes

The mountain ranges I traversed were nothing short of spectacular. In Canada, I drove through or over the Norwegian, Rocky, Columbia, Coast, Insular, and St. Elias Mountains, each with its own distinct charm. In the USA, I encountered the Alaska, Chugash, Cascade, Wasatch, Uinta, Rockies, Appalachian, and Adirondack ranges. Sometimes, the drive offered breathtaking panoramic views; other times, the snowy, blinding conditions reduced visibility to mere feet, reminding me of the precarious nature of my journey along the cliff edges with drops of over two thousand feet. Each range presented its own unique geographical, climatic, and ecological characteristics, adding to the rich tapestry of the North American landscape.

Before embarking, I had researched those passes renowned for their extreme winter conditions; at the time, their descriptions were mere words on paper. Having now navigated these passes, they've come alive with vivid, sometimes nerve-wracking, experiences. I prepared by upgrading to winter/ all-terrain tires and carrying the necessary equipment like snow chains, shovels, winches, and tow ropes. Yet, the weather's capricious nature still caught me off-guard at times. Some of the more difficult passes I traveled include:

1. **Summit Pass** (British Columbia, Canada): Known for being one of the highest points on the Alaska Highway. Elevation: Approximately 4,250 feet. When I traveled through this pass, it was so foggy I drove with my hazard lights on and went twenty miles per hour. I continued to travel because there had been no one on the road for hours before the fog set in. I was more worried about wildlife (moose, elk, or deer) than other vehicles, though.

2. **Thompson Pass** (Alaska, USA): One of the snowiest places in Alaska, it is known for avalanche risks, extreme cold, and severe winter storms. Elevation: Approximately 2,678 feet. When I started through the pass, it was overcast, and a storm was supposed to be a few hours away. As I drove through the pass, a snow squall with whiteout conditions came roaring through. At one point, I had to stop and pull over to what I hoped was the side of the road because the severity of the

snow made it impossible to see and, consequently, drive. Thankfully, there were no other vehicles on the road.

3. **Teton Pass** (Wyoming, USA): Known for steep grades (10%), sharp curves, and avalanche risks. Elevation: Approximately 8,431 feet. When I started going through the pass (west to east), I did not realize that you were not supposed to use this road if you were towing another vehicle. I did not notice the signs until it was too late. While the weather was a bluebird day, the steepness and the worry that the rig would jackknife if a curve was too tight or I stopped too suddenly left me at my wit's end when done. When I finally left Jackson Hole on my way to my next destination, I made certain that I took the longer and less stressful route.

4. **Rogers Pass** (British Columbia, Canada): Known for high avalanche risk, heavy snowfall, and complex terrain. Elevation: Approximately 4,364 feet. It was snowing quite heavily when I passed through. I kept my speed to twenty miles per hour and the hazards on. I am always surprised at how some drivers think that they are immune from skidding as they drive past me at forty or fifty miles per hour. There were a few pull-offs in the event that I had to stop, unlike many other passes that I drove through.

5. **Kicking Horse Pass** (Alberta/British Columbia, Canada): Known to be challenging during winter due to snow, ice, and steep grades. Elevation: Approximately 5,338 feet. When I drove through this pass, it was quite cold, and the roads were extremely icy. There were several autos and even eighteen-wheelers that had skidded off the road and abandoned. Others had pulled to the side of the road, waiting for it to get warmer. Again, I had my hazards on, kept my speed to twenty miles per hour, and labored along the pass.

Appendix M: Hot Springs

Throughout my journey along this storied route and beyond, I encountered a series of remarkable natural havens, each distinctively embodied by a variety of hot springs.

- In Laird, the hot springs stood as serene sanctuaries amidst the untamed wilderness, offering moments of peaceful retreat.
- Chena Hot Springs captivated me with its mesmerizing outdoor pools and the mountains in the backdrop.
- Manly Hot Springs, nestled in a more secluded spot, felt like stumbling upon a hidden gem, a secret garden of warmth and serenity. Aiyansh, with its primitive and untouched charm, seemed to connect me to the ancient rhythms of the land.
- Lava Hot Springs in Idaho and Bozeman Hot Springs in Montana were delightful interludes with their outdoor odor-free mineral-rich pools.

Each of these hot springs emerged as oases, their healing waters soothing the physical journey. They were not merely stops along the road but offered a profound connection to nature and a much-needed retreat from the endless stretches of highway.

Appendix N: Rock Climbing Terms

Rock climbing involves a variety of key terms that are essential to understand for anyone interested in the sport. Here are some of the most important ones:

1. **Belay:** The technique of managing the rope to safeguard the climber during their ascent or descent. The person doing this is called the belayer.

2. **Harness:** A piece of equipment worn by climbers around the waist and thighs. It's where the rope is attached and helps to distribute the force of a fall or hang.

3. **Carabiner:** A metal loop with a spring-loaded gate used to connect components in the climbing system, like the rope to the harness or the rope to an anchor point.

4. **Anchor:** A secure point where the rope is attached, typically using bolts, nuts, or other natural features. Anchors are crucial for belaying and rappelling.

5. **Pitch:** A section of a climb between two rest points or belay stations. Multi-pitch climbs involve several of these segments.

6. **Rappel (Abseil):** The act of descending a rock face using a rope and belay device.

7. **Chalk:** Used on climbers' hands to absorb moisture and improve grip.

8. **Quickdraw:** A set of two carabiners connected by a stiff fabric loop, used to connect the climbing rope to bolts or other protection.

9. **Protection (Pro):** Equipment placed in cracks or other natural features to protect against falls. This includes items like nuts, cams, and sometimes bolts.

10. **Route:** The path a climber takes up a climbing area or wall.

11. **Crimp:** A small edge where only fingertips can grip.

12. **Jug:** A large, easy-to-hold grip.

13. **Dyno:** A dynamic move to reach a hold that's too far away to grip from a static position.

14. **Bouldering:** Climbing on small rocks or boulders, usually without ropes, but with crash pads for protection.

15. **Lead Climbing:** A type of climbing where the climber ascends with the rope below them, clipping into protection as they go.

16. **Top-Roping:** Climbing where the rope is already set up through an anchor at the top of the climb.

17. **Crux:** The most difficult part of a climbing route.

18. **Redpoint:** Successfully climbing a route without falling or resting on the rope after having previously attempted it.

19. **Bitter End**: Simply the end of the rope.

20. **Onsight:** Successfully climbing a route on the first attempt without prior knowledge or watching others climb it.

These terms represent the basics of climbing terminology, but there are many more specialized terms that can be learned as one gets more involved in the sport.

Appendix O: Micro Breweries

Here's a summary of various breweries I visited while traveling.

1. **Farmery Estate Brewery (Neepawa, Manitoba):** Canada's first estate craft brewery, where the ingredients for its beers are grown on the farm, offering a unique farm-to-beer experience. Brewing excellence:
   - **Product Line:** Farmery Estate Brewery produces a variety of beers, including premium lager, Blonde Canadian Pale Ale, Prairie Berry Ale, and other malt-based coolers, such as pink lemonade and hard iced tea.
   - **Seasonal Brews:** They offer a range of seasonal beers, including Pioneer Harvest Stout, Fresh Hop Ale, Robbie Scotch Ale, Hop Bine Rye IPA, and Wind Chill Lager.
   - **Ingredients:** The beers are crafted using three strains of hops, prairie-grown barley, yeast, water, and wheat protein, all cultivated on their farm.

2. **Coast Mountain Brewing (Whistler, BC):** Known for a range of brews like Hero Dirt, Hazy IPA, Mahalo Fruited Sour, and Death Before Download Hazy IPA. It's situated in Function Junction, south of Whistler's Village, embracing the region's outdoor enthusiasm.

3. **Howe Sound Brewery (Squamish, BC):** Famous for its Devil's Elbow India Pale Ale, Rail Ale Nut Brown, and Pothole Filler Imperial Stout. It was voted "Brewery of the Year" at the Canadian Brewing Awards 2022 and is in Squamish, offering great views and a warm atmosphere.

4. **Pemberton Brewery (Pemberton, BC):** Located north of Whistler, it offers a relaxed, woodsy cabin feel. They are known for IPAs and pale ales, with the Cream Puff NE Pale Ale being a standout. The brewery is popular among mountain bikers and outdoor enthusiasts.

5. **Gladstone Brewing Company (Courtenay, BC):** Specializes in Belgian-style ales, European lagers, and Pacific Northwest-style India pale ales. Known for its cozy, community-focused atmosphere and often hosts events and live music.

6. **Batch 44 Brewery (Sechelt, BC):** Known for its diverse range of beers and a focus on quality ingredients. It's a popular spot for locals and tourists alike, offering a welcoming environment and often featuring seasonal brews.

7. **White Tooth Brewing Company (Golden, BC):** Offers a variety of beers with a focus on adventurous, bold flavors. The brewery has a modern taproom and often collaborates with local businesses and artists.

8. **Mt. Begbie Brewing Company (Revelstoke, BC):** Known for award-winning beers like Cream Ale and Tall Timber Ale. The brewery is named after a nearby mountain and reflects the adventurous spirit of the area.

9. **Fernie Brewing Company (Fernie, BC):** This brewery is known for a wide range of beers, including IPAs, stouts, and lagers. They are committed to the local community and often participate in local events and initiatives.

10. **Over Time Beer Works (Kimberley, BC):** A small brewery known for its handcrafted beers and a cozy taproom. They focus on quality over quantity, producing small batches of distinct beers.

11. **Rumpus Beer Company (Revelstoke, BC):** Known for their unique and experimental brews, often incorporating unusual ingredients and techniques. The brewery has a friendly, relaxed atmosphere.

12. **Fisher Peak Brewing Company (Cranbrook, BC):** This brewery offers a range of traditional and innovative beers, often inspired by the local environment and community.

13. **Big Delta Brewing Company (Delta Junction, AK):** This brewery features a selection of craft beers like BIG D IIPA, Alaska Sunrise—Cranberry Lime, Just Bluffin', and Trippin' on Sunshine. Big Delta Brewing is known for its various flavors and has become a notable destination in Delta Junction.

14. **Homer Brewing Company (Homer, AK):** Opened in 1996, it specializes in unfiltered, unpasteurized, cask-conditioned beers. Known beers include Old Inlet Pale, Broken Birch Bitter, Red Knot Scottish, and Odyssey Oatmeal Stout. The brewery is a staple in Homer, serving the local community with its traditional brewing techniques.

15. **St. Elias Brewing Company (Soldotna, AK):** A family-owned and operated full-service restaurant and brewpub. They offer hand-tossed pizzas, sandwiches, salads, homemade soups, and house-made desserts alongside a variety of red and white wines and handcrafted ales created in their seven-barrel brewhouse.

16. **49th State Brewery (Anchorage, AK):** This brewery is known for its diverse range of beers and a commitment to local ingredients and sustainable brewing practices. They have locations in Anchorage and Healy, offering a blend of traditional and innovative brews.

17. **Cooper Landing Brewing Company (Cooper Landing, AK):** This brewery is recognized for its quality craft beers and scenic location, often attracting outdoor enthusiasts.

18. **Bear Paw River Brewing Company (Wasilla, AK):** This brewery is known for its wide range of beers catering to different palates, from IPAs to stouts, and for its local community involvement.

19. **Valdez Brewing Company (Valdez, AK):** This brewery offers a variety of beers and is known for its unique location amidst the beautiful Alaskan landscapes.

20. **Last Frontier Brewing Company (Wasilla, AK):** This brewery is known for its blend of traditional and unique brews and its role as a community gathering spot.

21. **Salty Dawg Saloon (Homer, AK):** This is not a brewery but is well known for its unique atmosphere and historical significance. They serve various local and popular beers.

22. **Girdwood Brewing Company (Girdwood, AK):** This brewery is appreciated for its quality craft beers and the beautiful natural scenery.

23. **Heber Valley Brewing Company (Heber City, UT):** Recognized as the first craft brewery in Heber Valley, Utah, specializing in small-batch, quality beers. It opened in 2019 and quickly became a beloved spot in the community. The brewery is known for its relaxed setting and various beers catering to different palates.

24. **Moab Brewery (Moab, UT):** Renowned for being Moab's original microbrewery and the largest restaurant in the area, it also operates as the only microbrewery and distillery in Moab, Utah. Established in 1996, it has become a staple destination for locals and visitors, especially those looking to unwind after outdoor adventures. Key highlights:
    - **Unique Beer Inspirations:** The beers at Moab Brewery are inspired by Moab's individual and beautiful landscape, reflecting a strong connection with the local environment. This inspiration is evident in the distinct flavors and styles of their beers.
    - **Award-Winning Products:** The brewery prides itself on offering award-winning beer and distilled spirits, catering to various tastes and preferences.

25. **Proper Brewing and Burger (Moab, UT):** A significant player in Utah's craft beer scene, known for its quirky and inclusive approach to brewing and dining. It started as Avenues Proper in Salt Lake City and has since expanded to multiple locations, including Moab. Key highlights:
    - **Establishment and Growth:** Founded in 2013 in Salt Lake City, Proper Brewing started focusing on handcrafted cuisine and beer. The original location, Avenues Proper, was Utah's smallest commercial brewery. The company expanded in 2016 to include Proper Brewing Company and Proper Burger Company Downtown.

26. **Copper Club Brewing Company (Fruita, CO):** Has established itself as a significant community hub since its inception in 2012. It focuses on creating traditional-style beers along with seasonal and experimental brews. Brewing excellence:
    - **Brew House:** Copper Club operates a seven-barrel brew house and is proud to offer tours to visitors.

- **Beer Range:** They specialize in traditional-style beers and include seasonal and experimental brews. They make efforts to use Colorado-grown ingredients, with most base malts sourced from Proximity Malt in Monte Vista, Colorado.
- **Awards:** The brewery has received recognition for its F-Town Amber Ale and other beers.

27. **Bozeman Brewing Company, also known as "The Bozone" (Bozeman, MT):** Bozeman's oldest operating brewery, is recognized for its commitment to quality brewing and its significant role in the local community. Brewing excellence:
    - **Production:** Brewed approximately 5400 barrels in 2021.
    - **Sour Program:** Boasts the largest souring facility in Montana, with over 285 barrels in its cellar.
    - **Innovative Beers:** Offers a diverse range of beers, including year-round favorites, limited releases, and a notable sour barrel program.
    - **Sustainability:** Engages in sustainable practices, including solar energy usage and repurposing spent grain for agricultural use.

28. **Outlaw Brewing Company (Bozeman, MT):** It has established itself as a critical player in the local craft beer scene with its innovative brewing approach and strong community ties. Beer Production: Outlaw Brewing is known for its wide range of forty to forty-five seasonal and experimental beers annually, with sixteen tap handles in its tasting room.
    - **Specialties:** The brewery is recognized for its unique beers, such as Hop Mullet IPA, Patio Pounder IPA, Pot Shot Pilsner, Snail Mail Mountain Pale Ale, and Summit Dog Double IPA.
    - **Brewing Approach:** Emphasizing exploration and experimentation, Outlaw Brewing often releases a new beer approximately every ten days.

29. **Burnt Tree Brewing (Ennis, MT):** A relatively new addition to the state's thriving craft beer scene, known for its distinct beer offerings and community-centered approach. Brewing excellence:
    - **Beer Selection:** Burnt Tree Brewing prides itself on its diverse range of beers, including the Flying Ant golden honey ale and

the Black Dog Porter. They also recommend The Other One Hazy IPA and their Raspberry Sour.

- **Craftsmanship:** The brewery is noted for beers that balance flavor, catering to enthusiasts and those new to craft beers.

30. **Sleeping Giant Brewing Company (Thunder Bay, Ontario):** It is named after the nearby Sleeping Giant, a large formation on the North shore of Lake Superior. The brewery showcases a deep love for the city and region, which is evident in its beer names and use of local ingredients. Brewing philosophy and offerings:
   - **Beer Varieties:** They produce a distinctive lineup of easy-drinking, full-flavored beers. Some notable beers include Northern Logger, a Golden Ale, and Mr. Canoehead.
   - **Community Focus:** The brewery has strong local ties, with products and collaborations reflecting their love for Thunder Bay and a commitment to the local community.

31. **Century Barn Brewing & Beverage Company (Devlin, ON):** A family-owned business in Devlin, Ontario, dedicated to producing premium quality craft beer and other beverages. It is a part of the Cornell Farms, a 6th generation family farm, and aims to provide a full-circle experience "from our farm to your glass back to our farm." Key features:
   - **Diverse Product Line:** Their product line includes beer, sparkling hop water, craft soda, ciders, and non-alcoholic beer.
   - **Farm-to-Glass Approach:** They use grains and hops grown on their family farm, emphasizing the connection between agriculture and brewing.
   - **Location:** Situated in Fort Frances in Northwestern Ontario, the company is set to begin beverage production in the spring of 2024.
   - **Farm Story:** Century Barn Brewing & Beverage Company is deeply connected to its farm roots, offering a unique blend of agricultural heritage and beverage innovation.

32. **Lake of the Woods Brewing Company (Kenora, ON):** It has a storied history that traces back to its establishment in 1898 by entrepreneur Abraham Kingdon in Kenora, Ontario. This historical

brewery experienced closures during prohibition but was reopened by Stanley Drewery in 1927. Despite its efforts, it couldn't withstand competition from large national breweries and closed its doors in 1954. Reopening: The brewery was revitalized and reopened on June 29th, 2013, marking Kenora's first brewery in fifty-nine years. Location: It is situated in Kenora's Historic Firehall, which adds to its charm and heritage.

- **Brewing Philosophy:** Committed to its heritage, the brewery uses simple ingredients like fresh Canadian Shield water, malt, yeast, and hops, mirroring the practices of past brewers.

Acknowledgments

This book, a testament to the adventures and reflections gathered along the way, would not have reached your hands without the invaluable contributions of several key individuals.

To my beta readers—Tom Dunn, Annika Richter, and Steve McCarthy—your insights and feedback have been nothing short of transformative. Your keen observations and thoughtful suggestions have deeply enriched this work, pushing me to refine and elevate my narrative in ways I could not have achieved alone. Your dedication to the craft and your willingness to engage with my stories have been instrumental in bringing this project to fruition.

To Jeannie, my editor, whose skill and patience transformed a collection of thoughts and experiences into a coherent and engaging tome: your magic touch has made all the difference, turning raw text into readable sense, and for that, I am eternally grateful. Your guidance and expertise have not only polished this manuscript but have also taught me invaluable lessons about the art of writing.

And to Dexter, my silent yet ever-present travel companion, whose presence has been a constant source of comfort and joy on our overlanding journeys. Though you do not speak in words, your companionship speaks volumes. Your unwavering loyalty and adventurous spirit have been a source of inspiration and courage, reminding me of the importance of companionship, even in the most remote corners of the world.

Each of you has played a pivotal role in this journey, offering support, wisdom, and companionship through every word written and mile traveled. My heartfelt thanks to you all for being part of this adventure, for your contributions have been indispensable in bringing these pages to life.

About the Author

Thom, a former PwC partner with a remarkable 35-year tenure, has always been driven by an insatiable sense of adventure. Now retired and residing in Cape Cod, he dedicates his summers to crafting custom furniture in his workshop and spends the rest of the year exploring new horizons with his loyal companion, Dexter. His explorations have led him across Europe and, more recently, throughout North America. Thom's future is equally ambitious, aiming to experience the wonders of Antarctica and then traverse the western coast of South America, from Ushuaia, Argentina, to Colombia, and the following year, to undertake a full circumnavigation of Australia.

Amidst these adventures, Thom has been courageously battling cancer for eight years and is currently stage IV. It is incurable and, they believe, terminal. Through this blog, www.livinglifewhiledying.com, he offers insights into living with this relentless disease while continuing to embrace life's full spectrum. Thom's journey is not just about his own experiences, but also serves as a beacon of hope and inspiration. His goal is to encourage readers to cherish every moment, whether they are personally navigating a cancer journey or supporting a loved one on theirs.

Thom released his first book in January 2024, *Living While Dying*.

Dear Readers,

As you turn the final page of *Chasing My Northern Lights*, I hope the book has sparked a unique perspective on finding beauty in uncertainty and strength in struggle and it has inspired you to seize every moment with courage and grace.

To continue being reminded of the power of staying positive and mastering the art of living fully in the midst of illness, I invite you to visit my website: www.livinglifewhiledying.com. Here, I offer inspiration and support to those on a similar path and those supporting a loved one through their battle.

For daily doses of adventure and updates on my journey to living life to the fullest, follow me on Instagram at @Thom.Barrett. Join me in celebrating a life of courage and zest, navigating through the toughest challenges with a spirit of hope and adventure.

Thom

PS. If Thom's story and travels have inspired or motivated you, we invite you to share your thoughts with other readers by leaving a review at the retail outlet where you purchased the book. Your feedback helps others discover Thom's impactful narrative and fosters a community of support and understanding. We value your perspective and welcome your insights. Please don't hesitate to contact us today to share your thoughts. Your feedback is invaluable as we continue to strive for meaningful connections through Thom's story.

.

www.ingramcontent.com/pod-product-compliance
Lightning Source LLC
Chambersburg PA
CBHW060857120626

46553CB00001B/110